1

REAL ESTATE

THE BASICS

9th Edition

BY

JOHN ROSICH, PH.D.

© 2017 Real Estate – The Basics, 9th Edition.
1494 East Camero Avenue
Las Vegas, Nevada 89123
Email john.rosich@csn.edu

Real Estate – The Basics, 9th Edition
Publication Date: June 2017

Printed in the United States

TABLE OF CONTENTS

COPYRIGHT PAGE

INTRODUCTION

Chapter 1 REAL PROPERTY CHARACTERISTICS, LEGAL DESCRIPTION, AND PROPERTY USE

Chapter 2 OWNERSHIP, ESTATES, RIGHTS AND INTERESTS

Chapter 3 POLICE POWERS

Chapter 4 DEED, TITLE, TRANSFER OF TITLE, AND RECORDING OF TITLE

Chapter 5 PROPERTY VALUE AND APPRAISAL

Chapter 6 REAL ESTATE CONTRACTS

Chapter 7 AGENCY

Chapter 8 REAL ESTATE PRACTICE

Chapter 9 REAL ESTATE PRACTICE

Chapter 10 FNANCING AND SETTLEMENT

Chapter 11 REAL ESTATE MATH CALCULATIONS

GLOSARRY

Introduction

My goals in writing this book is to provide a comprehensive introduction to the field of real estate, and give more than enough information for real estate pre-licensure test preparation.

The study of real estate is endless, though fortunately well signposted by the national real estate testing services and licensing laws of individual states. These signposts are the eleven chapters in the book.

There are many people that were instrumental in the preparation of this book; however I want to particularly thank the two people from the Greater Las Vegas Board of Realtors, Mrs. Irene Vogel, and Mr. Dale Henson for their help in making available the majority of forms and contracts presented in this book.

Chapter 1 – Real Property Characteristics, Legal Descriptions and Property Use

Learning Objectives

Real property vs. personal property
    Fixtures, Trade fixtures, emblements
    Attachment, severance, and bill of sale
Characteristics of real property
    Economic characteristics
    Physical characteristics
    Legal description
    Methods used to describe real property
     Survey
    Public and private land use controls - encumbrances
    Public control – governmental powers
        Police power, eminent domain, taxation, escheat
            Zoning ordinances
        Private controls, restrictions, and encroachments
            Covenants, conditions, and restrictions
            Easements
            Licenses and encroachments
Ownership, estates, rights, and interests
    Forms of ownership
    Freehold estates
        Fee simple absolute
        Fee simple defeasible, determinable, and condition
        subsequent
         Life estate
         Bundle of rights
        Leasehold estates and types of leases
            Estate for years and from period to period
            Estate at will and estate at sufferance
            Gross, net and percentage leases
        Leans and lean priority
        Surface and subsurface rights
Deed, title, transfer of title, and recording of title
        Elements of a valid deed
        Types of deeds

Title transfer
    Voluntary alienation
    Involuntary alienation
Recording the title
    Constructive and actual notice
    Title abstract and chain of title
    Marketable title and cloud on title
    Attorney title opinion, quiet title opinion, quiet title
    lawsuit, and title insurance

-Property Ownership

Property ownership is the primary reason for the study of real estate. Ownership of property is usually divided into two broad classes: real and personal. The study of real estate deals with characteristics affecting the acquiring of real property. Included in property ownership is an understanding of classes of property, land, characteristics, encumbrances, and types of ownership.

This includes understanding classes of property, land characteristics, encumbrances, and types of ownership.

Classes of Property

Classes of property are divided into two broad areas:
1. Real property or real estate
2. Personal property, or personality.

Real Property

Real property is described as the land along with any improvements plus *appurtenances* that include rights, privileges, and *fixtures,* which is anything permanently affixed to the land.

As mentioned above property ownership is the primary reason for the study of real estate, and it deals with characteristics that affect the acquisition and transfer of real estate. A simple definition of real estate includes the land, and any improvements, and/or appurtenances.

Land

Land is what we picture when we consider real estate. However, we also need to envision what is above the land - the air up to the heavens - and what is beneath the land - subsurface rights, i.e. mineral rights. In essence, the landowner's property takes the shape of an inverted pyramid that reaches to the very center of the earth.

Inverted Pyramid

Attachments

All things permanently attached to the land are included in real estate ownership. These encompass both natural and manmade attachments. Naturally growing attachments to the land and those affixed to the land by their roots are called *fructus naturales*. Things that someone has planted, *fructus industriales*, are also part of the real estate. There can be confusion as to whether the planted crops should be considered real property, or personal property. If the landowner planted the crops, they're considered real property. If a tenant farmer plants the crops, then they are considered part of the personal property of the farmer.

Doctrine of Emblements

A legal rule, called the doctrine of emblements, allows a tenant farmer access to the crops at harvest time even if that date exceeds the expiration of the lease (held by the tenant farmer).

Fixtures

Manmade attachments that are affixed to the land are called fixtures. A fixture is something, (i.e. wood, etc.), considered personal property at the time of purchase. However, once attached to the property by nail, or whatever it becomes part of the real property. Attachments could also be considered improvements when affixed to the land with the intent of being permanent. These can include a house, garage, fence, landscaping, etc.

The method of attachment is one factor used to define an item as realty or the personal property of the tenant. However, an item does not have to be physically attached to be part of the realty. (See Constructive Annexation)

Constructive Annexation

The doctrine of constructive annexation identifies items such as a pool sweep or keys as part of the realty even though they aren't permanently affixed to the land.

Items such as mobile homes can be problematic when determining if they are realty or personal property. Mobile homes that meet city or county codes when affixed to the land are considered realty. Mobile home with the wheels attached, are defined as personal property.

Appurtenances

Appurtenances include certain rights and privileges that go with the real property and are included in property ownership even if they aren't always part of the property. For example, air, water oil, gas, and mineral rights are appurtenances.

Air Rights

As stated previously, the landowner's property takes on the shape of an inverted pyramid that extends from the center of the earth to the heavens above it. However, U.S. law gives the government complete control over airspace. Subsequently, landowners can do nothing to impede air traffic. But they do have the right to seek compensation if they can prove such traffic substantially reduces property values.

Water Rights

Water rights are property rights that are called *riparian rights*. *Riparian waters* refer to rivers and streams while *littoral waters* are lakes property owners have frontage or access to. Both come under the category of riparian rights. Riparian rights state that owners may not divert these waters to non-riparian land.

Appropriate Rights

It is also necessary to consider *appropriate rights* when water is an issue.

Prior appropriation is the system used to determine water rights. It uses the following two factors to do so:

- The purpose for which the water will be used.
- Who was the first to take the water and apply it to a particular use?

Owners must obtain a permit from the state to establish appropriative rights for water use. Applicants do not have to own property adjacent to the water they use. Once the state determines ownership, water rights may be sold and used on any property the owner chooses.

All waterways that are navigable, rivers, lakes, etc., are owned and controlled by the government. The public is granted an easement right to use waterways for transportation.

Oil, Gas and Minerals

Oil and gas are in their natural state below the earth's surface. Oil and gas are tapped by drilling wells. Oil and gas are under great pressure and once they are tapped they flow in the direction of the well. The landowner could remove all of the oil and from the reservoir including the oil and gas under adjoining property owners.

Rule of Capture

The *rule of capture* legally enables a landowner to tap adjacent underground mineral deposits. Once they come to the surface, and are removed they become personal property, rather than real property. The rule of capture allows a land owner to remove as much of the valuable oil and gas as he can, regardless of whether some of product actually is under adjoining owner's land. The landowner has the right to mine any minerals on the land's surface and beneath it. However, these rights become somewhat murky with oil and gas. For example: once tapped, oil and gas will migrate. This migration may end up beneath the land of an adjacent property owner. The landowner who drilled the well has the right under *the rule of capture* to remove migrating minerals.

Support Rights

The landowner has the right to natural support of land by the surrounding land. The right of support includes both the *lateral support and subjacent support* under the land's surface.

Personal Property/Chattel

Civil law identifies personal property as "movable property" or "movables" because the personal property can be moved from place to place. Everything that is not real estate is considered personal property or chattel and is transferred by a bill of sale at closing.

It is possible to place a mortgage on real property. This mortgage requires payment or the lender can seek foreclosure. Personal property can often be secured with similar kind of device, known as a *chattel* or trust *mortgage,* and/or *security interest*. Article 9 of the U.S. Uniform Commercial Code governs the creation and enforcement of security interest in most types of personal property. Personal property can be labeled in a variety of ways, including goods, furniture, refrigerators, ranges, etc.

It is imperative for real estate agents to clearly identify personal items when listing both real and personal property. If they fail to do so, they could find themselves incurring costly out-of-pocket expenses. Problems arise when items aren't accurately described allowing for a substitution that buyers find unacceptable. For example: a sale may include a double-door refrigerator equipped with an ice and water-

12

maker on one of the doors, but the seller replaces that model with an antiquated refrigerator of lesser value before the buyer moves in. Oftentimes, the only remedy is for the agent to use his own funds to purchase a new model. To avoid such problems, agents should always describe all personal property included with real property as accurately as possible using photos and serial numbers when possible.

Land Characteristics

One of the physical characteristics of land is that it is immobile. The geographic location of a piece of land is fixed and can never be changed. Land is indestructible. The long-term nature of improvements and the permanence of land tend to create stability in land development. Land is unique or "non-homogeneous" since each parcel differ, geographically from another and has its own location

Allodial

In the United States, all land is allodial. Allodial title is real property that is owned free and clear of any liens.

Accretion

Accretion is the natural growth in land that results either from alluvium or dereliction. Alluvion, (also known as alluvium), is the deposit of suspended soil by flowing water. It usually occurs along a river or seacoast.

Dereliction

Dereliction is the exposure of formerly submerged land that appears when water retreats below its previous waterline. Natural processes may cause a loss of property, either through erosion, the gradual wearing away by wind or rain, or avulsion, or violent tearing away by flowing water

Economic Characteristics of Land

Although there is a substantial amount of unused land, supply of certain quality of land can be limited. The placement of an improvement on a parcel of land affects its value and the use of neighboring parcels of land. The improvements represent a large fixed investment economically. Land is not a liquid asset since it is not easily converted into cash. Location or area preference for a specific parcel of land is referred as a *site or situs*. The site is an individual's choice and represents the desire for a given area.

Legal Description

Although any description of land does not have to be exact, it cannot be ambiguous. An adequate description of land is one that allows a qualified surveyor to locate the boundaries of the parcel or site.

Types of Legal Description of Land

There are three basic legal descriptions of land: the metes-and-bounds system, the government survey system, and the maps and plats system.

Metes and Bounds

The oldest method of land description is referred to as the metes and bounds method. All of the parcels of land in the original colonies were described by metes and bounds. Metes refer to bearings and distances cited by course measurements. Bounds refer to the monuments that describe boundaries or limits to the property. The key thing to remember is to begin and end the legal description at the *point of beginning (POB)* and measure clockwise. The metes and bounds system refer to three things – *monuments, courses, and distances.* A *monument* is a natural or manmade landmark such as a river, tree, road, or marker. *Courses* are directions in the form of compass bearings. A metes and bounds system of description will start at some well described point along a boundary of a tract of land and gives directions that enable a surveyor to completely follow the boundaries of the tract and return to its point of origin *(distances)*. Remember, a metes and bounds description must end at the point of beginning in order to be a totally enclosed tract.

Rectangular or Government Survey

The *Government Survey System (GSS)* is also called the rectangular or quadrangular survey system. This system incorporates all land west of the eastern boundary of Ohio that was acquired during the presidential term of Thomas Jefferson, in addition to California and Alaska. Note however, that Texas developed its own type of subdivision through grants of league.

Aliquot Parts

The method of land division in the rectangular survey system is called *aliquot parts*. This is defined by (as) forming an exact proper divisor (See next paragraph for further details).

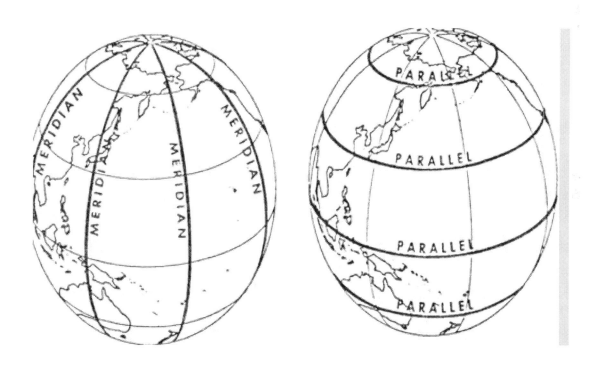

Although the system was designed for rectangular lot size there was a need to regularly adjust the entire township grid to account for distortions caused by the curvature of the Earth and the convergence of meridians toward the poles. These lots that have been adjusted are referred to as government lots.

SUBDIVISION OF CHECKS INTO TOWNSHIPS

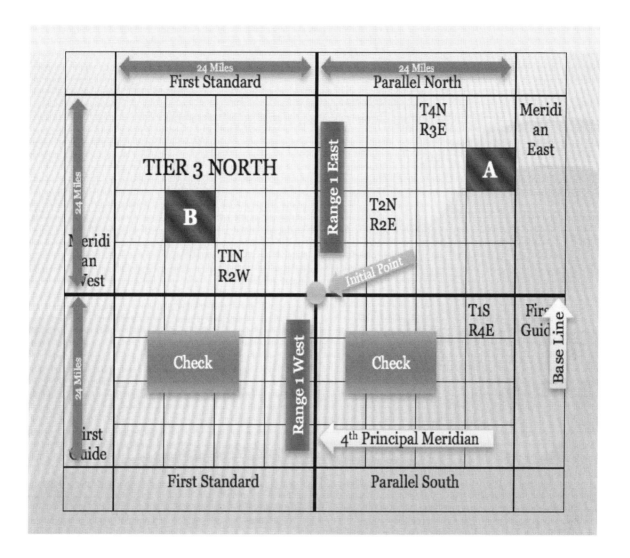

The system is a grid of north/south and east/west lines. The north/south lines are called *meridians* and east/west lines are called *parallels*. Twenty-four miles separate meridians from parallels. These distances are referred to as *checks*. Since the checks are too large an area (576 square miles) to be used for any purposeful survey, _the government allowed checks to be reduced to 16 townships. A township is formed by the meeting, (intersection) of principal meridian and base lines (6 x 6 miles = 36 sq. mi.)._

Ranges and Townships

As mentioned previously, ranges are vertical rows of townships (north/south), and tiers are horizontal (east/west) rows of townships. _Each township contains 36 sections._

17

And each section is one mile by one mile, equaling one square mile, or 640 acres. Township sections are numbered in a serpentine method beginning in the northeast corner with Section No. 1, and ends in the southeast corner with Section No. 36.

NUMBER SECTIONS OF A TOWNSHIP

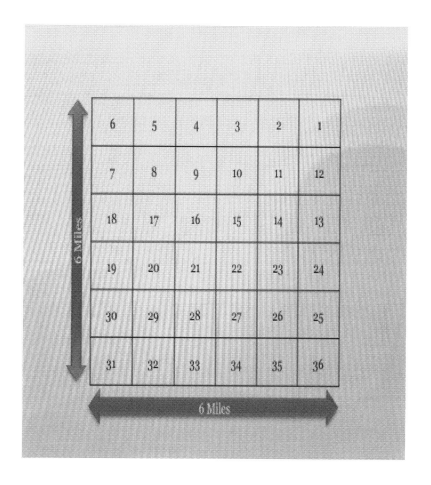

Township sections are then further divided into quarters, i.e. a quarter section is 160 acres. Each quarter section can be divided into quarters, i.e. 40 acres; each quarter of a quarter section can be divided into quarters, i.e. 10 acres. That quarter of a quarter of a quarter of a quarter section can be divided into quarters, i.e. 2.5 acres, and each quarter of a quarter of a quarter of a quarter section can then be split in halves resulting 1.25 acres. These quarter divisions are noted in their individual north, south, east or west areas. In other words, if there were no city or county restrictions a person could sell a parcel of land by simply writing out the location of the land within a section. See next page.

SUBDIVISION OF SECTION 8 OF T3NR2W, 4TH PM.

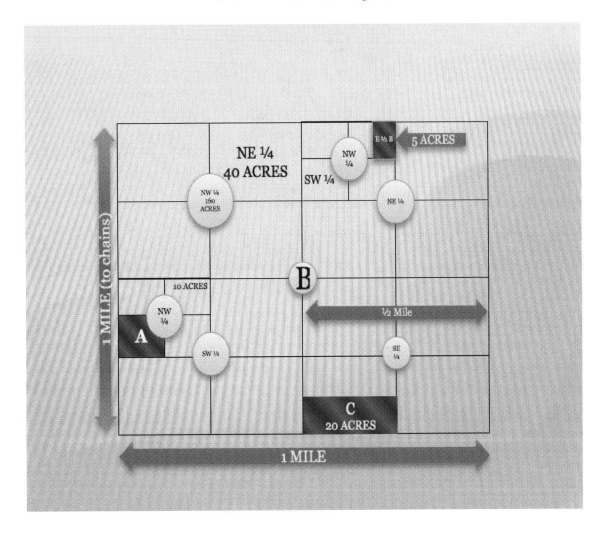

Measurements to Remember

Township – 36 square miles
Acre – 43,560 sq. ft.
640 acres – 1 square mile
1 section – 1 square mile – 640 acres
¼ section – 160 acres
¼ of ¼ section – 40 acres
¼ of ¼ of ¼ section – 10 acres
1 linear mile – 5,280 feet

Benchmarks and Datum

Survey teams in the description of land use *benchmark and datum*.

Benchmarks

Benchmarks are geodetic control points that are permanently affixed objects at locations throughout the United States. They enable land surveying, civil engineering and mapping to be done efficiently. Although these objects are usually metal disks, they can be any objects that serve as a control point. A benchmark is a reference point that is permanent in nature and can be natural or artificial. Its elevation is known with respect to a reference datum from which other elevations can be established.

Datum

A datum is a reference from which measurements are made. In surveying, a datum is a reference point on the earth's surface from which position measurements are made. *Horizontal datum*'s are used for describing a point on the earth's surface, in latitude and longitude or another coordinate system. *Vertical datum*'s are used to measure elevations or underwater depths. A datum is a level surface used to reference elevations. Sea level is generally used as a reference datum.

Platting

The third major system of land description is called platting. This is sometimes called the *map-and-plats-system*. Platting is basically a formal contract between the developer and the public entity, including the city or county. Platting is used to describe the location of lots, easements, and rights-of-way for the public record. A legal lot is a lot that has been plated and can be described as a lot out of a particular subdivision. For example, Lots 3, 4, and 5, block 10, Desert Springs Subdivision.

In this system land is described with reference to lots and blocks that have been mapped out by a surveyor in a subdivision plat. These plats are recorded in the county where the land is located. A reference to a numbered lot on a specific plat is considered a legal description of the lot since a detailed description of that lot is on file at the Recorder's office. These lot and block identifications (street addresses) can be incorporated into any legal document simply by reference. The plat maps can include measurements of: an area, the location of easements and survey markers, and right of way dimensions. Plat maps also contain the location of survey markers, records of any conditions, covenants, and restrictions that apply to the particular parcel of land and its improvements.

Torrens System

Some governmental recording agencies have adopted the Torrens System to record or register land titles. These titles are settled consequent to establishment and validation of ownership. The system was named after Sir Robert Torrens (1814-84). Lenders may require a survey to reveal encroachments or zoning violations.

Property Ownership Quiz

1. The removal of land when a stream suddenly changes its channel is:

    (A) Adverse possession.
    (B) Accretion.
    (C) Avulsion.
    (D) Breach.

2. Trees and crops:

    (A) Are real property.
    (B) Are personal property.
    (C) May be real or personal property.
    (D) None of the above.

3. Appurtenances refer to as:

    (A) Those rights that go with the land.
    (B) Contractual limitations.
    (C) Proposed easements.
    (D) Encumbrances on the use of the property.

4. The system of land ownership whereby the land is owned and controlled by individuals is known as:

    (A) Feudal system.
    (B) Commercial system.
    (C) Allodial system.
    (D) Torrens system.

5. In real estate terms improvements most nearly means:

    (A) Fences, wells, drains, and roadways.
    (B) Additions to the original structure.
    (C) Outbuildings.
    (D) Everything artificial or constructed on the land.

6. The right of alienation is defined as:

    (A) The right to execute and deliver a deed.
    (B) The right to make a will.
    (C) The right to transfer an interest in land.
    (D) Statutes of decent and distribution.

7. Which of the following could not be real estate?

(A) Growing trees.
(B) Coal in the ground.
(C) Air rights.
(D) Lessee's interest under a year-to-year lease.

8. The transferring of title to real property to another is defined as:

(A) Proration.
(B) Alienation.
(C) Prescription.
(D) Consideration.

9. The right of ownership, including the right to use, possesses, enjoy and dispose of a thing:

(A) Corporeal ownership.
(B) Incorporeal ownership.
(C) Survivorship.
(D) Bundle of rights.

10. All of the following are tests to determine whether personal property becomes a fixture, except:

(A) Cost of the item.
(B) Intent of the person placing the item.
(C) Manner of annexation.
(D) Nature of use or adaptation.

11. Personal property is conveyed using:

(A) A bill of sale.
(B) A deed.
(C) An encumbrance.
(D) A partial release for blanket encumbrances.

12. Which of the following is correct?

(A) Property is either real or personal.
(B) A fixture is personal property.
(C) A trade fixture is real property.
(D) Only the surface element of land is real property.

13. The three tests of annexation, adaption, and intention enable one to determine if an item is:

   (A) Littoral property.
   (B) An emblements.
   (C) A fixture.
   (D) An encumbrance.

14. Rights in personal property are called:

   (A) Estates.
   (B) Common estates.
   (C) Fee simple estates.
   (D) Chattel interests.

15. All of the following are factors generally applied when determining whether an item of personal property has become real property, except:

   (A) Cost of the article.
   (B) Permanence of annexation.
   (C) Agreement of the parties.
   (D) Relationship between the parties.

16. Which of the following is not an appurtenance?

   (A) A fence.
   (B) A barn.
   (C) An orchard.
   (D) A trade fixture.

17. In law, a trade fixture is:

   (A) Real property.
   (B) Personal property.
   (C) An easement.
   (D) Both real and personal property.

18. The word emblements means:

   (A) Improvements to buildings.
   (B) Farm machinery.
   (C) Additional provision in a contract.
   (D) Annual crops.

19. Smith owned 40 acres of land on which he grew potatoes. He sold the crop of potatoes to Williams who agreed to harvest the potatoes. Before the potatoes were harvested, Smith sold his land to Jones and the deed was recorded. The crops belong to:

   (A) Smith.
   (B) Jones.
   (C) Williams.
   (D) Williams and Jones in joint tenancy.

20. Which of the following are an encumbrance, but not a lien?

   (A) Mortgage.
   (B) Deed restriction.
   (C) Trust deed.
   (D) Property taxes.

LAND DESCRIPTION QUIZ

1. Land sells for $1,200 an acre. What is the price of the E 1/2 of the NE ¼ of the SW ¼ of Section 10?

   (A) $9,000.
   (B) $12,000.
   (C) $24,000.
   (D) $48,000.

2. A land parcel measures 220 yards by 220 yards contains?

   (A) 1.1 acres.
   (B) 5.0 acres.
   (C) 10.0 acres.
   (D) 302.5 acres.

3. If a quarter section of land is divided into four equal parcels, each parcel would contain:

   (A) 10 acres.
   (B) 30 acres.
   (C) 40 acres.
   (D) 60 acres.

4. Which of the following is larger than a standard section?

   (A) 16 parcels, 40 acres each.
   (B) 5,000 feet by 6,000 feet.
   (C) 1/36th of a township.
   (D) 5,280 feet by 5,280 feet.

5. Which of the following contains the smallest parcel of land?

   (A) 640 acres.
   (B) 9 square miles.
   (C) ½ of a section.
   (D) 36 sections.

6. A normal size section in the Government Rectangular Survey System contains:

   (A) 160 acres.
   (B) One square mile.
   (C) Six square miles.
   (D) 36 square miles.

7. All of the following are types of property descriptions, except:

   (A) Lot and block.
   (B) Allodial system.
   (C) Metes and bounds.
   (D) Rectangular survey.

8. The legal description method that uses angles, terminal points, and established lines the:

   (A) Government survey.
   (B) Metes and bounds description.
   (C) Lot and block.
   (D) Allodial system.

9. What would the section number be of the section directly south of section 16?

   (A) 15.
   (B) 17.
   (C) 21.
   (D) 22.

10. What are the east west rows of townships called?

   (A) Ranges.
   (B) Tiers.
   (C) Sections.
   (D) Parallel.

CHAPTER 2 - OWNERSHIP, ESTATES, RIGHTS AND INTERESTS

Types of Ownership

There are several types of ownership interests a person may have in a particular piece of property. Those include estates and encumbrances. Estates are interests in land. However, there are land interests that may not be estates. Generally, estates have two categories, freehold and non-freehold.

Freehold Estates

Freehold estates are measured by their duration, use and possession. *Estates* refer to the ownership interest a person has in a specific property. Freehold estates are defined as estates where land is inherited or held forever. Estates are described as if they were in layers or hierarchies. The highest and best estate is the fee simple absolute. Some authors attempt to make a distinction between fee and fee simple. However, in this text we will consider fee and fee simple to be synonymous. Remember that there can be non-possessory estates such as a lien.

Bundle of Rights

Use of an estate is usually called a "bundle of rights," with the preeminent right being "the right to use." Other rights included in this bundle are the right to own, sell, enjoy, and the right to do nothing at all.

Fee Simple Estates

A fee or fee simple estate lasts forever and features the maximum control of use.

Fee Simple Defeasible

Fee simple defeasible is a lesser estate than fee simple because defeasible means there is something in the present owner's title that can be defeated in the estate. A determinable fee lasts "so long " as any condition is met.

Life Estate

An even lesser estate is the life estate. This estate lasts the entire life of the *"life tenant"*. While the life tenant has lifetime ownership and use, the original grantor has *reversionary interest*. This means that upon the death of a life estate owner, title will revert back to the person giving the life estate. Since the holder of the life estate may out live the original grantor, the grantor will usually name a *remainder man* or third person. A remainderman holds a remainder estate and gets a fee simple estate when a life tenant dies.

Profits

Life tenants have the same rights as the fee simple owners. These include the right to profits or rents and the right to lease or mortgage the property. Life tenants have the same duties as fee owners. An example of profits would be removal of coal, timber etc. They must pay taxes, assessments and liens. In addition, there are other duties for life tenants since there is a remainderman (third person) who has future promissory interest in the property.

Waste

Life tenants must not commit waste. This means life tenants can't engage in acts that permanently damage the property, or harm the interest of the reversionary, or remainder estates. However, these factors cease upon the death of any life tenancy.

Severalty

Ownership in severalty is the condition where *one person owns property solely and separately* or one entity such as a corporation owns property.

TYPES OF OWNERSHIP

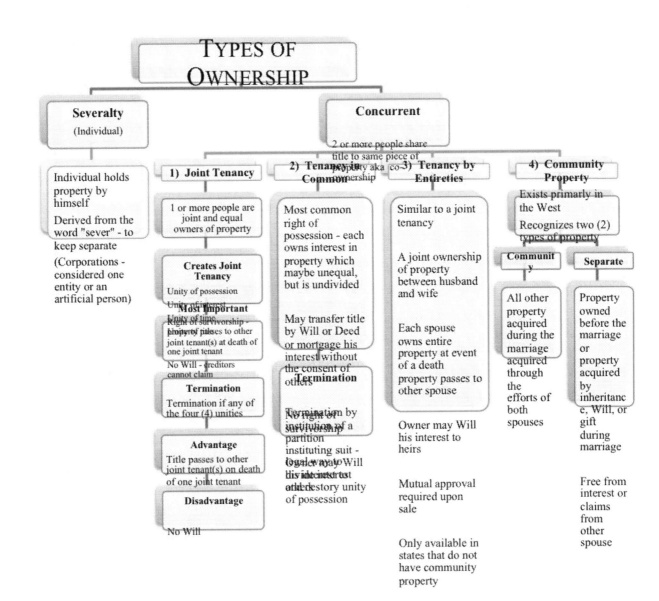

Severalty
(Individual)

Concurrent

2 or more people share title to same piece of property aka co-ownership

Individual holds property by himself

Derived from the word "sever" - to keep separate

(Corporations - considered one entity or an artificial person)

1) Joint Tenancy

1 or more people are joint and equal owners of property

Creates Joint Tenancy

Unity of possession
Unity of interest
Unity of time
Unity of title

Most Important

Right of survivorship - property passes to other joint tenant(s) at death of one joint tenant

No Will - creditors cannot claim

Termination

Termination if any of the four (4) unities

Advantage

Title passes to other joint tenant(s) on death of one joint tenant

Disadvantage

No Will

2) Tenancy in Common

Most common right of possession - each owns interest in property which maybe unequal, but is undivided

May transfer title by Will or Deed or mortgage his interest without the consent of others

Termination

No right of survivorship

Termination by institution of a partition instituting suit - legal way to divide interest

May Will his interest to others

Statutory unity of possession

3) Tenancy by Entireties

Similar to a joint tenancy

A joint ownership of property between husband and wife

Each spouse owns entire property at event of a death property passes to other spouse

Owner may Will his interest to heirs

Mutual approval required upon sale

Only available in states that do not have community property

4) Community Property

Exists primarily in the West

Recognizes two (2) types of property

Community

All other property acquired during the marriage acquired through the efforts of both spouses

Separate

Property owned before the marriage or property acquired by inheritance, Will, or gift during marriage

Free from interest or claims from other spouse

Concurrent Ownership

Concurrent ownership is the opposite condition of single ownership in severalty. Concurrent ownership occurs when more than one party owns real estate.

Tenancy in Common

Tenancy in common is the most typical way to take concurrent title to a property where each owner having an undivided fractional share without right of survivorship. After the death of an owner all interests will pass to heirs or *devisees*. A devisee is a person or entity that inherits real estate under the terms of a will. If no form of ownership is indicated, law presumes tenancy in common. Ownership shares don't have to be equal. Should a divorce occur for one owner, ownership can be terminated and the divorced-owner share of the property can be legally divided by *partition suit.*

Joint Tenancy

Joint tenancy is co-ownership with the *right of survivorship.* This allows the interest, of any concurrent owner, who dies, to pass to co-owners without the delay of probate. *This signifies that the heirs of the deceased owner do not have any interest in the property.*

Four Unities

Joint tenancy must have four unities at the time the property is purchased. Those include

- Possession,
- Interest,
- Time, and
- Title

If any one of the four unities *do not exist at the time of purchase*, the joint tenancy ownership automatically becomes tenancy in common.

Tenancy by the Entireties

Tenancy by the entirety applies exclusively to married couples in some states that do not have community property. Tenancies of the Entireties spouses have the right of survivorship.

Community Property

Community (marital) property is any property acquired during the marriage. The husband and wife are equal partners in this property. Property acquired before the marriage, and during marriage through gift or inheritance is sole and separate property. Written agreements can also signify sole and separate property.

COMMON FORMS OF CO-OWNERSHIP AND THEIR CHARACTERISTICS

Parties	Joint Tenancy	Tenancy in Common	Community Property
	Any number of persons – including husband and wife.	Any number of persons – including husband and wife.	Husband and wife only.
Ownership Interest/ Possession	Equal ownership interest. Equal right of possession of whole property. Key characteristic is right of survivorship.	Equal right to possession, an undivided share in whole property. No right of survivorship.	Ownership is equal.
Creation	Must be created on purpose, right of survivorship must be specifically stated. Must have four unities for creation. Not favored by law.	May be created on purpose or by accident, such as where parties fail to legally create a joint tenancy. Favored by law, except in community property states as between husband and wife.	Presumption that all property acquired after marriage is community property.
Title	One title for the whole property.	Title is separate in each individual tenant in common.	Title is in community, although each spouse has a separate interest in the property.
Conveyance	Conveyance will destroy joint tenancy if made by one without other tenants. Purchaser becomes tenant in common with other co-owners.	Each tenant may convey his own separate interest. Purchaser is tenant in common with other co-owners.	Both husband and wife must convey, neither may convey their separate interest. Purchaser must take title to whole property, cannot hold as community property with co-owner.
Termination	Conveyance by one without other tenants will destroy the four unities and terminate joint tenancy.	Conveyance does not terminate tenancy in common.	One spouse cannot convey title alone. Property held as tenants in common after divorce.

Effect of Death	Upon death of joint tenant, interest passes to surviving tenant. Heirs of deceased have no interest in property.	Tenant's interest passes to heirs as tenants in common. No right of survivorship.	One-half interest goes to surviving spouse, one-half passes by devise or intestate succession. If interest passes by will, they devise and surviving spouse are tenants in common.
Creditors	Co-owner's interest may be executed upon to satisfy his creditors, who take interest as tenants in common.	Co-owner's interest may be executed upon creditor takes as tenant in common.	Property may be sold at execution safe to satisfy community debts.

Other Types of Concurrent Ownership

Syndication

Another type of concurrent ownership is syndication. Syndication is used to purchase raw land by a group of owners. A syndication can be a general partnership. This is an association where all partners who participate in business operations may be held personally liable for business losses and obligations.

Limited Partnership

Sometimes a limited partnership or limited liability partnership (LLP) includes general partners who may be held liable for losses, while the investors, are liable only to the extent of their investment.

Joint Venture

A joint venture is a general partnership for a project, corporation, or limited liability company that is formed for investment purposes. The number of investors in a joint venture determines whether it requires a securities license and is governed by the Securities and Exchange Commission (SEC) at the federal level and the Blue Sky Laws at the local level.

Encumbrances

An encumbrance is an interest or right other than the owner of record-on the title of a property. *An encumbrance can be financial or non-financial.* For example, the titleholder may have taken a loan out on the property that appears as an encumbrance in the recorders office. If the titleholder tries to sell the property, the records would indicate the encumbrance (lien) and the lender would require payment to remove the lien.

Voluntary Liens or Encumbrances

A voluntary lien occurs with the consent of the property holder. This would be a lien that has resulted from a new loan, etc. In such an instance, the lender is said to have a *security interest* in the property.

Involuntary Encumbrances or Liens Taxes

Taxes imposed on the titleholder are considered to be an *involuntary lien* because they are the result of laws and titleholders do not have to agree or consent to the encumbrance or lien. Liens can be specific to a particular property or can be general in nature and apply to all of the individual's assets. The Internal Revenue Service can impose a general lien on all of the individual's assets.

The lien itself doesn't prevent the titleholder from selling a property. But the titleholder must have the lien paid before the titleholder can receive money from the sales transaction.

Clouds on the Title

Clouds on titles are things that may impair or lessen an owner's rights. For example, sometimes a name change has occurred. But at time of sale, the title of property reflects a former name. To solve this problem, it is necessary to file a *quitclaim deed* showing the change. Once this is done the cloud on the title is removed.

Encroachments

An encroachment is the unauthorized use of another person's land that is usually proven by survey and which title insurance or attorney's opinion may not protect. Most properties have set back requirements, and are there to insure that the titleholders don't build anything within the setback area, where most encroachment problems occur.

License

A license is a revocable permission to use the real property of another without creating an estate in land, i.e. a movie ticket.

Easements

An easement is a right to use the land of another for a specific purpose. Most easements have a dominant tenement and a survient tenement. For example, a landlocked titleholder, (dominant tenement) must have access to the nearest roadway even if it requires going through another's property, (survient tenement). The easement should appear on the servient tenement's title.

Easement in Gross

An easement in gross has no dominant tenement, only servient tenement (e.g. utility easement).

Any easement can cease to exist when a merger, release, or abandonment terminates it.

CC& R's – Covenants, Conditions, and Restrictions

Condominium or townhouse homeowner's association can record a specific lien to collect monies owed the association for dues and/or fines. Deed restrictions, restrictive covenants, subdivision deed restrictions, condominium bylaws or CCRs, are privately created limitations on land use. They are designed to protect property values and the interests of property owners.

Other Liens

There are other liens that attach to and are binding on property to secure debt repayment. For example a property tax or special assessment is a specific lien that takes priority over all other liens, even those previously recorded. Mechanics and material mans liens are involuntary specific lien that may be filed by subcontractors to collect money due them for work that has been completed.

Court Action - Lis Pendens

Lis pendens is a recorded document that gives constructive notice of a pending lawsuit.

A winner of a court case may file a judgment, which is a general lien against the loser.

Non-Freehold Estates – Leasehold Estates

A non-freehold or less than freehold estate, is a leasehold estate, usually some type of rental agreement.

Tenancy for Years

An estate/tenancy for years is a leasehold estate of a predetermined termination date or definite period. Remember, there can be a lease that extends for less than one year and still be an estate for years. For example, a three-month lease with a specific start and end date meets the definition of an estate for years.

Periodic Tenancy

Periodic estate/tenancy continues from period to period, such as month-to-month. This lease exists until proper notice is given, and the rental agreement renews under the same conditions and terms upon payment of rent.

Estate at Will

An estate at will and an estate at sufferance are situations where the actual lease term has expired and is no longer paying the required rent.

A tenancy at will continues for an indefinite duration, assuming that rents continue to be paid, after the lease has expired at the owner's consent. In this instance a commercial lease may have certain penalties if the tenant doesn't renegotiate a lease extension.

Estate at Sufferance

An estate/tenancy at sufferance is a "holdover tenant" who stays beyond termination and is about to be evicted, but is not a trespass.

Chapter - 3 – Police Powers - Public and private land use controls

Learning Objectives

Public control – governmental powers
Police power, eminent domain, taxation, escheat
Zoning ordinances
Private controls, restrictions, and encroachments
Covenants, conditions, and restrictions
Easements

There are three powers of government that restrict a private property owner's rights:

1. Police powers
2. Eminent domain
3. Taxation

Police Powers

Police Powers are those powers granted to individual states to adopt and enforce laws and regulations required to protect the public health, safety and general welfare. States often delegate these powers to local governments. Specifically, police powers allow governments to regulate the use of a titleholder's property.

Police Powers also include the enactment and enforcement of laws governing land use to promote and support the public safety, health, morals, and general welfare. These include zoning, building codes, and subdivisions.

Planning

State laws require that local government agencies prepare and adopt a comprehensive master plan into a community's intentions, aspirations, and interests.

Local governments have the primary responsibility to implement and administer comprehensive plans. Tools used to implement a master plan include zoning codes, subdivision ordinances, design reviews, building codes, environmental programs, and capital improvements plans and budgets.

Master Plan

The purpose of the master plan defines community's intentions, aspirations, and interests. It also serves as a framework for more specific planning, a decision making guide for local officials. The plan is comprehensive because it addresses a host of inter-related topics pertaining to local government agencies.

Zoning

Planning and zoning usually follow a local government's master plan that may be developed by the city or county planning agency. This is done in conjunction with community input, and approved by a local governing council or commission.

Zoning ordinances are local government requirements that control land use. The zoning regulation should outline the purposes, and intensity requirements for the various zoning base districts. These local laws may divide the community into user classifications by density such as:

R-E - Rural Estates, Residential District
R-1 - Single Family Residential District
R-T - Manufactured Home Residential District
R-2 - Medium Density Residential District
RUD - Residential Urban District
R-3 - Multi-Family Residential District
R-4 - Multi-Family Residential District (High Density)
R-5 - Apartment Residential District
CRT - Commercial Residential Transitional District
C-P - Office and Professional District
C-1 - Local Business District
C-2 - General Commercial District
MD - Designed Manufacturing and Industrial District
M-1 - Light Manufacturing District
M-2 - Industrial District
U-V - Urban Village (Mixed Use) District
H-1 - Limited Resort and Apartment District

Zoning Exceptions

Nonconforming Use

When local governments adopt new zoning regulations, there will be some areas in the new zone that do not meet the new requirements. It would not be fair to expect property owners to change their property to conform to the new use. The result is that these non-conforming properties are allowed to remain in their present state and are "grandfathered in" as a non-conforming use. It is likely that certain restrictions will be placed on these properties if the titleholders attempt to make any improvements to the property.

Variance

The variance allows individual owners to vary or deviate from the master plan in order to prevent economic hardship. Certain conditions must exist before a variance is granted. For example, the need for the change should not be to increase the economic development of the property. Rather, the property owner must show a hardship where the zoning regulations restrict the intended use of the property. A variance permits the owner to build a building or conduct a use otherwise not permitted. A common example is a patio cover that infringes on a property's side set back requirement.

Conditional Use

The conditional use is a special use necessary for the community welfare that may not be allowed within the zoning requirements. Conditional use permits are used for cemeteries, schools, hospitals, churches, etc. Conditional use permits do not require a hardship situation such as a variance.

Rezone or Zoning Amendment

Property owners may recognize that the present use of their property is improper. Hence, they may petition local governing agencies for a rezone. This is sometimes referred to as a zoning amendment. Proper notice should be given to surrounding property owners about the proposed zone change. Up zoning is the usual request for most property owners seeking a zone change. Up zoning is a zone change from less dense to more dense usage. There may be occasions where the property owner requests a zone change from dense to less dense usage. This is called a down zoning.

Eminent Domain

Eminent domain is the government's right to take private land for public use.

Police power is not the power of eminent domain. Eminent domain takes private property for governmental use. Police power only denies some use or uses of private property to its owner. Eminent domain is exercised because property is useful to the public. Police power is exercised because some use of private property is harmful to the public.

Condemnation

Condemnation is the process governments use to seize the land. Compensation should be fair and is usually based on the appraised value of the property plus damages. The Taking Clause of the Fifth Amendment to the U.S. Constitution specifies that that the government may take private property for public use so long as the government pays the private owner just compensation

Inverse Condemnation

Inverse condemnation is when the owner initiates court action to seek fair compensation from the government when the owner's property has been substantially interfered with.

Taxation

There are two types of real estate property taxes:

1. General real estate taxes based on the value of the property called *ad valoreum taxes*.
2. *Special assessments* that benefit a particular parcel of land also called improvement districts.

General Real Estate Taxes

General real estate taxes are also called *ad valorem taxes* "Ad valorem" is a Latin term meaning according to value. Ad valorem taxes are levied on individual property owners. The total tax paid on the property is determined by the property value. The appraised value of the property is determined by the market value method or replacement cost method. State regulation usually determines the method of appraisal.

The governmental authority may have a number of taxing districts within the general tax. These districts may include tax rates that result in tax income for libraries, fire departments, local schools, etc.

Assessed Value

The process of determining general real estate taxes is the taxing district uses mathematical methods to determine tax charges. This involves, multiplying the *appraised value* by an *assessment percentage* to arrive at the *assessed value*.

Mills

Then the assessed value is multiplied by the tax rate. In some cases the assessed value is multiplied by some *"millage value."* A mill is one tenth of a penny or one-one thousandth of a dollar. Millage is defined as the tax rate, for real property, assessed in mills per dollar. Most people do not have a clue as to how a can real estate tax system works.

General real estate taxes automatically become a specific involuntary lien on the owner's property. Payment of the tax releases the lien from the property. General real estate taxes usually have priority over most liens that have been recorded prior to the recording of the tax lien.

Tax Foreclosure

The taxing authority has the power of foreclosure. This is similar to mortgage foreclosure, but the time period is usually much longer. For example, let's assume property taxes have not been paid for some time, say three years. The taxing authority then puts the property in a taxing authority's name, such as the county treasurer. The county treasurer auctions the property. The auctions are usually held annually on a specific date. The list of the properties to be auctioned is published in a local newspaper for a specific time period. That can extend for several weeks. When it expires, the property is auctioned at a public auction held by the local governing authority. Each property will probably have a minimum bid consisting of all delinquent taxes, penalties, interest and costs.

Redemption Period

In most cases, there is a *redemption period*, (two years), where the previous owner may protest the sale. During the redemption period the previous owner may come up with the balance owed plus any fees and take back his property. t

Escheat

Escheat is the government's reversionary right on abandoned property or property of intestate owners with no heirs. Property ownership reverts to the government.

Special Assessments or Improvement Districts

The second type of taxation power that local governments have is to levy special assessments or improvement districts. Special assessments are improvement taxes used to pay for improvements that benefit a specific property. Examples of such improvements include installation of sewers, street improvements, etc. The special improvement district tax is a specific involuntary lien.

IRS Liens

The federal income tax is considered a personal property tax since income is personal property. The unpaid income taxes can become a lien on real property. However, income tax liens have no special priority, and upon any sale of property, the IRS liens are paid according to their recorded priority.

Environmental Hazards and Regulations

An *Environmental Impact Statement (EIS)* is a report that assesses the probable impact of a proposed project on the environment. An EIS is required by federal agencies in advance of any major government actions such as new highway or bridge construction.

Lead Based Paint

Federal government regulations require owners of most housing built before 1978 to provide information regarding lead based paint usage in their buildings to all prospective buyers and/or renters. 1978 is the year use of lead based paint in residential housing was phased out. Note that foreclosure sales of studio apartments, and property that has been tested and found to be free of lead based paint are exempted from these regulations. For all other property, owners must comply with the following four requirements:

1. Provide buyers and lessees with a specific federally approved lead based paint information pamphlet.

2. Disclose the presence of any known lead based paint hazards in the housing. Hazards include lead-based paint, contaminated soil, and lead in household dust.

3. Provide buyers and lessees with any available records or reports pertaining to the presence of lead based paint or hazards.

4. Provide buyers with a 10-day opportunity to conduct a risk assessment or inspection before the buyers are obligated under any purchase contract.

Lead-Based Paint Renovation, Repair and Painting Program

As of April 22, 2010 Lead Based Paint Renovation, Repair and Painting Program is intended to make home renovation safer by ensuring that lead-based paint is contained and cleaned up so as to minimize exposure. Renovation is broadly defined as any activity that disturbs painted surfaces and includes most repair, remodeling, and maintenance activities, including window replacement.

Radon Gas

Radon gas is an odorless radioactive gas that enters through cracks in the basements and/or foundations. Studies indicate the gas is the second leading cause of lung cancer, in the United State causing more than 15,000 deaths each year. One of every fifteen homes in this county is found to contain greater than 4 pico curies per liter, a radon level the U.S. Environmental Protection Agency (EPA) considers dangerous. The EPA has determined that the results of radon testing are not required to be disclosed in real estate transactions.

Asbestos

Asbestos is a material used for many years in the insulation process. When disturbed, asbestos dust is considered extremely dangerous and life threatening.

Water

Groundwater contaminants come from several sources, common pesticides used on farms, leaks from underground storage tanks (gas and oil), septic tanks and waste disposal sites. *Prior appropriation* is a concept that gives states the right to use water for more than limited domestic use. This power rests with the states and not adjacent landowners. Certain states rely on the doctrine of prior appropriation. Prior appropriation simply means that the first owner has the power to determine the water usage allocated to the property.

48

Private Controls

Private controls for real estate use are the most common land use restrictions. Private controls are often called proprietary controls because they use traditional property law devices such as deed restrictions, restrictive convents, and easements to restrict land use.

Deed Restriction

A deed restriction places limits on the use and conveyance of land. Deed restrictions generally include traditional proprietary controls such as restrictive covenants and easements. Although deed restrictions operate like traditional property law devices, the term "deed restriction" has no clear meaning in traditional property law.

Restrictive Covenants

A restrictive covenant is a traditional provision in a deed that limits and prohibits certain property uses. For example; landowners may promise or "covenant" not to develop residential housing on their properties but use it for industrial purposes only. Restrictive covenants are a form of private control.

Common Elements

Common elements in a condominium include those portions of the property not owned individually by unit owners, but in which an indivisible interest is held by all unit owners, Common elements generally include the grounds, parking areas, recreational facilities, and external structure of the building.

For example, in a condominium building, each resident unit owner owns the interior space within that unit. The remainder of the building site is common elements enjoyed by each resident according the condominium bylaws. The common elements are maintained by the owners' association, to which each owner pays a fee.

Reversionary Interests

Reversionary interests restrict the owner to uses that are compatible with intended future uses of the site. If the current property owner violates the land use restrictions, ownership of the site reverts to the previous owner. Reversionary interests are a form of private control.

Easement

An easement is a right granted to use a part of his land for a specific purpose to another property owner. The holder of the easement can access the property detailed in the easement or preclude certain uses to it. An easement is a form of private control.

Easement Appurtenant

An easement appurtenant is one that benefits a parcel of land and burdens another. The parcel with the benefit is called the *dominant tenement;* the parcel with the burden is called *the servient tenement.* Probably the most common example of an easement appurtenant is a driveway easement that provides access across one parcel of land to another. An easement appurtenant passes with the sale of the land, and the new owner becomes the dominant or servient tenement, whichever the case may be.

Easement in Gross

An easement in gross benefits a person rather than a parcel of land. Most easements in gross are commercial in nature such as the power company's right to install and service its lines.

Easement by Prescription

An easement by prescription is created when there is long and continued use of land without the landowner's permission.

Consent Decrees

Consent degrees are legal agreements between regulatory agencies and private parties in which private parties agree to do – or refrain from doing certain activities. Once entered, a consent decree is binding on the consenting parties and cannot be reviewed except on a showing that the consent was obtained by fraud or that the decree was based on mutual error or a failure of consent. Consent decrees are used most commonly in criminal law and family law, and sometimes in United States antitrust law.

Police Powers Quiz

1. When legal private restrictions on building uses conflict with the public restrictions _____ will prevail. The words to complete the above sentence are

   (A) The legal private
   (B) The less stringent
   (C) The public
   (D) The more stringent

2. Required zoning set backs are 10 feet from the edge of a building to the lot line. If approval were to be obtained to build to seven feet from the lot line, it would be called a

   (A) Nonconforming use
   (B) Spot zone approval
   (C) Variance
   (D) Conditional use permit

3. A zoning ordinance is

   (A) A restriction
   (B) An easement
   (C) A lien
   (D) A reservation

4. An area of land set off by a local ordinance for specific use is called

   (A) Subdivision
   (B) Zone
   (C) Public improvement
   (D) Cul-de-sac

5. Buildings which are erected before the enactment of a zoning ordinance and do not comply with zoning limitations are called

   (A) Nonconforming uses
   (B) Outlawed classifications
   (C) Dilapidated structures
   (D) Depreciated improvements

6. Zoning ordinances control the use of private land through several kinds of restrictions. Which of the following is not a zoning restriction?

   (A) Building height limitations
   (B) Nonconforming uses
   (C) Setback requirements for buildings
   (D) Designation of land area which building may occupy

7. Who normally puts deed restrictions on property in a subdivision?

   (A) The developer
   (B) The Real Estate Agency
   (C) The purchaser
   (D) The local planning board

8. Deed restrictions are considered to be

   (A) Encumbrances
   (B) General liens
   (C) Constrictive notice
   (D) Enforceable only by the property's owners

9. Restrictive covenants that run with the land

   (A) Expire when the property is sold
   (B) Are enforceable only against past owner
   (C) Apply only to the first owner of the property
   (D) Are applicable to all owners of the property

10. Restrictions on property owners in a subdivision development are sometimes called

   (A) Covenants
   (B) Encroachments
   (C) Easements appurtenant
   (D) Zoning constraints

11. Deed restrictions are created by

   (A) Covenants
   (B) Encroachments
   (C) Easement appurtenant
   (D) Zoning constraints

12. A customary procedure to enforce deed restrictions on real property is

   (A) Equitable estoppel
   (B) A writ of mandamus
   (C) An injunction
   (D) A writ of execution

13. A community planning board is established to

   (A) Stimulate wider interest in community problems
   (B) Coordinate civic developments
   (C) Stabilize property values and city growth
   (D) Do all of the above

14. In a subdivision the units of land are referred to as

    (A) Sections
    (B) Parcels
    (C) Lots
    (D) Partitions

15. A man owning an acre of ground with five rental houses on it decides to divide the property and sell the houses to the tenants. He must

    (A) File a subdivision plat
    (B) Have a real estate license
    (C) Pay a fine to the real estate commissioner
    (D) Do nothing

16. A public report, when it is required, must be given to the purchaser of a lot prior to

    (A) Negotiation of the sale
    (B) Execution of the binding sale agreement
    (C) Closing
    (D) Viewing the property

17. Condominiums may be

    (A) Residential property
    (B) Resort property
    (C) Industrial property
    (D) All of the above

18. The term "common elements" are most often associated with what type of real estate?

    (A) Condominiums
    (B) Cooperative
    (C) Corporate headquarters
    (D) Leasehold estates

19. Johnson bought, for his use, an apartment in a large building and received a deed conveying to him a fee simple estate and also a tax bill on his ownership. His apartment ownership is called a

    (A) Real estate investment trust
    (B) Cooperative
    (C) Corporation
    (D) Condominium

20. A person who owns a fee title to air space within a residential, industrial, or commercial building   together with an undivided interest in common in the common areas usually has an interest in an

    (A) Community apartment project
    (B) Planned development project
    (C) Condominium project
    (D) Stock cooperative project

CHAPTER - 4 – DEEDS – TRANSFER OF TITLE

Learning Objectives

- Title Insurance
    - What is Insured Against
    - Title Searches/Title Abstracts/Chain of Title
    - Cloud on Title/ Suit to Quiet Title
- Conveyances After Death
    - Types of Wills
    - Testate vs. intestate Succession
- Deeds
    - Purpose of Deed, when Title Passes
    - Types of Deeds (General Warranty, Special Warranty, Quitclaim) and when used
    - Essential Elements of a Deed
    - Importance of Recording
- Escrow or Closing
    - Responsibilities of Escrow Agent
    - Prorated Items
    - Closing Statements/HUD-1
    - Estimated Closing Costs
- Foreclosure, Short Sales
- Tax Aspects of Transferring Title to Real Property

Topics included in this category are title insurance, deeds, settlement procedures, and tax aspects of real estate transactions. In addition, brokers will be asked questions about legal vs. equitable title and special processes involved in probate and foreclosure.

Title Insurance

The most effective way to protect title, and the method that is used almost universally is to obtain a policy of title insurance.

Title insurance is a contract whereby the title insurance company agrees to reimburse the policyholder for any losses, which is caused by defects in the title, except for those certain defects, which are specified in the policy. The title insurance company will also provide the legal defense for any claims based on defects, which are covered by the policy. Both the buyer and the seller of the property are required purchase title insurance. Presently both buyer and seller are required to purchase in order for the escrow company to close escrow. The responsibility for paying for the policy is usually defined in the contract of sale.

The procedure for obtaining title insurance involves two steps:

1. First the owner or buyer pays a fee to the title company to cover the costs of the title search. Most title companies have their own set of records called title *plat*s so they do not have to bother searching the files in the recorder's office. After the title search is completed the title company issues a report as to the condition of the title. This report is called the *preliminary title report* and it lists all defect and encumbrances. The listed items will be excluded from the policy.

2. If the owner is satisfied with the report he will purchase a policy of insurance by paying the required premium. One payment covers the entire life of the policy.

There are two basic forms of title insurance *standard coverage and extended coverage.*

Owners of residential property normally use standard coverage. It protects against defects in the chain of title such as forged deeds, incompetent grantors and improperly delivered deeds.

Lending institutions that give mortgages on land prefers the extended coverage title policy. This policy provides the same coverage as the standard policy; buy also covers any defects that could be discovered by an *inspection and survey* of the property. Examples of such defects are adverse possessors and erroneous property description.

Alienation

The process of transferring real property is called alienation. Alienation may be voluntary or involuntary. Voluntary alienation is done mostly by deed, but can be done by a patent, or will. Involuntary alienation is done by rules of law, or adverse possession.

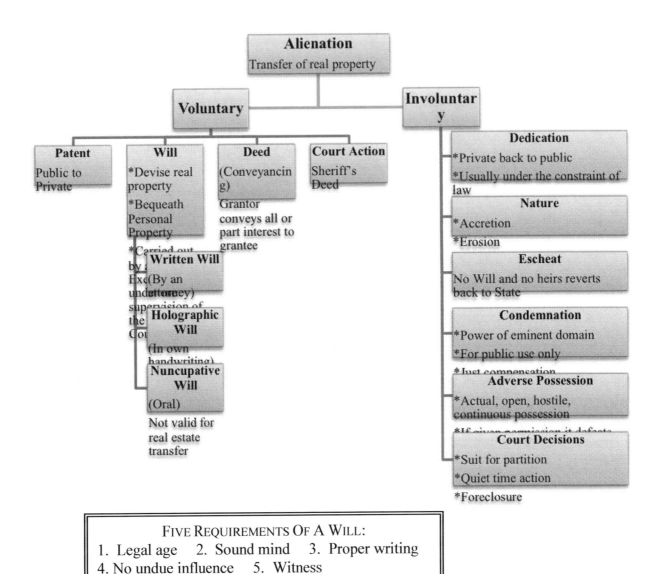

Alienation
Transfer of real property

Voluntary

Involuntary

Patent
Public to Private

Will
*Devise real property
*Bequeath Personal Property
*Carried out by Executor under supervision of the Court

Deed
(Conveyancing)
Grantor conveys all or part interest to grantee

Court Action
Sheriff's Deed

Written Will
(By an attorney)

Holographic Will
(In own handwriting)

Nuncupative Will
(Oral)
Not valid for real estate transfer

Dedication
*Private back to public
*Usually under the constraint of law

Nature
*Accretion
*Erosion

Escheat
No Will and no heirs reverts back to State

Condemnation
*Power of eminent domain
*For public use only
*Just compensation

Adverse Possession
*Actual, open, hostile, continuous possession
*If given permission it defeats

Court Decisions
*Suit for partition
*Quiet time action
*Foreclosure

FIVE REQUIREMENTS OF A WILL:
1. Legal age   2. Sound mind   3. Proper writing
4. No undue influence   5. Witness

The Deed

The most common form of alienation is the deed. The deed is a document that conveys, (demises); the grantor may hold whatever interest, unless it specifically states that it is conveying a lesser interest. The major difference between types of deeds lies in the extent of the promises given by the grantor to the grantee.

Types of Deeds

There are many types of deeds used in private grants, (voluntary alienation), but the ones used most often are the warranty deed, special warranty deed, quitclaim deed, grant bargain and sale deed, grant deed, trustee's deed and the deed executed under court order.

Warranty Deed

Warranty deed is used in most states, and is the best for the grantee because the seller guarantees the title. The warranty deed has 5 basic covenants.

1. Covenant of seisen - grantor has right to convey.
2. Covenant of quiet enjoyment– grantee will not be "disturbed" by others.
3. Covenant against encumbrances – no unspecified encumbrances.
4. Covenant of further assurance - cooperation in signing additional documents.
5. Warranty forever– guarantee of defense.

A limited warranty deed guarantees related only to grantor's period of ownership.

A copy of a basic warranty deed follows on the next page.

Warranty Deed

[list name of person conveying the property], an individual with an address of **[list address of grantor]**, being married, ("Grantor"), in consideration of $**[e.g. 100,000.00]** and other good and valuable consideration to Grantor paid, the receipt of which is acknowledged, does hereby grant, bargain, sell, convey and warrant to **[list name of person receiving property]**, an individual with an address of **[list address of grantee]**, ("Grantee"), all the following real estate:

[enter the exact legal description].

Subject to: [list encumbrances the property will be subject to, e.g. mortgages, easements, etc.].

Subject to real estate taxes and assessments for the current year and subsequent years.

Subject to all valid easements, rights of way, covenants, conditions, reservations and restrictions of record, if any, and also to applicable zoning, land use and other laws and regulations.

To have and to hold the same, together with all the buildings, improvements and appurtenances belonging thereto, if any, to the Grantee and Grantee's heirs, successors and assigns forever.

Grantor, for Grantor and Grantor's heirs and successors, covenants with Grantee and Grantee's heirs, successors and assigns, that:

1. Grantor is lawfully seized in fee simple of the above property, and has good right to convey the same;

2. The above property is free from all encumbrances, except as set forth above;

3. Grantee shall quietly enjoy the above property; and

4. Grantor will forever warrant and defend the title to the above property against the lawful claims and demands of all persons.

This property was acquired by the Grantor by: [statement explaining how grantor acquired the property].

I, [list name of grantor's spouse], of [list address of grantor's spouse], spouse of [list name of person conveying the property], in consideration of the above sum and other good and valuable consideration received, do hereby waive and release to Grantee all rights of dower, curtesy, homestead, community property, and all other right, title and interest, if any, in and to the above property.

IN WITNESS WHEREOF, this Warranty Deed is executed under seal on this **[day]** day of **[month]**, **[year]**.

Signed, sealed and delivered in the presence of:

WITNESS   GRANTOR

_____   _____ (Seal)

[witness]   **[grantor]**

WITNESS   GRANTOR'S SPOUSE

_____   _____ (Seal)

[witness]   **[spouse, if applicable]**

Notarized, Delivered, and Accepted

Notary publics are commissioned in their counties of residence. After receiving and approving an applicant for a notary public commission, the Secretary of State forwards the commission, the original oath of office and the signature of the notary public to the appropriate county clerk. The county clerk maintains a record of the commission and signature. The public may then access this record and verify the "official" signature of the notary at the county clerk's office.

Upon request, county clerks will authenticate the signature of the notary on a document and will attest to the notary's authority to sign.

Most people assume that when a real estate deed is signed, it is effective. However, there is one more essential part of the process. Even if a deed is properly executed, *it is not effective until it has been delivered to and accepted by the buyer.*

Until the deed is delivered, the title remains with the seller, who could change his mind at any time and destroy the deed. But once the deed has been properly delivered and accepted, the title passes and cannot be revoked. Thus the old, old saying: signed, sealed, notarized and delivered.

MERS

MERS is a national electronic registration and tracking system that tracks the beneficial ownership interests and servicing rights in mortgage loans. MERS eliminates the need to prepare and record assignments when trading residential and commercial mortgage loans. MERS is being sued in a number of states in regard to validity of the system.

Grant, Bargain and Sale Deed

The Grant, Bargain and Sale deed contains only implied warranties that the grantor actually holds the title and the possessions of the property. This type of deed has a *granting clause* in it, with words such as *grant and release, or grant, bargain and sale.*

Some states use a grant, bargain and sale deed which is defined by state statute, and contains two warranties: that grantor has not previously conveyed title to another and that there are no unspecified encumbrances.

There is an implied warranty in this type of deed, but it is difficult to prove. Most people use title insurance to insure the grantor has ownership in the real property that is being transferred.

A copy of a basic Grant, Bargain and Sale deed follows on the next page.

Affix R.P.T.T., $ _____   APN _____

GRANT, BARGAIN, SALE DEED

THIS INDENTURE WITNESSETH: That _____

_____

FOR A VALUABLE CONSIDERATION, the receipt of which is hereby acknowledged, do hereby Grant,

Bargain, Sell and Convey to _____

_____

all that real property situated in the _____ County of _____

State of Nevada, bounded and described as follows:

SUBJECT TO: 1. Taxes for the fiscal year.
               2. Covenants, conditions, restrictions, reservations, rights-of-way and easements of record.

Together with all and singular the tenements, hereditaments and appurtenances thereunto belonging or in anywise appertaining.
Witness _____ hand _____ this _____ day of _____, 19 _____

STATE OF NEVADA   }
COUNTY OF _____   } SS.

On _____   _____
Before me, a Notary Public, personally appeared   _____

_____   _____
_____
_____   _____

personally known to me (or proved to me on the basis of   ESCROW NO:
satisfactory evidence) to be the person whose name is   _____
subscribed to this instrument and acknowledged that he   MAIL TAX STATEMENTS TO: _____
(she or they) executed it.   _____

                                                                 _____

63

Quitclaim Deed

The quitclaim deed is the best for grantor, and is used as problem solver and to terminate deed restrictions referred to as clouds on the title. There may be defects in the title as a result of technical flaws in an earlier conveyance. *No after acquired title* and no promises or guarantees come with a quitclaim deed. A copy of a basic quitclaim deed follows on the next page.

Sheriff's Deed

The Sheriff's Deed or certificate of sale goes to the high bidder at a sheriff's sale.

QUITCLAIM DEED

For a valuable consideration, receipt of which is acknowledged _____

_____

_____

do_____ hereby quitclaim to _____

_____

_____ the real property in the

City of _____ County of _____, State of Nevada, described as:

Witness_____ hand_____ this_____ day of_____, 19____

STATE OF NEVADA   } SS.
COUNTY OF _____ }

_____

_____

On _____

Before me, a Notary Public, personally appeared

_____

_____

_____

_____

_____

_____

Title Order No._____

personally known to me (or proved to me on the basis of

Escrow or Loan No._____

65

Patent

The Patent title to property originates with the sovereign government, i.e. the United States. The government holds absolute title to all lands within its boundaries. The process by which the government transfers land to private individuals is known as the patent. The patent is the highest form of title in the United States and is the ultimate source of title for all lands under private ownership.

Requirements of a valid deed

- Competent grantor, 18 years of age and sound mind.
- Identifiable grantee.
- Consideration, money or something of value.
- Granting clause (words of conveyance) followed by a *habendum clause*, (to have & to hold), which identifies the type of estate.
- Legal description.
- Executed by grantor(s).
- Delivered and accepted by grantee(s)—title and possession of property, (unless otherwise agreed), pass at this point.

Additional requirements of conveyance of a deed include a valid deed, acknowledgement, (notarization), delivery and acceptance.

Conveyance After Death

Probate is the process of distributing all of a deceased's assets.

Devise is the act of transferring deceased's (called the *devisor or testator*) interest in real estate to another (devisee) by will.

If *intestate, (no will)*, laws of descent and intestate succession determine heirs/descendants.

Bequest is the act of transferring deceased's interest in personal property to another. Title to any interest in land passes immediately to heirs or devisees upon death, although it is not final until probate is complete.

Other Ways of Transferring Rights (Involuntary Alienation)

Adverse Possession

Adverse possession is ownership granted by the courts due to actual, open, continuous, hostile, notorious, and exclusive possession of another's land for minimum statutory period.

Easement by Prescription

Easement by prescription/prescriptive easement is an easement prescribed by the courts due to actual, open, continuous, hostile, and notorious use of another's land for a minimum statutory period.

Easement by Necessity

Easement by necessity is an easement created by law to prevent landlocked property. Gives grantee an easement over grantor's land, but only if there is no other access to grantee's land.

Notarization/Acknowledgement

Notarization or acknowledgement is the process grantor's signature is witnessed and the signature is genuine and voluntary. Notarization is a procedure governed by the state in which the property exists. The witness is usually a notary public. In most states deeds are recorded by some city or county officer holding the title of Recorder.

Recording

Recording is generally not required for validity. Recording gives constructive (legal) notice to protect interests, and determines priority. State laws govern specifics of recording—generally include requirements that recorded deeds/mortgages must be executed by grantors/mortgagors, signatures must be acknowledged (notarized) to indicate that the signature is made voluntarily and under no duress. The document must be dated and recorded in the county where the property is located.

Settlement/Closing

Escrow/settlement procedures

Escrow or settlement is the means by which parties to a contract carry out the terms of their agreement.

Parties appoint a third party to act as an escrow agent.

Seller's deed and buyer's money are deposited with escrow agent according to an escrow agreement that sets forth conditions to be met before the sale will be consummated.

Closing statement-debits and credits

Credit to seller is anything that increases the amount of money seller takes from the closing. Example: Sale price, pre-paid taxes.

Debit to seller is anything that decreases amount of money seller takes from the closing. Example: Brokerage fee, mortgage payoff.

Credit to buyer is anything that decreases the amount of money buyer must bring to closing. Example: Earnest money, new mortgage, contract for deed.

Debit to buyer is anything that increases the amount of money buyer must bring to the closing. Example: Sale price, discount points (paid by the buyer).

Pro-ration based on 365-day year or 360-day year (30 day months). Rent is paid in advance; mortgage interest is paid in arrears.

Broker's responsibilities

- Account for all monies held in trust/escrow.
- Pay commissions to their salespeople and to co-brokers.

Tax Aspects

Property taxes – "At value"— "Ad valorem"

Tax rate may be expressed as mill rate, percentage rate, or decimal.

Properties can be re-assessed for current value. Re-assessments can be appealed to an Assessor's Appeal Board.

Special assessments

Pay for improvements or benefits received on front footage basis.

Paid along with property taxes and enforced by a lien.

Capital gains

There is no Capital Gains tax on the first $250,000 of profit (single) or $500,000 of profit (married) from sale of principal residence.

Must reside in residence for 2 out of last 5 years.

Exemption from the Capital Gains tax can be taken every two years.

Deductible Items

Mortgage interest, property taxes (ad valorem taxes), discount points, and certain loan origination fees are deductible.

Foreclosure

Short Sale

A short sale is a contract to relieve a mortgage lien. When an owner chooses a Short Sale, they have to provide the bank with a Short Sale package that may include financial statements as well as a "hardship letter" that explains why the Short Sale is necessary. The bank may not even review the package and approve/disapprove the package until they have received an offer to purchase. In most cases the bank is not a part of the process of determining the list process of the property.

The homeowner and the listing agent set the list price. Once the bank has received the purchase offer, the purchase offer is assigned to a negotiator. The negotiator reviews the purchase offer and Short Sale package, and has 30 days to respond to the package. The negotiator will order a current BPO, (Broker Price Option) from a different agent. The BPO is similar to a normal market analysis that provides information as to other comparable properties in the area, and is to determine what the bank may decide to be a fair market value.

The negotiator may accept or counter offer.

Tax Aspects of a Short Sale

If the lender cancels or forgives a some debt, they may have to include the canceled amount as income for tax purposes, depending on the circumstance. The Mortgage Debt Relief Act of 2007 generally allows taxpayers to exclude income from discharge of debt on their principal residence. Debt reduced through mortgage restructuring, as well as mortgage debt forgiven in connection with a foreclosure, qualifies for relief.

A 1099-C is issued to a borrower by the lender for cancelled debt. The debt is generally taxable income to he borrower.

A concern is that the mortgage debt must have been to buy, build, or substantially improve the principal residence, or to refinance debt incurred for those purposes. All tax questions should be referred to a qualified CPA.

Recourse Loans – The Recourse

Recourse loans are loans that allow the lender to come after the borrower in case of default. Recourse loans get their name from the fact that lenders have power. The lenders are allowed to come after the borrower for what he owes even after haven taken his collateral, (house, autos, etc.). If a borrower defaults on a loan the lender can take court action that could result in the garnishment of wages, to try to collect the amount owed.

Non-Recourse Loans

A non-recourse loan does not allow the lender to go after anything other than the collateral. If a borrower defaults on home loan, the lender is limited to the property, and nothing else. The bank is out of luck even if the sale proceeds do not repay the loan.

Applicable State Laws

A borrower should consult an attorney and/or tax advisor to be certain whether they have a recourse, non-recourse loan. State laws often dictate whether a loan is recourse or not. California is best known as a non-recourse state that makes it hard for lenders to sue. Some states give lenders flexibility in how they pursue defaults, but many lenders choose not to sue because defaulting borrowers often don't have much to sue for.

Recourse States

Recourse states leave the door open for mortgage lenders and collection agencies to pursue homeowners with deficiency judgments, going after assets and income years after a foreclosure or short sale, or bank approved short sale. Mortgage holders sometime sign a promissory note and the contract details the penalty for non-payment. Regardless their credit rating will also be affected.

Deficiency Judgments

Lenders are selling their deficiency judgments to collection agencies for much less than the judgment. These agencies may wait for a sufficient time for the debtor to recover financially to take legal action.

Anti-Deficiency /Non-Recourse States

Alaska, Arizona, California, Connecticut, Florida, Idaho, Minnesota, North Carolina, North Dakota, Texas, Utah and Washington.

One Action States

In some states, lenders are only permitted a single lawsuit to collect mortgages debt.

TRANSFER OF PROPERTY QUIZ

1. Title insurance is:

    (A) Not required by law
    (B) Protection against false impersonations
    (C) Issued to insure the named party only
    (D) All of the above

2. The cost of the owner's title insurance policy is based primarily on:

    (A) Age of the property
    (B) Cost of the property
    (C) The number of covenants in the deed
    (D) All of the above

3. Abstract of title is a

    (A) Contract for a deed
    (B) Condensed history of the title
    (C) Guarantee of title
    (D) Survey of the subject property

4. To remove a cloud from the title of a property an owner would most likely

    (A) An assessment
    (B) A quitclaim deed
    (C) A trusts deed
    (D) An option

5. Which of the following documents will transfer title to real property

    (A) Trust deed
    (B) Bargain and sale deed
    (C) Purchase money mortgage
    (D) Both (A) and (B) above

6. When court orders a person to sell property it issues

    (A) An attachment
    (B) A foreclosure
    (C) A writ of execution
    (D) A deficiency judgment

7. To be legal a deed must have

       (A) Acknowledgement
       (B) Verification
       (C) The grantee's signature
       (D) A granting clause

8. The best deed a grantee can receive is ordinarily the
       (A) Special warranty deed
       (B) General warranty deed
       (C) Bargain and sale deed
       (D) Quitclaim deed

9. A reconveyance deed is signed by the

       (A) Grantee
       (B) Grantor
       (C) Beneficiary
       (D) Trustee

10. In the transfer of real property by deed, ownership changes hands when the deed has been

       (A) Signed
       (B) Delivered
       (C) Recorded
       (D) Notarized

11. The main purpose of a deed is to

       (A) Provide a written instrument for recording

       (B) Identify the party to whom the taxes are sent

       (C) Evidence the terms of a property transaction

       (D) Evidence the change in title

12. First grant or patent in a chain of title is issued by
       (A) A sovereign power
       (B) U.S. Government Patent Office
       (C) The recorder
       (D) The recorder of deeds

13. Voluntary alienation

     (A) Sale or gift
     (B) Adverse possession
     (C) Eminent domain
     (D) Descent

14. A deed executed and delivered, but not recorded

     (A) Void
     (B) Avoidable
     (C) Valid
     (D) Unenforceable

Chapter 5 – Appraisal - Valuation and Market Analysis

Learning Objectives

A. Concept of Value
1. Market value vs. market price
2. Characteristics of value
3. Principals of value
B. Appraisal process
1. Purpose and steps to an appraisal
2. Federal oversight of the appraisal process
C. Methods of estimating value and Broker price opinion (BPO)
1. Sales comparison approach (market data)
2. Cost approach
a. Improvements and depreciation
b. Physical deterioration, functional and economic obsolescence
c. Reproduction and replacement costs.
3. Income approach
4. Gross rent and gross income multiplier
5. Comparative market analysis (CMA)
6. Broker price opinion (BPO)
7. Assessed value and tax implications

Appraisal

Appraisal deals with knowledge of methods used to estimate real estate prices. This involves understanding how economic and financial conditions impact real estate prices.

An appraisal is an *estimate or opinion* of market value supported by an analysis of relevant property data. Appraisers must comply with the Uniform Standards of Professional Appraisal Practice (USPAP). An appraiser's compensation is based on the time and effort that goes into an appraisal. Compensation may not be based on a percentage of the appraised value.

A consumer seeking an appraisal should provide the appraiser with as much information as possible, and be prepared to answer the following questions:

- What is the purpose of the appraisal?
- What is the required completion date of the appraisal?
- Do you have a copy of the deed, survey, purchase agreement, or other papers that may be important to the subject property?
- What is the mortgage amount? What company has the loan? What is the start date, amount owed, loan type, (FHA, VA, Conventional, etc.), and interest rate? Are there any other types of financing?
- Do you have a copy of the current real estate tax billing, statement of special assessments, and balance owed?
- Is the property listed for sale? If so, for how much and with whom?
- What personal property is included?

Market Value

Market value is the highest price in terms of cash or its equivalent that a property will bring when:

- A willing seller sells and a willing buyer buys.
- The property has been exposed in the marketplace for a reasonable time.
- Buyer and seller are familiar with the property's uses.
- Neither the buyer nor seller is under abnormal pressure to sell or buy.

Highest and Best Use

- The highest and best use refers to the most profitable use; one that produces greatest net return over time.
- Highest and best use may not necessarily be the present use.
- Highest and best use must be financially feasible, legally permitted, and considerate of adjacent land uses.

Supply and Demand

Supply is the amount of properties available. Prices move opposite of supply. If there are large quantities of properties for sale, prices go down. Demand is the amount of properties that will be purchased. Prices move with demand. If properties are scarce and desired, prices go up. Increasing returns occur when the improvements add more value than cost. Decreasing returns occur when the *building improvements* add less value than their cost.

Conformity

Conformity is the concept that values tend to move toward surroundings.

Regression is when the value of over-improved property declines. *Progression* is when the value of under-improved property increases. A usual neighborhood life cycle is growth/stability/decline/rejuvenation.

Plottage & Assemblage

Plottage is the increased value resulting from assemblage. Assemblage is combining adjacent lots into one larger lot.

Economic Life

Economic life is the period of time that site improvements contribute to value. Effective age is based upon a property's physical condition and usefulness. Chronological age is the actual age of the property.

Principal of Substitution

Appraisers use the principal of substitution. This suggests that if there are several similar properties for sale, the lowest priced has greatest demand.

Market Value Approach

The market value approach is the primary method used to appraise residential properties. Residential appraisers must analyze selling prices of comparable properties and consider the same factors that buyers consider: location, size, quality, design, age, condition, desirability, and usefulness. When using the market data approach, appraisers compile sales figures and compare the subject property with similar properties that have recently sold.

Appraiser must take large numbers of sales and select only those that are truly comparable with the appraised property. Appraisers set parameters for comparison by using a specially designed computer program that searches the sales files, specifically for sales that match up with the subject property. The ability to select comparable sales from this sales file is significant because it produces estimates of value that directly reflect the attitude of the market. This approach to value makes use of matching the subject property with recently sold comparable properties of similar size, quality and location.

A comparison is made to the subject property. The property being evaluated is the subject property. Similar properties recently sold are comparables or comps. *Adjustments are made to comparables not to the subject property.* If the comparable property is better, a deduction is made to comparable property. If the comparable property is worse, an addition of value is made to comparable property, and not the subject property.

Comparable Market Analysis

A Comparable Market Analysis (CMA) uses a similar market value approach, but is not considered an appraisal.

Cost Approach

The replacement cost approach, or cost approach, involves making an estimate of the depreciated cost of reproducing, and/or replacing the building and site improvements. Reproduction refers to the cost at a given point in time of reproducing a replica property. Replacement cost refers to the cost of reproducing improvements of equal utility. *From the reproduction cost new, is deducted any depreciation for loss in value caused by physical depreciation, functional or economic obsolescence.* The estimated land value is an indication of market value (since land never depreciates), and is added to the depreciated cost to arrive at the appraised value using the replacement cost method. The cost approach is significant because it is the only approach that can be applied to all types of construction.

The cost approach is most frequently used to appraise property when the lack of adequate market and income data preclude the reasonable application of more traditional approaches.

The cost approach is the most effective appraisal method for new construction and special purpose or single purpose buildings. As previously mentioned, the cost approach to value is what it costs to replace or reproduce the improvements at the appraisal date, minus the physical deterioration and/or functional obsolescence. The remainder is added to the land value that has been estimated using the market value approach.

Step 1

The first step is to estimate new construction costs and be sure to replace with the same or mostly similar materials, so that the improvement is the same function or utility.

Step 2

The second step is to subtract accrued depreciation (loss in value to the building). The first definition of depreciation found in the dictionary is a decrease in value due to wear and tear, decay, decline in price, etc. The second definition is to claim depreciation on a property for tax purposes. The difference between the two definitions above may seem confusing for some students, and they may have to take a course or two in accounting to clearly understand the difference between the two definitions. As properties mature, the decline in value due to wear and tear, etc., results in a lower value compared to newer properties of similar kind and condition.

The strange thing is that depreciation for tax purposes suggests book values of properties are declining when in reality the property's market value may be increasing.

Depreciation

There are three basic types of depreciation:

1. Physical deterioration, wear and tear, deferred maintenance, which can be *curable*, correctable at an economically feasible cost, or *incurable*.
2. Functional obsolescence, inadequate design or equipment, can *be curable or incurable*.
3. Economic or location obsolescence is due to external forces that are generally *incurable*.

Physical Deterioration

Physical deterioration is the wear and tear or breaking down of a physical structure. It may include decay, dry rot, or damage caused by the elements or vandalism. Physical deterioration is categorized as curable or incurable.

In analyzing physical deterioration, the appraiser must distinguish among the following:

- Deferred maintenance, involves curable items in need of immediate repair. They are either short lived or long lived.
- Short-lived items can be replaced later. They include roofing, paint, floor covering, water heater, etc.
- Long-lived items are expected to last for the remaining economic life of the building. Long-lived items include framing, wiring, plumbing, etc.

Curable Physical Deterioration

Physical deterioration is measured by the cost to cure the problem. Physical deterioration is curable if the costs to repair or replace the items are less than the value added to the property by their replacement. These include items such as leaky roofs, broken windows, etc.

Functional Obsolescence

Functional obsolescence is the loss in value due to *super adequacy* or deficiency within the property. Super adequacy is the component or system that exceeds market requirements and adds less value than the cost of the component. Examples include:

- Oversized heating systems;
- Excess plumbing features;
- Oversized structural support; and
- Any items that exceed reasonable requirements.

Deficiency is described as a component or system that is substandard or lacking. Examples include:

- Components smaller than normal;
- Poor design. Lack of closet space, ceilings that are too low or too high, poor room arrangements, etc., would all be considered "poor design"; and
- An architectural style that is not compatible with other buildings in the area.

Like physical deterioration, functional obsolescence is either curable or incurable depending on whether the "cost to cure" is economically justified.

Curable Functional Obsolescence

Functional obsolescence is considered curable when the increase in value gained by correcting the problem exceeds the cost to cure it. For example, if the cost to add a second bath is less than the added value the improvement would make to the appraised value the improvement would be justified.

Incurable Functional Obsolescence

Functional obsolescence is considered incurable when it is possible and reasonable to cure an item, but there is no economic advantage in doing so. Incurable functional obsolescence is considered poor room arrangement or a design feature that cannot be corrected without excessive costs.

External obsolescence

External obsolescence is a loss in value resulting from conditions outside the property. There are many causes of external obsolescence. These include:

- Deterioration of a neighborhood due to social changes;
- Oversupply of houses;
- Changing traffic patterns;
- High unemployment;
- Proximity of a home to sewage treatment plant; and
- Any other condition outside the property that causes a loss in value.

External obsolescence can be temporary or permanent but is always *incurable.*

Step 3

Add the totals arrived at in step 1 and 2 together with the estimated land value that was derived using the market value approach to arrive at the appraised value using the replacement cost approach. This is why the replacement cost approach is also called the *summation* approach.

The Income Approach

The income approach is frequently used when appraising commercial or industrial properties. The strength of this method is its ability to measure a property's value based on the property's ability to generate and maintain a stream of income for the owner. To be effective, this method requires appraisers to have the ability to gather basic information, analyze the income yields in terms of their relative quality and durability, and relate all of the information gathered and analyzed to the changing economic environment of the area studied. This approach lends itself best to the appraisal of commercial or industrial properties because prospective buyers of commercial properties are primarily interested in the potential net return and tax shelter the properties should provide. The prices used to justify a purchase are a measure of the prospects of the net return from their investment in the property.

The income approach to value is most important when ascertaining the value of income producing properties. The income approach provides an objective estimate of what a knowledgeable investor pays for the property based on any income the property generates. This approach is used to complete a more sophisticated analysis of properties using formulas, such as *the internal rate of return, return on the investment, and return of the investment.* These concepts are beyond the introductory appraisal information provided in this text.

Step 1: Estimate Potential Gross Income

Economic Rent

To estimate gross income, forecast the income a typical investor expects to receive from the property from the present date forward and is referred to as *economic rent*. Past income is referred to as *contract rent* and may be a guide to the expected future income.

Potential gross income is the market rent that would be collected if the property were fully occupied. In estimating potential gross income, appraisers distinguish between *market rent, or economic rent, and contract rent*. Market rent is the prevailing rent received for comparable properties. Contract rent is the actual amount agreed to by a landlord and tenant. It may or may not be the same as market rent, depending on various factors. Contract rents should be analyzed to determine if the lease amount is typical for the type of property to be appraised.

Step 2: Deduct for Vacancy and Collection Loss

Vacancy and collection loss is an allowance for reductions in potential income due to vacancies, tenant turnover, and nonpayment of rents. Vacancy allowance for older motels/hotels may be as high as 50 to 60 percent, while for newer, well located, and well-managed office structures, it may be as low as 1 to 3 percent. As buildings age, vacancy rates generally increase because of physical deterioration and functional and/or external obsolescence.

Step 3: Add Miscellaneous Income

Miscellaneous income may come from several sources including parking, vending machines, and laundry services.

Step 4: Estimate Expenses Before Discount, Recapture, and taxes

Net Operating Income (NOI) is estimated by subtracting operating expenses and reserves for replacement from Estimated Gross Income (EGI). Appraisers would determine operating expenses and replacement reserve by reviewing the last three years of expenses for the property. Appraisers must also estimate future expenses buyers will incur.

Operating expenses are the costs necessary to maintain the property so it can continue to produce rental income.

Expenses Not Included

The following are frequently reported as expenses to be excluded for appraisal purposes:

- Property taxes are a legitimate property expense. However, property taxes should *not* be included as an operating expense.
- Depreciation is *not* a separate deduction. But it is taken into consideration in the income approach by the recapture component of the capitalization rate.
- Income taxes are *not* allowed in the income approach because these taxes are based on the personal incomes of the individuals and not on the income produced by the property.
- Debt service is the amount of payment made toward principal and interest on the loan for the purchase of the property. It is an expense of the buyer, *not* of the real estate.
- Capital improvements are long-lasting additions to the property that usually increase income, total value, or economic life of the property. But they are *not* considered operating expense.

Included Expenses

Operating expenses typically include:
- Insurance,
- Management,
- Salaries,
- Utilities,
- Supplies and Materials,
- Repairs and Maintenance, and
- Reserves for Replacement.

Reserves for replacement are funds set aside for replacing short-lived items that will not last for the remaining economic life of a building. Reserves for replacements include roof and floor coverings, heating and air conditioning systems, kitchen appliances, water heaters, painting, decorating, etc. Replacing these items usually requires spending large sums of money.

Step 5: Deduct Expenses from Effective Gross Income to Determine Net Operating Income

> After estimating all operating expenses and appropriate reserves for replacements, subtract Expenses from the Effective Gross Income to determine Net Operating Income.

Step 6: Capitalization: Selecting the Proper Capitalization Rate

> Capitalization is the process of converting anticipated future income into an indication of present value. The principal of anticipation states that present value is determined by future benefits.

Capitalization Rate

> The capitalization rate converts net operating income to an estimate of value. It reflects the relationship between income and value. The capitalization rate includes the following components:
>
> - Discount rate,
> - Recapture rate, and
> - Effective tax rate.

Return On/Of Investment

> The capitalization rate used in real estate appraisal includes both a return of and a return on investment and is similar to the prevailing interest rates charged for mortgages. Return of the investment or recapture is recovery of invested capital. Return on investment is compensation to an investor for the risk, time value of money, non-liquidity, and other factors associated with investment.

Recapture Rate

> Recapture rate provides for the recovery of capital on an annual basis. It is called the rate of return of investment.

Step 7: Capitalization Application

> Once the appraiser estimates annual net operating income before discount, recapture and taxes, he can use several methods and techniques to capitalize that income to an estimate of market value. Proper rate selection is necessary to correctly estimate value. Small variations in the capitalization rate will result in substantial differences in value estimates.

For example, if the net operating income is $39,035 and the capitalization rate is 10%; the appraised value is determined by dividing the $39,035 by .10, which equals $390,350. Increasing the capitalization rate to 11% would result in an appraised value of $354,864. As the capitalization rate increases the value of the property decreases. As the capitalization rate decreases the value of the property increases. As the capitalization rate increases and decreases the value of property follows accordingly.

Reconciliation Process

The reconciliation includes analyzing and weighing the three approaches, but not averaging estimates of value from market, cost, and income approach.

The Appraisal Report

Each comprehensive appraisal report for a commercial development should contain the following items:

1. A statement of purpose or the objective for the appraisal, with value defined.
2. A legal description or adequate identification of the property.
3. The date of the value estimate.
4. An adequate description of the physical characteristics of the subject property.
5. A statement to the known and observed encumbrances on the subject property.
6. A statement and analysis of the highest and best use of the subject property.
7. A statement as to the property rights appraised.
8. A market value approach and analysis.
9. A cost approach and analysis, if applicable.
10. An income approach and analysis, if applicable.
11. A statement of the conclusions reached in the appraisal report.
12. Documentation requirements: the appraiser must have the minimum data requirements in the file to properly support the final estimate of value.
13. A statement of the assumptions and limiting conditions that affect the subject property.
14. The signature of the responsible appraiser and particular designation.
15. A statement concerning the confidentiality regarding the appraisal itself.

Gross Income Multipliers

A gross income multiplier (GIM) is a factor calculated when dividing the sale price of a property by its gross income. Gross income is normally defined as the annual income prior to any deduction for services or expenses. Using a GIM assumes that any differences between the subject and comparables are reflected in the rents of each property. If the sales used to extract a GIM from the market are valid and the properties are comparable the resulted GIM should produce a reliable indicator of value for the subject property.

The following example shows how to develop a gross income multiplier from a sold property.
A typical neighborhood home rents for $10,000 per year and is sold for $150,000. This results in a ratio of 15 to 1. If a home rents for $14,000 per year with the same multiplier (15 to 1), it would result in an estimated value of $210,000.

The gross income multiplier is an alternative to capitalization that takes into account gross income, but not expenses.

Zillow.com

Zillow.com is a beta real estate site, offering free valuations on more than millions of homes across the U.S. The listing of homes is not limited to presently listed homes or those that are for sale. All consumers need to do is enter an address. In addition to finding a value for homes, consumers can access:

- The historical value changes for each home, charted over the past year, five years, or ten years.
- Comparable home sales in an area.
- Satellite, aerial, and parcel views of homes.
- Individual home data, such as: number of bedrooms/bathrooms, square footage, lot size, stories, and year built.

Consumers should be aware that not all of the information is up to date. But Zillow.com is an interesting website.

HVCC

The Home Value Code of Conduct was developed by the Federal Housing Finance Agency to strengthen appraisal independence and improve the appraisal process. HVCC was announced by Fannie Mae and Freddie Mac in December 2008, and was deployed in May 2009. The Code expanded on existing appraisal standards, seeking to redress problems that contributed to the mortgage crisis. Unfortunately, during the 2005 to 2007 periods, mortgage lending was much too aggressive and placed pressure on the appraisers, and the appraisal process. In some cases, that resulted in unrealistically high appraisals. The HVCC is designed to promote professional appraisals free from inappropriate pressure from lenders, borrowers or brokers.

APPRAISAL QUIZ.

1. The list price of houses is in most cases:

    (A) The ceiling price for a residential listing.
    (B) Are lower that market value.
    (C) Are over the market price.
    (D) None of the above.

2. The net income divided by the capitalization rate would generate?

    (A) Value.
    (B) Expenses.
    (C) Interest rate.
    (D) None of the above.

3. Which appraisal approach determines the present worth of future benefits?

    (A) Income approach.
    (B) Cost approach.
    (C) Market data approach.
    (D) None of the above.

4. The capitalization approach is:

    (A) Return of investment.
    (B) Return on investment.
    (C) Return of and on investment.
    (D) None of the above.

5. Which in not an example of functional obsolescence?

    (A) Outmoded kitchen appliances.
    (B) Leaking roof.
    (C) One car garage.
    (D) None of the above.

6. Which type of depreciation is incurable?

    (A) Functional obsolescence.
    (B) Economic obsolescence.
    (C) External obsolescence.
    (D) None of the above.

7. When using the income approach which of the following would be considered an operating expense?

    (A) Property taxes.
    (B) Mortgage payments.
    (C) Interest expenses.
    (D) None of the above.

8. Which of the following is considered an example of economic obsolescence?

    (A) Paint that is peeling.
    (B) Odd design.
    (C) Sagging roof.
    (D) Run down neighborhood.

9. Depreciation can be:

    (A) Curable.
    (B) Loss of value due to any cause.
    (C) Incurable.
    (D) None of the above.

10. Which is true about fee appraisers?

    (A) There is no fee for the appraisal.
    (B) They are self-employed.
    (C) The appraiser is employed by the lender.
    (D) None of the above.

11. Another term for the income approach is?

    (A)\ Replacement cost approach.
    (B) Correlation approach.
    (C) Capitalization approach.
    (D) Commercial approach.

12. The unit of comparison for a home using the market data approach is the:

    (A) Using only the lot size.
    (B) The lot and the building.
    (C) The location.
    (D) The entire property.

13. A good guesstimate to convert gross income to the approximate value is:

    (A) The gross rent multiplier.
    (B) The mortgage calculator.
    (C) The gross expense multiplier.
    (D) All of the above.

14. Which of the following is not a type of depreciation?

    (A) Physical deterioration.
    (B) Functional obsolescence.
    (C) Economic obsolescence.
    (D) None of the above.

15. The approach that takes the selling of similar properties and adjusts these prices for any difference is known as?

    (A) Income approach.
    (B) Cost approach.
    (C) Comparative approach.
    (D) None of the above.

16. The replacement cost approach to appraisal is best used for:

    (A) Land.
    (B) Apartments.
    (C) New construction.
    (D) Single family residences.

17. Which appraisal approach uses the principal of substitution?

    (A) Cost approach.
    (B) Income approach.
    (C) Market data approach.
    (D) All of the above.

18. Capitalization is a process to:

    (A) Convert income into value.
    (B) Establish loan value.
    (C) Determine net income.
    (D) Find the interest rate.

19. When comparing the cost method to the income method of appraising:

    (A) The income method develops the upper limits of value.
    (B) The cost method develops the lower limits of value.
    (C) The income method provides the higher limit of value.
    (D) The reproduction method provides the upper limits of value.

20. A post office of unique construction and design is best appraised by which of the following methods?

(A) Cost.
(B) Income.
(C) Land residual.
(D) Market data.

CHAPTER – 6 - CONTRACTS

Learning Objectives

A. Types of contracts
   1. Express or implied
   2. Unilateral vs. bilateral
B. Required elements of a valid contract
C. Contract performance
   1. Executed vs. executor
   2. Valid vs. void
   3. Voidable vs. unenforceable
   4. Breach of contract, rescission, and termination
   5. Liquidated, punitive, or compensatory damages
   6. Statute of Frauds
   7. Time is of the essence.
D. Sales contracts
   1. Offer and counter offer
   2. Earnest money and liquidated damages
   3. Equitable title
   4. Contingencies
   5. Disputes and breach of contract
   6. Option contracts and installment sales contracts
E. Types of agency and licensee-client relationships
F. Creation and termination of agency
G. Licensee obligations to parties of a transaction

Contract basics

A contract is defined as a legally binding and enforceable agreement to do or not to do a specific thing. General contract principals apply to all real estate purchase agreements. A contract is also defined as a promise or set of promises for breach of which, gives a remedy, or the performance of which, the law recognizes as a duty.

Essential Elements of a Valid Contract

1. Offer and Acceptance

Offer and acceptance is also known as mutual agreement or meeting of the minds. The offer and the communication of acceptance must be made before offer has been withdrawn. Qualified acceptance, and counteroffer is, in effect, rejection and the original offer is *destroyed*. If both parties sign the counteroffer, it usually meets the agreement requirements of a contract.

2. Competent Parties

18 is the age of majority. A contract with minor is voidable, on the part of the minor. The parties must be mentally sound, and not in prison.

3. Lawful Objective

Contracts must be lawful and for legal purposes. There can be no mistake of material fact and must be genuine with no undo influence, no duress. Duress is force, threat or unfair advantage.

4. Consideration

There must be consideration, usually money or something of value.

5. Real Estate Contracts

The Statute of Frauds requires real estate contracts include the four elements mentioned previously plus a *fifth requirement, that is real estate contracts must be in writing.* The statute of Frauds requires, that real estate contracts, or any promise or agreements involving contracts for real property are not enforceable unless the agreement is in writing and signed by the person(s) involved in the agreement or by persons lawfully authorized to sign for them. The *exception* to the Statute of Frauds is a lease of 12 months or less.

Purpose of the Statute of Frauds

The purpose of the Statute of Frauds is to prevent fraud by someone seeking enforcement of an executory contract that was never made and to protect spouses' rights to property. It is not designed to prevent the performance of oral contracts.

Required Signatures

Certain agreements must be signed by the parties to be charged with the responsibility to perform. Both spouses must sign to release community property and homestead rights.

Conditions of a Contract

The four *conditions* of a contract are valid, voidable, void and unenforceable.

Valid

A valid contract contains all the essential elements, is binding on both parties and is enforceable by the court

Voidable

a voidable contract appears to be valid, but one party may disaffirm because the party is a minor, or was subject to duress, fraud or misrepresentation. Or the contract has a condition allowing one of the parties back out of the agreement.

Void

A void contract is not enforceable due to failure to contain all essential elements.

Unenforceable

An unenforceable contract was valid when made but either it cannot be proved or will not be enforced by the courts, e.g. certain oral contracts.

Unilateral Contract

A unilateral contract is an agreement to pay in exchange for performance. A real estate listing contract may be an example of a unilateral contract.

Bilateral Contract

A bilateral contract is an exchange of one promise to another. The difference between a unilateral contract and bilateral contract is normally only of interest to academics.

Executed Contract

An executed contract is one where the duties have been completed or performed by both parties.

Executor Contract

An executor contract is an agreement where one, or both parties need to complete a part of the contract. In effect, the contract has yet to be performed.

Assignment

An assignment is the transfer of rights held by one party, the assignor, to another party the assignee. Common law favors the freedom of assignment, so an assignment will be generally allowed unless the contract language specifically prohibits assignment. Almost all mortgage loans are not assignable.

Due on Sale

Contracts may have non-assignment or due on sale clauses, which prohibits the assignment of the contract. These clauses do not prevent assignment. It merely gives lenders the ability to sue for breach of contract if assignments are made. The other method to prevent assignment in a contract is a recession clause or a clause creating a *condition subsequent*, which would rescind the contract automatically if an assignment, is made.

Novation

Novation can be broadly defined as a substitution of a new contract for an old one. Because of the broad reaching effect of a novation, it is necessary that there be a mutual agreement among the parties to the old and new obligation.

Performance

Performance means that all terms of the contract have been fully carried out or executed. Partial performance is a contact, which has not sufficiently been completed to force payment. Substantial performance is where the contract may be sufficient to force payment.

Impossibility of Performance

Impossibility of performance is a contract that cannot be legally accomplished.

Amendments

Amendments are changes or modifications to a contract, which must be in writing and signed by all parties. Real estate agents to insure all parties understand the contract changes use the following form "Addendum to Purchase Agreement".

Types of Real Estate Contracts

There are as many types of purchase agreements as there are different types of real estate transactions, such as commercial, residential, industrial, hotel, etc. An example of the standard agreement used by some professionals is the "Residential Purchase Agreement," that follows. As you can see the contact is presently ten pages long, not including any required disclosure forms, and may be changed as the need occurs.

Uniform Vendor and Purchase Act

The Uniform Vendor and Purchase Act make a contract voidable by the buyer if the property is destroyed prior to closing. Death does not terminate contract. The heirs must perform.

Contingency Clause

A real estate contract may contain contingency clauses allowing the buyer to terminate under certain conditions.

Time is of the Essence Clause

A time is of the essence clause requires performance within the time specified. If time is not specified, the contract must be performed within a reasonable time. Earnest money is not required to create a valid purchase agreement.

Land Contract or Contract for Deed

The contract for deed, land contract, and an agreement for sale deed are, essentially, the same thing. These types of contracts are used as a form of *owner financing* in real estate. The contact requires the buyer (*Vendee*) to make payments over time usually with interest and principal included. The owner agrees to give the buyer a deed upon completion of the total payments and/or contract requirements. During the contract period the buyer has possession of the real property and may be required to pay real estate taxes, etc. The seller, (*Vendor*) retains legal title, and the buyer has equitable title.

When a person buys a home the transaction usually has the buyer receiving the deed. The lender has a promissory note that can used to foreclose on the property in case of default. Land contracts have the seller keeping the deed and only releasing the deed to the buyer upon completion of all the payments. This is very similar to the process used in purchasing cars. Land contracts are weak forms of ownership.

The following Residential Purchase Agreement is eleven pages long and it takes a profession real estate agent who has specific training in purchase contracts to complete the agreement.

RESIDENTIAL PURCHASE AGREEMENT

1
2 (Joint Escrow Instructions and Earnest Money Receipt)
3
4 Date: _____
5 _____ ("Buyer"), hereby offers to purchase
6 _____ ("Property"),
7 within the city or unincorporated area of _____, County of _____ ,
8 State of Nevada, A.P.N. # _____ for the purchase price of $ _____
9 (_____ dollars) ("Purchase Price") on the terms
10 and conditions contained herein:
11 BUYER ☐ does -OR- ☐ does not intend to occupy the Property as a residence.
12

Buyer's Offer

13
14 1.   FINANCIAL TERMS & CONDITIONS:
15 $_____   A. EARNEST MONEY DEPOSIT ("EMD") is ☐ presented with this offer -OR- ☐ _____
16
17   *(NOTE: It is a felony in the State of Nevada–punishable by up to four years in prison and a $5,000 fine–to write a*
18   *check for which there are insufficient funds. NRS 193.130(2)(d).)*
19
20 $_____   B. ADDITIONAL DEPOSIT to be placed in escrow on or before (date) _____ . The
21   additional deposit ☐ will -OR- ☐ will not be considered part of the EMD. (Any conditions on the additional
22   deposit should be set forth in Section 28 herein.)
23
24 $_____   C. THIS AGREEMENT IS CONTINGENT UPON BUYER QUALIFYING FOR A <u>NEW LOAN</u> ON
25   THE FOLLOWING TERMS AND CONDITIONS:
26   ☐ Conventional, ☐ FHA, ☐ VA, ☐ Other (specify) _____
27   Interest: ☐ Fixed rate, _____ years -OR- ☐ Adjustable Rate, _____ years. Initial rate of interest not to
28   exceed _____ %. Initial monthly payment not to exceed $ _____ , not including taxes, insurance
29   and/or PMI or MIP.
30
31 $_____   D. THIS AGREEMENT IS CONTINGENT UPON BUYER QUALIFYING TO <u>ASSUME THE</u>
32   <u>FOLLOWING EXISTING LOAN(S):</u>
33   ☐ Conventional, ☐ FHA, ☐ VA, ☐ Other (specify) _____
34   Interest: ☐ Fixed rate, _____ years -OR- ☐ Adjustable Rate, _____ years. Initial rate of interest not to
35   exceed _____ %. Monthly payment not to exceed $ _____ , not including taxes, insurance and/or PMI or MIP.
36
37 $_____   E. BUYER TO EXECUTE A <u>PROMISSORY NOTE SECURED BY DEED OF TRUST</u> PER TERMS
38   IN "FINANCING ADDENDUM."
39
40 $_____   F. BALANCE OF PURCHASE PRICE (Balance of Down Payment) in cash or certified funds to be paid
41   at Close of Escrow ("COE").
42
43 $_____   G. TOTAL PURCHASE PRICE. (This price DOES NOT include closing costs, prorations, or other fees
44   and costs associated with the purchase of the Property as defined herein.)
45

Each party acknowledges that he/she has read, understood, and agrees to each and every provision of this page unless a particular paragraph is otherwise modified by addendum or counteroffer.

Buyer's Name: _____   BUYER(S) INITIALS: _____ / _____

Property Address: _____   SELLER(S) INITIALS: _____ / _____

Rev. 6/09   ©2009 Greater Las Vegas Association of REALTORS®   Page 1 of 11

Encore Realty Group 6596 McLeod Dr Ste 9 Las Vegas, NV 89120   Phone: (702)735-7799   Fax: melody
Juliana Solash   Produced with ZipForm® by zipLogix 18070 Fifteen Mile Road, Fraser, Michigan 48026   www.zipLogix.com

2. ADDITIONAL FINANCIAL TERMS & CONTINGENCIES:

   A. NEW LOAN APPLICATION: Within _____ business days of Acceptance, Buyer agrees to (1) submit a completed loan application to a lender of Buyer's choice; (2) authorize ordering of the appraisal (per lender's requirements); and (3) furnish a preapproval letter to Seller based upon a standard factual credit report and review of debt to income ratios. If Buyer fails to complete any of these conditions within the applicable time frame, Seller reserves the right to terminate this Agreement. In such event, both parties agree to cancel the escrow and return EMD to Buyer. Buyer

☐ does -OR- ☐ does not

authorize lender to provide loan status updates to Seller's and Buyer's Brokers, as well as Escrow Officer. Buyer agrees to use Buyer's best efforts to obtain financing under the terms and conditions outlined in this Agreement.

   B. CASH PURCHASE: Within _____ business days of Acceptance, Buyer agrees to provide written evidence from a bona fide financial institution of sufficient cash available to complete this purchase. If Buyer does not submit the written evidence within the above period, Seller reserves the right to terminate this Agreement.

   C. APPRAISAL: If an appraisal is required as part of this agreement, or requested by Buyer, and if the appraisal is less than the Purchase Price, the transaction will go forward if (1) Buyer, at Buyer's option, elects to pay the difference and purchase the Property for the Purchase Price, or (2) Seller, at Seller's option, elects to adjust the Purchase Price accordingly, such that the Purchase Price is equal to the appraisal. If neither option (1) or (2) is elected, then Parties may renegotiate; if renegotiation is unsuccessful, then either Party may cancel this Agreement upon written notice, in which event the EMD shall be returned to Buyer.

3. SALE OF OTHER PROPERTY:

   A. This Agreement
   ☐ is not -OR-
   ☐ is contingent upon the sale (and closing) of another property which address is

   _____.

   B. Said Property
   ☐ is currently listed
   ☐ is not -OR- ☐ is
   presently in escrow with _____ ;
   Escrow Number: _____ . Proposed Closing Date: _____ ;

When Buyer has accepted an offer on the sale of this other property, Buyer will promptly deliver a written notice of the sale to Seller. If Buyer's escrow on this other property is terminated, abandoned, or does not close on time, this Agreement will terminate without further notice unless the parties agree otherwise in writing. If Seller accepts a bona fide written offer from a third party prior to Buyer's delivery of notice of acceptance of an offer on the sale of Buyer's property, Seller shall give Buyer written notice of that fact. Within three (3) days of receipt of the notice, Buyer will waive the contingency of the sale and closing of Buyer's other property, or this Agreement will terminate without further notice. In order to be effective, the waiver of contingency must be accompanied by reasonable evidence that funds needed to close escrow will be available and Buyer's ability to obtain financing is not contingent upon the sale and/or close of any other property.

4. FIXTURES AND PERSONAL PROPERTY: The following items will be transferred, free of liens, with the sale of the Property with no real value unless stated otherwise herein. Unless an item is covered under Section 7(E) of this Agreement, all items are transferred in an "AS IS" condition.

   A. All EXISTING fixtures and fittings including, but not limited to: electrical, mechanical, lighting, plumbing and heating fixtures, ceiling fan(s), fireplace insert(s), gas logs and grates, solar power system(s), built-in appliance(s), window and door screens, awnings, shutters, window coverings, attached floor covering(s), television antenna(s), satellite dish(es), private integrated telephone systems, air coolers/conditioner(s), pool/spa equipment, garage door opener(s)/remote control(s), mailbox, in-ground landscaping, trees/shrub(s), water softener(s), water purifiers, security systems/alarm(s);

   B. The following additional items of personal property: _____

   _____

Each party acknowledges that he/she has read, understood, and agrees to each and every provision of this page unless a particular paragraph is otherwise modified by addendum or counteroffer.

Buyer's Name: _____   BUYER(S) INITIALS: _____ / _____

Property Address: _____   SELLER(S) INITIALS: _____ / _____

5. **ESCROW:**

   A. **OPENING OF ESCROW:** The purchase of the Property shall be consummated through Escrow ("Escrow"). Opening of Escrow shall take place by the end of one (1) business day after execution of this Agreement ("Opening of Escrow"), at _____ title or escrow company ("Escrow Company" or "ESCROW HOLDER") with _____ ("Escrow Officer") (or such other escrow officer as Escrow Company may assign). Opening of Escrow shall occur upon Escrow Company's receipt of this fully accepted Agreement and receipt of the EMD (if applicable). ESCROW HOLDER is instructed to notify the Parties (through their respective Brokers) of the opening date and the Escrow Number.

   B. **EARNEST MONEY:** Upon Acceptance, Buyer's EMD as shown in Section 1(A), and 1(B) if applicable, of this Agreement, shall be deposited per the Earnest Money Receipt Notice and Instructions contained herein

   C. **CLOSE OF ESCROW:** Close of Escrow ("COE") shall be on (date) _____ . If the designated date falls on a weekend or holiday, COE shall be the next business day.

   D. **IRS DISCLOSURE:** Seller is hereby made aware that there is a regulation which became effective January 1, 1987, that requires all ESCROW HOLDERS to complete a modified 1099 form, based upon specific information known only between parties in this transaction and the ESCROW HOLDER. Seller is also made aware that ESCROW HOLDER is required by federal law to provide this information to the Internal Revenue Service after COE in the manner prescribed by federal law.

   E. **FIRPTA:** If applicable, Seller agrees to complete, sign, and deliver to ESCROW HOLDER a certificate indicating whether Seller is a foreign person or a nonresident alien pursuant to the Foreign Investment in Real Property Tax Act (FIRPTA). A foreign person is a nonresident alien individual; a foreign corporation not treated as a domestic corporation; or a foreign partnership, trust or estate. A resident alien is not considered a foreign person under FIRPTA. Buyer and Seller understand that if Seller is a foreign person then the Buyer must withhold a tax in an amount to be determined by ESCROW HOLDER in accordance with FIRPTA, unless an exemption applies. Seller agrees to sign and deliver to the ESCROW HOLDER the necessary documents, to be provided by the ESCROW HOLDER, to determine if withholding is required. (See 26 USC Section 1445).

6. **TITLE INSURANCE:** Upon COE, Buyer will be provided with the following type of title insurance policy:
   ☐ CLTA; ☐ ALTA-Residential; -OR- ☐ ALTA-Extended (including a survey, if required).

7. **PRORATIONS, FEES AND EXPENSES (Check appropriate box):**
   A. **TITLE AND ESCROW FEES:**

TYPE	PAID BY SELLER	PAID BY BUYER	50/50	N/A
Escrow Fees	☐	☐	☐	☐
Lender's Title Policy	☐	☐	☐	☐
Owner's Title Policy	☐	☐	☐	☐
Real Property Transfer Tax	☐	☐	☐	☐
Other: _____	☐	☐	☐	☐

   B. **PRORATIONS:**

TYPE	PAID BY SELLER	PRORATE	N/A
CIC (Common Interest Community) Assessments	☐	☐	☐
CIC Periodic Fees	☐	☐	☐
SIDs / LIDs / Bonds / Assessments	☐	☐	☐
Sewer Use Fees	☐	☐	☐
Real Property Taxes	☐	☐	☐
Other: _____	☐	☐	☐

All prorations will be based on a 30-day month and will be calculated as of COE. Prorations will be based upon figures available at closing. Any supplementals or adjustments that occur after COE will be handled by the parties outside of Escrow.

Each party acknowledges that he/she has read, understood, and agrees to each and every provision of this page unless a particular paragraph is otherwise modified by addendum or counteroffer.

Buyer's Name: _____ BUYER(S) INITIALS: _____ / _____

Property Address: _____ SELLER(S) INITIALS: _____ / _____

1   **C. INSPECTIONS AND RELATED EXPENSES (See also Section 12):**

2 Acceptance of this offer is subject to the following reserved right. Buyer may have the Property inspected and select the
3 licensed contractors, certified building inspectors and/or other qualified professionals who will inspect the Property. Seller will
4 ensure that necessary utilities (gas, power and water) are turned on and supplied to the Property within two (2) business days
5 after execution of this Agreement, to remain on until COE. (It is strongly recommended that Buyer retain licensed Nevada
6 professionals to conduct inspections.)

TYPE	PAID BY SELLER	PAID BY BUYER	50/50	WAIVED
8 Appraisal	☐	☐	☐	☐
9 CIC Capital Contribution	☐	☐	☐	☐
10 CIC Transfer Fees	☐	☐	☐	☐
11 CLUE Report ordered by Seller	☐	☐	☐	☐
12 Fungal Contaminant Inspection	☐	☐	☐	☐
13 Home Inspection	☐	☐	☐	☐
14 Mechanical Inspection	☐	☐	☐	☐
15 Oil Tank Inspection	☐	☐	☐	☐
16 Pool/Spa Inspection	☐	☐	☐	☐
17 Roof Inspection	☐	☐	☐	☐
18 Septic Inspection (requires pumping)	☐	☐	☐	☐
19 Septic Lid Removal	☐	☐	☐	☐
20 Septic Pumping	☐	☐	☐	☐
21 Soils Inspection	☐	☐	☐	☐
22 Structural Inspection	☐	☐	☐	☐
23 Survey _____ (type)	☐	☐	☐	☐
24 Termite/Pest Inspection	☐	☐	☐	☐
25 Well Inspection (Quantity)	☐	☐	☐	☐
26 Well Inspection (Quality)	☐	☐	☐	☐
27 Wood-Burning Device/Chimney Inspection 28 (includes cleaning)	☐	☐	☐	☐
29 Other: _____	☐	☐	☐	☐
30 Re-Inspections	☐	☐	☐	☐

32 If any inspection is not completed and requested repairs are not delivered to Seller within the Due Diligence Period, Buyer is
33 deemed to have waived the right to that inspection and Seller's liability for the cost of all repairs that inspection would have
34 reasonably identified had it been conducted, except as otherwise provided by law.

36   **D. CERTIFICATIONS:**

TYPE	PAID BY SELLER	PAID BY BUYER	50/50	WAIVED
39 Fungal Contaminant	☐	☐	☐	☐
40 Roof	☐	☐	☐	☐
41 Septic	☐	☐	☐	☐
42 Well	☐	☐	☐	☐
43 Wood-Burning Device/Chimney Certification	☐	☐	☐	☐
44 Other: _____	☐	☐	☐	☐

47 The foregoing expenses for inspections and certifications will be paid outside of Escrow unless the Parties present instructions
48 to the contrary prior to COE (along with the applicable invoice). A certification is not a warranty. Notwithstanding the above
49 elections, in the event an inspection reveals problems with any of the foregoing, Buyer reserves the right to require a
50 certification.

52   **E. SELLER'S ADDITIONAL COSTS AND LIMIT OF LIABILITY:** Seller agrees to pay a maximum
53 amount of $ _____ to correct defects and/or requirements disclosed by inspection reports, appraisals,
54 and/or certifications. It is Buyer's responsibility to inspect the Property sufficiently as to satisfy Buyer's use. Buyer reserves
55 the right to request additional repairs based upon the Seller's Real Property Disclosure. Items of a general maintenance or

Each party acknowledges that he/she has read, understood, and agrees to each and every provision of this page unless a particular paragraph is otherwise modified by addendum or counteroffer.

Buyer's Name: _____ BUYER(S) INITIALS: _____ / _____

Property Address: _____ SELLER(S) INITIALS: _____ / _____

1 cosmetic nature which do not materially affect value or use of the Property, which existed at the time of Acceptance and which
2 are not expressly addressed in this Agreement are deemed accepted by the Buyer, except as otherwise provided in this section.
3 The Brokers herein have no responsibility to assist in the payment of any repair, correction or deferred maintenance on the
4 Property which may have been revealed by the above inspections, agreed upon by the Buyer and Seller or requested by one
5 party.
6
7   **F.**   **LENDER'S FEES: In addition** to Seller's expenses above, Seller will contribute $ _____
8 to Buyer's Lender's Fees and Buyer's Title and Escrow Fees ☐ **including -OR-** ☐ **excluding** costs which Seller must pay
9 pursuant to loan program requirements. Different loan types (e.g., FHA, VA, conventional) have different appraisal and
10 financing requirements, which will affect the parties' rights and costs under this Agreement.
11
12   **G.**   **HOME PROTECTION PLAN:** Buyer and Seller acknowledge that they have been made aware of Home
13 Protection Plans that provide coverage to Buyer after COE. Buyer ☐ **waives -OR-** ☐ **requires** a Home Protection Plan with
14 _____ ☐ **Seller -OR-** ☐ **Buyer** will pay for the Home Protection
15 Plan at a price not to exceed $ _____ . **Buyer** will order the Home Protection Plan. Neither Seller nor Brokers make
16 any representation as to the extent of coverage or deductibles of such plans. ESCROW HOLDER is not responsible for
17 ordering the Home Protection Plan.
18
19   **H.**   **OTHER FEES:** Buyer will also pay $ _____ to Buyer's Broker for _____ .
20
21 **8.**   **TRANSFER OF TITLE:** Upon COE, Buyer shall tender to Seller the agreed upon Purchase Price, and Seller shall
22 tender to Buyer marketable title to the Property free of all encumbrances other than (1) current real property taxes,
23 (2) covenants, conditions and restrictions (CC&R's) and related restrictions, (3) zoning or master plan restrictions and public
24 utility easements; and (4) obligations assumed and encumbrances accepted by Buyer prior to COE. Buyer is advised the
25 Property may be reassessed after COE which may result in a real property tax increase or decrease.
26
27 **9.**   **COMMON-INTEREST COMMUNITIES:** If the Property is subject to a Common Interest Community ("CIC"),
28 Seller or his authorized agent shall request the CIC documents and certificate listed in NRS 116.4109 (collectively, the "resale
29 package") within two (2) business days of Acceptance and provide the same to Buyer within one (1) business day of Seller's
30 receipt thereof. Buyer may cancel this Agreement without penalty until midnight of the fifth (5th) calendar day following the
31 date of receipt of the resale package. If Buyer does not receive the resale package within fifteen (15) calendar days of
32 Acceptance, this Agreement may be cancelled in full by Buyer without penalty. If Buyer elects to cancel this Agreement
33 pursuant to this section, he must deliver, via hand delivery or prepaid U.S. mail, a written notice of cancellation to Seller or his
34 authorized agent identified in the Confirmation of Representation at the end of this Agreement. Upon such written cancellation,
35 Buyer shall promptly receive a refund of the EMD. The parties agree to execute any documents requested by ESCROW
36 HOLDER to facilitate the refund. If written cancellation is not received within the specified time period, the resale package
37 will be deemed approved. Seller shall pay all outstanding CIC fines or penalties at COE.
38
39 **10.**   **DISCLOSURES: Within five (5) calendar days of Acceptance of this Agreement,** Seller will provide the
40 following Disclosures and/or documents (each of which is incorporated herein by this reference). **Check applicable boxes.**

41   ☐ **Construction Defect Claims Disclosure,** if Seller has marked "Yes" to Paragraph 1(d) of the
42   Seller Real Property Disclosure Form (NRS 40.688)

43   ☐ **Fungal (Mold) Notice Form** (not required by Nevada law)

44   ☐ **Lead-Based Paint Disclosure and Acknowledgment,** required if constructed before 1978 (24 CFR 745.113)

45   ☐ **Methamphetamine Lab Disclosure,** if applicable (NRS 40.770, NRS 489.776)

46   ☐ **Pest Notice Form** (not required by Nevada law)

47   ☐ **Promissory Note and the most recent monthly statement** of all loans to be assumed by Buyer

48   ☐ **Rangeland Disclosure** (NRS 113.065)

49   ☐ **Seller Real Property Disclosure Form** (NRS 113.130)

50   ☐ **Other** (list) _____

51

Each party acknowledges that he/she has read, understood, and agrees to each and every provision of this page unless a particular paragraph is otherwise modified by addendum or counteroffer.

Buyer's Name: _____   BUYER(S) INITIALS: _____ / _____

Property Address: _____   SELLER(S) INITIALS: _____ / _____

1 adequacy of law enforcement; proximity to commercial, industrial, or agricultural activities; crime statistics; fire protection;
2 other governmental services; existing and proposed transportation; construction and development; noise or odor from any
3 source; and other nuisances, hazards or circumstances. If Buyer cancels this Agreement due to a specific inspection report,
4 Buyer shall provide Seller at the time of cancellation with a copy of the report containing the name, address, and telephone
5 number of the inspector.
6
7   C.   **PRELIMINARY TITLE REPORT:** Within ten (10) business days of Opening of Escrow, Title Company
8 shall provide Buyer with a Preliminary Title Report ("PTR") to review, which must be approved or rejected within five (5)
9 business days of receipt thereof. If Buyer does not object to the PTR within the period specified above, the PTR shall be
10 deemed accepted. If Buyer makes an objection to any item(s) contained within the PTR, Seller shall have five (5) business
11 days after receipt of objections to correct or address the objections. If, within the time specified, Seller fails to have each such
12 exception removed or to correct each such other matter as aforesaid, Buyer shall have the option to: (a) terminate this
13 Agreement by providing notice to Seller and Escrow Officer, entitling Buyer to a refund of the EMD or (b) elect to accept title
14 to the Property as is. All title exceptions approved or deemed accepted are hereafter collectively referred to as the "Permitted
15 Exceptions."
16
17 **13.** **WALK-THROUGH INSPECTION OF PROPERTY:** Buyer is entitled under this Agreement to a walk-through of
18 the Property within _____ calendar days prior to COE to ensure the Property and all major systems, appliances,
19 heating/cooling, plumbing and electrical systems and mechanical fixtures are as stated in Seller's Real Property Disclosure
20 Statement, and that the Property and improvements are in the same general condition as when this Agreement was signed by
21 Seller and Buyer. To facilitate Buyer's walk-through, Seller is responsible for keeping all necessary utilities on. If any
22 systems cannot be checked by Buyer on walk-through due to non-access or no power/gas/water, then Buyer reserves the right
23 to hold Seller responsible for defects which could not be detected on walk-through because of lack of such access or
24 power/gas/water. The purpose of the walk-through is to confirm (a) the Property is being maintained (b) repairs, if any, have
25 been completed as agreed, and (c) Seller has complied with Seller's other obligations. If Buyer elects not to conduct a walk-
26 through inspection prior to COE, then all systems, items and aspects of the Property are deemed satisfactory, and Buyer
27 releases Seller's liability for costs of any repair that would have reasonably been identified by a walk-through inspection,
28 except as otherwise provided by law.
29
30 **14.** **DELIVERY OF POSSESSION:** Seller shall deliver the Property along with any keys, alarm codes, parking permits
31 (if freely transferable), gate transponders and garage door opener/controls outside of Escrow, upon COE. Seller agrees to
32 vacate the Property and leave the Property in a neat and orderly, broom-clean condition and tender possession no later than
33 ☐ COE -OR- ☐ _____ . In the event Seller does not vacate the Property by this time, Seller shall be
34 considered a trespasser and shall be liable to Buyer for the sum of $ _____ per calendar day in addition to
35 Buyer's legal and equitable remedies. Any personal property left on the Property after the date indicated in this section shall be
36 considered abandoned by Seller.
37
38 **15.** **RISK OF LOSS:** Risk of loss shall be governed by NRS 113.040. This law provides generally that if all or any
39 material part of the Property is destroyed before transfer of legal title or possession, Seller cannot enforce the Agreement and
40 Buyer is entitled to recover any portion of the sale price paid. If legal title or possession has transferred, risk of loss shall shift
41 to Buyer.
42
43 **16.** **ASSIGNMENT OF THIS AGREEMENT:** Unless otherwise stated herein, this Agreement is non-assignable by
44 Buyer.
45
46 **17.** **CANCELLATION OF AGREEMENT:** In the event this Agreement is properly cancelled in accordance with the
47 terms contained herein, then Buyer will be entitled to a refund of the EMD. Neither Buyer nor Seller will be reimbursed for any
48 expenses incurred in conjunction with due diligence, inspections, appraisals or any other matters pertaining to this transaction
49 (unless otherwise provided herein).
50
51 **18.** **DEFAULT:**
52   A.   **MEDIATION:** Before any legal action is taken to enforce any term or condition under this Agreement, the
53   parties agree to engage in mediation, a dispute resolution process, through GLVAR. Not withstanding the foregoing,
54   in the event the Buyer finds it necessary to file a claim for specific performance, this section shall not apply.
55

Each party acknowledges that he/she has read, understood, and agrees to each and every provision of this page unless a particular paragraph is otherwise modified by addendum or counteroffer.

Buyer's Name: _____   BUYER(S) INITIALS: _____ / _____

Property Address: _____   SELLER(S) INITIALS: _____ / _____

B. IF BUYER DEFAULTS: If Buyer defaults in performance under this Agreement, Seller shall have one of the following legal recourses against Buyer (check one only):

☐ As Seller's sole legal recourse, Seller may retain, as liquidated damages, the EMD. In this respect, the Parties agree that Seller's actual damages would be difficult to measure and that the EMD is in fact a reasonable estimate of the damages that Seller would suffer as a result of Buyer's default. Seller understands that any additional deposit not considered part of the EMD in Section 1(B) herein will be immediately released by ESCROW HOLDER to Buyer.

-OR-

☐ Seller shall have the right to recover from Buyer all of Seller's actual damages that Seller may suffer as a result of Buyer's default including, but not limited to, commissions due, expenses incurred until the Property is sold to a third party and the difference in the sales price.

C. IF SELLER DEFAULTS: If Seller defaults in performance under this Agreement, Buyer reserves all legal and/or equitable rights (such as specific performance) against Seller, and Buyer may seek to recover Buyer's actual damages incurred by Buyer due to Seller's default.

Instructions to Escrow

19. ESCROW: If this Agreement or any matter relating hereto shall become the subject of any litigation or controversy, Buyer and Seller agree, jointly and severally, to hold ESCROW HOLDER free and harmless from any loss or expense, except losses or expenses as may arise from ESCROW HOLDER'S negligence or willful misconduct. If conflicting demands are made or notices served upon ESCROW HOLDER with respect to this Agreement, the parties expressly agree that Escrow is entitled to file a suit in interpleader and obtain an order from the Court authorizing ESCROW HOLDER to deposit all such documents and monies with the Court, and obtain an order from the Court requiring the parties to interplead and litigate their several claims and rights among themselves. Upon the entry of an order authorizing such Interpleader, ESCROW HOLDER shall be fully released and discharged from any obligations imposed upon it by this Agreement; and ESCROW HOLDER shall not be liable for the sufficiency or correctness as to form, manner, execution or validity of any instrument deposited with it, nor as to the identity, authority or rights of any person executing such instrument, nor for failure of Buyer or Seller to comply with any of the provisions of any agreement, contract or other instrument filed with ESCROW HOLDER or referred to herein. ESCROW HOLDER'S duties hereunder shall be limited to the safekeeping of all monies, instruments or other documents received by it as ESCROW HOLDER, and for their disposition in accordance with the terms of this Agreement. In the event an action is instituted in connection with this escrow, in which ESCROW HOLDER is named as a party or is otherwise compelled to make an appearance, all costs, expenses, attorney fees, and judgments ESCROW HOLDER may expend or incur in said action, shall be the responsibility of the parties hereto.

20. UNCLAIMED FUNDS: In the event that funds from this transaction remain in an account, held by ESCROW HOLDER, for such a period of time that they are deemed "abandoned" under the provisions of Chapter 120A of the Nevada Revised Statutes, ESCROW HOLDER is hereby authorized to impose a charge upon the dormant escrow account. Said charge shall be no less than $5.00 per month and may not exceed the highest rate of charge permitted by statute or regulation. ESCROW HOLDER is further authorized and directed to deduct the charge from the dormant escrow account for as long as the funds are held by ESCROW HOLDER.

Brokers

21. BROKER FEES: Buyer herein requires, and Seller agrees, as a condition of this Agreement, that Seller will pay Listing Broker and Buyer's Broker, who becomes by this clause a third party beneficiary to this Agreement, that certain sum or percentage of the Purchase Price (commission), that Seller, or Seller's Broker, offered for the procurement of ready, willing and able Buyer via the Multiple Listing Service, any other advertisement or written offer. Seller understands and agrees that if Seller defaults hereunder, Buyer's Broker, as a third-party beneficiary of this Agreement, has the right to pursue all legal recourse against Seller for any commission due.

22. WAIVER OF CLAIMS: Buyer and Seller agree that they are not relying upon any representations made by Brokers or Broker's agent. Buyer acknowledges that at COE, the Property will be sold AS-IS, WHERE-IS without any representations

Each party acknowledges that he/she has read, understood, and agrees to each and every provision of this page unless a particular paragraph is otherwise modified by addendum or counteroffer.

Buyer's Name: _____ BUYER(S) INITIALS: _____ / _____

Property Address: _____ SELLER(S) INITIALS: _____ / _____

1   or warranties, unless expressly stated herein. Buyer agrees to satisfy himself, as to the condition of the Property, prior to COE.
2   Buyer acknowledges that any statements of acreage or square footage by Brokers are simply estimates, and Buyer agrees to
3   make such measurements, as Buyer deems necessary, to ascertain actual acreage or square footage. Buyer waives all claims
4   against Brokers or their agents for (a) defects in the Property; (b) inaccurate estimates of acreage or square footage; (c)
5   environmental waste or hazards on the Property; (d) the fact that the Property may be in a flood zone; (e) the Property's
6   proximity to freeways, airports or other nuisances; (f) the zoning of the Property; (g) tax consequences; or (h) factors related to
7   Buyer's failure to conduct walk-throughs or inspections. Buyer assumes full responsibility for the foregoing and agrees to
8   conduct such tests, walk-throughs, inspections and research, as Buyer deems necessary. In any event, Broker's liability is
9   limited, under any and all circumstances, to the amount of that Broker's commission/fee received in this transaction.
10

Other Matters

11 **23.   DEFINITIONS:** "Acceptance" means the date that both parties have consented to and received a final, binding
12 contract by affixing their signatures to this Agreement and all counteroffers. "**Agent**" means a licensee working under a Broker
13 or licensees working under a developer. "**Agreement**" includes this document as well as all accepted counteroffers and
14 addenda. "**Bona Fide**" means genuine. "**Buyer**" means one or more individuals or the entity that intends to purchase the
15 Property. "**Broker**" means the Nevada licensed real estate broker listed herein representing Seller and/or Buyer (and all real
16 estate agents associated therewith). "**Business Day**" excludes Saturdays, Sundays, and legal holidays. "**Calendar Day**" means
17 a calendar day from/to midnight unless otherwise specified. "**CFR**" means the Code of Federal Regulations. "**CIC**" means
18 Common Interest Community (formerly known as "HOA" or homeowners associations). "**CIC Capital Contribution**" means
19 a one-time non-administrative fee, cost or assessment charged by the CIC upon change of ownership. "**CIC Transfer Fees**"
20 means the administrative service fee charged by a CIC to transfer ownership records. "**CLUE**" means Comprehensive Loss
21 Underwriting Exchange. "**Close of Escrow (COE)**" means the time of recordation of the deed in Buyer's name. "**Default**"
22 means the failure of a Party to observe or perform any of its material obligations under this Agreement. "**Delivered**" means
23 personally delivered to Parties or respective Agents, transmitted by facsimile machine, electronic means, overnight delivery, or
24 mailed by regular mail. "**Down Payment**" is the Purchase Price less loan amount(s). "**EMD**" means Buyer's earnest money
25 deposit. "**Escrow Holder**" means the neutral party that will handle the escrow. "FHA" is the U.S. Federal Housing
26 Administration. "**GLVAR**" means the Greater Las Vegas Association of REALTORS®. "**IRC**" means the Internal Revenue
27 Code (tax code). "**LID**" means Limited Improvement District. "**N/A**" means not applicable. "**NAC**" means Nevada
28 Administrative Code. "**NRS**" means Nevada Revised Statues as Amended. "**Party**" or "**Parties**" means Buyer and Seller.
29 "**PITI**" means principal, interest, taxes, and hazard insurance. "**PMI**" means private mortgage insurance. "**PST**" means
30 Pacific Standard Time, and includes daylight savings time if in effect on the date specified. "**PTR**" means Preliminary Title
31 Report. "**Property**" means the real property and any personal property included in the sale as provided herein. "**Receipt**"
32 means delivery to the party or the party's agent. "**Seller**" means one or more individuals or the entity that is the owner of the
33 Property. "**SID**" means Special Improvement District. "**Title Company**" means the company that will provide title insurance.
34 "**USC**" is the United States Code. "**VA**" is the Veterans Administration.
35
36 **24.   DELIVERY, FACSIMILE, COPIES AND NOTICES:**
37   A.   Delivery of all instruments or documents associated with this Agreement shall be delivered to the Agent for
38 Seller or Buyer if represented. This Agreement may be signed by the parties on more than one copy, which, when taken
39 together, each signed copy shall be read as one complete form. Facsimile signatures may be accepted as original.
40
41   B.   Except as otherwise provided in Section 9, when a Party wishes to provide notice as required in this
42 Agreement, such notice shall be sent regular mail, personal delivery, by facsimile, overnight delivery and/or by email to the
43 Agent for that Party. The notification shall be effective when postmarked, received, faxed, delivery confirmed, and/or read
44 receipt confirmed in the case of email. Any cancellation notice shall be contemporaneously faxed to Escrow.
45
46 **25.   IRC 1031 EXCHANGE:** Seller and/or Buyer may make this transaction part of an IRC 1031 exchange. The party
47 electing to make this transaction part of an IRC 1031 exchange will pay all additional expenses associated therewith, at no cost
48 to the other party. The other party agrees to execute any and all documents necessary to effectuate such an exchange.
49
50 **26.   OTHER ESSENTIAL TERMS:** Time is of the essence. No change, modification or amendment of this Agreement
51 shall be valid or binding unless such change, modification or amendment shall be in writing and signed by each party. This
52 Agreement will be binding upon the heirs, beneficiaries and devisees of the parties hereto. This Agreement is executed and
53 intended to be performed in the State of Nevada, and the laws of that state shall govern its interpretation and effect. The parties
54 agree that the county and state in which the Property is located is the appropriate forum for any action relating to this

Each party acknowledges that he/she has read, understood, and agrees to each and every provision of this page unless a particular paragraph is otherwise modified by addendum or counteroffer.

Buyer's Name: _____   BUYER(S) INITIALS: _____ / _____

Property Address: _____   SELLER(S) INITIALS: _____ / _____

Produced with ZipForm® by zipLogix 18070 Fifteen Mile Road, Fraser, Michigan 48026   www.zipLogix.com   melody

1 Agreement. Should any party hereto retain counsel for the purpose of initiating litigation to enforce or prevent the breach of
2 any provision hereof, or for any other judicial remedy, then the prevailing party shall be entitled to be reimbursed by the losing
3 party for all costs and expenses incurred thereby, including, but not limited to, reasonable attorneys fees and costs incurred by
4 such prevailing party.
5
6 **THIS IS A LEGALLY BINDING CONTRACT.** All parties are advised to seek independent legal and tax advice to review
7 the terms of this Agreement.
8
9 **NO REAL ESTATE BROKER/AGENT MAY SIGN FOR A PARTY TO THIS AGREEMENT UNLESS THE**
10 **BROKER OR AGENT HAS A PROPERLY EXECUTED POWER OF ATTORNEY TO DO SO.**
11
12 **THIS FORM HAS BEEN APPROVED BY THE GREATER LAS VEGAS ASSOCIATION OF REALTORS®**
13 **(GLVAR). NO REPRESENTATION IS MADE AS TO THE LEGAL VALIDITY OR ADEQUACY OF ANY**
14 **PROVISION IN ANY SPECIFIC TRANSACTION. A REAL ESTATE BROKER IS THE PERSON QUALIFIED TO**
15 **ADVISE ON REAL ESTATE TRANSACTIONS. IF YOU DESIRE LEGAL OR TAX ADVICE, CONSULT AN**
16 **APPROPRIATE PROFESSIONAL.**
17
18 This form is available for use by the real estate industry. It is not intended to identify the user as a REALTOR®.
19 REALTOR® is a registered collective membership mark which may be used only by members of the NATIONAL
20 ASSOCIATION OF REALTORS® who subscribe to its Code of Ethics.
21
22 **27.   ADDENDUM(S) ATTACHED:** _____
23 _____
24 _____
25 _____
26 _____
27 _____
28 _____
29 _____
30 **28.   ADDITIONAL TERMS:** _____
31 _____
32 _____
33 _____
34 _____
35 _____
36 _____
37 _____
38 _____
39 _____
40 _____
41 _____

Each party acknowledges that he/she has read, understood, and agrees to each and every provision of this page unless a particular paragraph is otherwise modified by addendum or counteroffer.

Buyer's Name: _____   BUYER(S) INITIALS: _____ / _____

Property Address: _____   SELLER(S) INITIALS: _____ / _____

Earnest Money Receipt

BUYER'S AGENT ACKNOWLEDGES RECEIPT FROM BUYER HEREIN of the sum of $ _____

evidenced by ☐ Cash,   ☐ Cashier's Check, ☐ Personal Check, or ☐ Other _____

payable to _____ . Upon Acceptance, Earnest Money to be deposited within ONE (1) business

day, with ☐ Escrow Holder, ☐ Buyer's Broker's Trust Account, - OR - ☐ Seller's Broker's Trust Account

Date: _____ Signed: _____ Buyer's Agent.

Buyer's Acknowledgement of Offer

Upon Acceptance, Buyer agrees to be bound by each provision of this Agreement, and all signed addenda, disclosures, and attachments.

_____   _____   _____ __:__ ☐ AM ☐ PM
Buyer's Signature   Buyer's Printed Name   Date   Time

_____   _____   _____ __:__ ☐ AM ☐ PM
Buyer's Signature   Buyer's Printed Name   Date   Time

Seller must respond by: _____ ☐ AM ☐ PM on (month) _____ , (day) _____ , (year) _____ . Unless this Agreement is accepted, rejected or countered below and delivered to the Buyer's Broker before the above date and time, this offer shall lapse and be of no further force and effect.

Confirmation of Representation: The Buyer is represented in this transaction by:

Buyer's Broker: _____   Agent's Name: _____
Company Name: _____   Office Address: _____
Phone: _____   Fax: _____
Email: _____

Seller's Response

☐ **ACCEPTANCE:** Seller(s) acknowledges that he/she accepts and agrees to be bound by each provision of this Agreement, and all signed addenda, disclosures, and attachments.

☐ **COUNTER OFFER:** Seller accepts the terms of this Agreement subject to the attached Counter Offer #1.

☐ **REJECTION:** In accordance with NAC 645.632, Seller hereby informs Buyer the offer presented herein is not accepted.

_____   _____   _____ __:__ ☐ AM ☐ PM
Seller's Signature   Seller's Printed Name   Date   Time

_____   _____   _____ __:__ ☐ AM ☐ PM
Seller's Signature   Seller's Printed Name   Date   Time

Confirmation of Representation: The Seller is represented in this transaction by:

Seller's Broker: _____   Agent's Name: _____
Company Name: _____   Office Address: _____
Phone: _____   Fax: _____
Email: _____

Each party acknowledges that he/she has read, understood, and agrees to each and every provision of this page unless a particular paragraph is otherwise modified by addendum or counteroffer.

Buyer's Name: _____   BUYER(S) INITIALS: _____ / _____

Property Address: _____   SELLER(S) INITIALS: _____ / _____

GREATER LAS VEGAS ASSOCIATION OF REALTORS®
ADDENDUM TO PURCHASE AGREEMENT

In reference to Agreement of Sale executed by _____

_____ , as Buyer(s), dated _____ , _____ , covering the real property

commonly known as

_____

It is further agreed by both parties as follows:

_____

_____

_____

_____

_____

_____

_____

_____

_____

_____

_____

_____

_____

This agreement, upon its execution by both parties, is herewith made an integral part of the aforementioned Agreement of Sale.

WHEN PROPERLY COMPLETED THIS IS A BINDING CONTRACT. IF NOT FULLY UNDERSTOOD, SEEK COMPETENT LEGAL AID AND/OR COUNSEL BEFORE SIGNING.

The undersigned Buyer, having inspected the above described property and its appurtenances, offers and agrees to purchase said property on the terms and conditions herein stated and acknowledges receipt of a copy of this agreement from the Agent.

BUYER	DATE
	☐ AM ☐ PM
BUYER	TIME

ACCEPTANCE OF OFFER TO PURCHASE

The undersigned Seller accepts the foregoing offer to purchase and agrees to sell the above described property on the terms and conditions as stated herein and acknowledges receipt of a copy of this agreement.

SELLER	DATE
	☐ AM ☐ PM
SELLER	TIME
AUTHORIZED AGENT	PHONE

Rev. 8/01

© GREATER LAS VEGAS ASSOCIATION OF REALTORS®

Option

The Optionor sells the right to purchase a property, to the optionee at a fixed price for designated period. Usually an option fee is paid by the optionee for the right to use the option. Optionor retains the option fee if the option is not performance by the optionee. This *unilateral* contract becomes a *bilateral* contract when the optionee exercises the option.

Lease purchase

A lease purchase agreement is really two contracts. A purchase agreement and lease. Sometimes portions of lease payment may be applied toward a down payment.

Lease

Elements of lease

1. Lessor and lessee names.
2. Physical description of property.
3. Rent terms.
4. Hold harmless clause to protect lessor from liability claims.
5. Lessor gives right to occupy to lessee and has reversionary interest to retake possession.
6. Lessee may transfer rights by assignment, unless language in lease restricts assignment.

Types of Leases

Gross Lease

A gross lease has tenant pays fixed rent; landlord pays all expenses (utilities, taxes, special assessments).

Net Lease

A net lease has the tenant pay a fixed rent plus expenses (utilities, taxes, special assessments). A net lease is common for commercial property.

Percentage Lease

A percentage lease has the tenant pay a percentage of income as rent.

Land Lease

A land lease or ground lease has the tenant rent unimproved property. Tenant improvements become the landlord's upon termination according to the lease agreement.

Graded Lease

A graded lease or step up lease has the tenant's rent increase or decrease at predetermined times and amounts.

Index Lease

An index lease has the tenant's rent adjusted based on some economic index.

Escalator Lease

Escalator lease increases taxes or other charges are passed along to tenant.

Sandwich Lease

A sandwich lease is named for the original lease between the landlord and tenant 1, and tenant 1 has sublet to tenant 2.

Sale and Lease Back

A sale lease back is a vehicle that converts equity to capital without giving up possession.

Constructive Eviction

Constructive eviction occurs when a lease is terminated and lessee must vacate due to acts or failure to act on the part of the lessor. Wrongful eviction.

Remedies for Breach of Contract/Default

Once a valid, mutually binding contract has been created, both the buyer, and the seller must perform or be discharged. If not, the contract.is breached. The remedy for breach is to put the non-breaching party in as good a position as performance.

Mutual Rescission

Mutual recession or cancellation of obligations and return of all parties to their original condition before the contract was executed. Buyer may recover earnest money upon escrow officer receiving original mutual release papers.

Remedies for Default

The standard real estate contract usually has a provision spelling out the legal remedy of the buyer or seller upon default of the agreement.

Damages

When a buyer defaults on a contract for the sale of real estate there are specific remedies courts may determine are applicable. For example one of the remedies is special damages, including consequential and incidental damages. These damages must be reasonably expected as a probable result of the breach at the time of the contract. An example of special damages is the recovery of the amount required for the removal of the cloud on the title of the property, because the purchase agreement was recorded, though not valid.

Liquidated Damages

A liquidated damages provision states that if the buyer breaches the contract by failing to close title, the seller's *sole legal remedy* s is to keep the buyer's earnest money. Without a liquidated damages provision, the seller could sue the buyer for actual, provable damages. The liquidated damages provision is an agreed upon estimated guess of the actual damages the seller would sustain if the buyer breached the agreement by failing to close. From the buyer's perspective liquidated damages limits his downside risk. In a breach of contract case, at worst he loses his deposit. From a seller's perspective it limits potential recovery, but greatly simplifies smaller disputes.

Specific Performance

As an alternative to damages for breach of a real estate contract, courts have the discretion to award specific performance. Specific performance is the court-ordered performance of each party's duties under a contract. Courts often award specific performance as an alternative to damages when the subject matter of the contract is unique. This is true in real estate because each parcel is unique. Courts are reluctant to decree specific performance, especially when the results would be oppressive or inequitable. Courts do not often force parties into relationships with each other.

Arbitration

If buyers or sellers discover small problems arbitration is recommended. It may not be worth filing lawsuit. Lawsuits are long, expensive, and stressful. Often they could have been prevented by better paperwork or written disclosures. Sometimes they are inevitable, but settlement is almost always better. Each party must initial arbitration in a contract or it does not apply. As general rule arbitrations is less costly and faster than litigation.

Contingencies and Negotiations in a Real Estate Contract

Buyers make offers on homes prior to having sold their own home. They make the offer "contingent" or "conditional" on the sale of their own home.

Contingencies or conditions in real estate contracts limit the completion of the contract and closing. It makes the contract voidable by the buyer.

Some contingencies are normal because most home purchase offers are predicated on financing. If the buyer cannot get a loan, they cannot buy the house. So this type of contingency makes sense.

Inspections make offers conditional. Usually there is a financial limit in the offer, say a $500 limit to cure any defects found in the inspection process. If these defects exceed the $500 limit the seller may choose not to make the repairs and therefore not sell the house, or the buyer may choose to accept the home with the defects.

CONTRACTS QUIZ

1. The transfer of rights under a contract without the release from obligation by the transferor is known as

>   (A) Assignment
>   (B) Novation
>   (C) Succession
>   (D) Supersedure

2. If the sales contract does not specify otherwise, real estate sales contracts

>   (A) Are assignable
>   (B) May be valid at the option of the buyer
>   (C) May be oral
>   (D) Can only be assigned with the consent of the seller

3. An illiterate person is considered

>   (A) Insane
>   (B) Incompetent to contract
>   (C) One who cannot speak
>   (D) One who can't read or write

4. A binder given by a buyer in a real estate transaction

>   (A) May be monetary
>   (B) Must be in the form of a check
>   (C) Must be in cash
>   (D) May be withdrawn by the buyer an time before the seller accepts

5. The printed matter in a sales contract will usually include some reference to all of the following except

>   (A) Evidence of title
>   (B) Assessments of liens
>   C) Prorating of taxes
>   (D) Amount of discount points

6. An offer that does not describe the method and terms of financing, but does state the price

>   (A) Voidable
>   (B) Valid
>   (C) One lacking legal principal
>   (D) Not binding

7. Each of the following is an essential element of a real estate contract except

(A) Legality of object
(B) Valuable consideration
(C) Words of conveyance
(D) Offer and acceptance

8. Which of the following is true about valid contracts

(A) Money must be the consideration
(B) Earnest money is essential consideration
(C) The date must be written in the contract
(D) The consideration can be the mutual promises to perform

9. Which of the following best describes a clause in a sales contract providing for the buyer to obtain a new first mortgage, or the contract may be terminated if it cannot be obtained

(A) Defeasance clause
(B) Subordination clause
(C) Habendum clause
(D) Contingency clause

10. The interest a purchaser acquires when the offer to purchase has been accepted is

(A) Freehold estate
(B) An estate in fee simple
(C) Equitable title
(D) Legal title

11. Realty of consent is lacking in a contract due to all of the following except

(A) Duress
(B) Misrepresentation
(C) Mistake
(D) Illiteracy

12. A person must be of the age of majority in order to do which of the following

(A) Hold title to real property
(B) Pay federal income tax
(C) Appoint an agent
(D) Contract to buy necessities

13. Smith agrees to buy Brown's property and the written agreement was placed in escrow. Smith deposited the full purchase price but Brown refused to sign the deed. Brown's actions is an example of

       (A) Breach
       (B) Recession
       (C) Tender
       (D) Rejection

14. Which is the most essential element for an enforceable real estate purchase contract

       (A) Witnessed
       (B) Being in writing
       (C) Date of the contract
       (D) Time of closing

15. All of the following would constitute a type of consideration required to enforce a real estate contract to purchase a $250,000 property except

       (A) A $250,000 cashier's check
       (B) An earnest money deposit with a written offer
       (C) An oral offer to purchase
       (D) A written promise to pay $250,000 over five years at 7 percent interest

16. All of the following are an essential element of every real estate sales contract except

       (A) Legality of object
       (B) Consideration
       (C) Acknowledgment
       (D) Reality of consent

17. A contract in which Samuel agrees to purchase Rick's property in 60 days is

       (A) An option
       (B) A deed
       (C) A lease
       (D) A contract of sale

18. A real estate contract signed by an unmarried minor is

       (A) Void
       (B) Unenforceable
       (C) Voidable
       (D) Indefeasible

19. If it is to be a bilateral contract the listing must be signed by

       (A) Buyer and seller
       (B) Seller and broker
       (C) Buyer
       (D) Husband and wife

20. A vendee is best described as one whom

       (A) Sells or offers to sell
       (B) Buys or offers to buy
       (C) Borrows money
       (D) Loans money

Chapter - 7 – Laws of Agency

Learning Objectives

A. Types of agency and licensee-client relationships
B. Creation and termination of agency
C. Licensee obligations to parties of a transaction

Agency

Agency is defined as a relationship where one person has the legal authority to act on behalf of another. It defines whom a professional represents and how that representation will be employed. Agency carries *a fiduciary responsi*bility requirement putting clients interests above the agents. Notice that only when an agency relationship exists is the term *client* appropriate. If no agency exists then the customer is just - a *customer*. A real estate agency relationship is a voluntary legal relationship in which a real estate licensee, the agent, agrees to act on behalf of a buyer or seller, or the client in a real estate transaction.

Principals

The sellers and buyers themselves are the principals in the sale, and real estate brokers, (and their broker's agents) are the agents as defined by the law. Although a real estate agent commonly fills out the real estate contract form, agents are typically not given power of attorney to sign the real estate contract or the deed; the principals sign these documents.

The use of a real estate broker is not required for the sale or conveyance of real estate.

Education

In most states real estate licensing is a 3-step procedure:

1. Enrolls in a pre-licensing educational program.

2. Pass a test administered by the state for a real estate agent's licensure.

3. Upon passing, the new licensee must place their license with an established real estate firm, managed by a broker.

Requirements vary by state but after some period of time working as an agent, the licensee may return to the classroom and test to become a broker. Brokers may manage or own firms. Each branch office of a real estate firm must be managed by a broker.

States issue licenses for a multi-year period and require real estate agents and broker to complete continuing education courses prior to renewing their license. Many states recognize licenses from other states and issue licenses upon request to existing agents and firms upon request, however the license must be granted before real estate service is provided in the state.

Three Types of Agency Agreements

State laws provide for three types of agency relationships between real estate agents and their clients:

1. Seller's agent
2. Buyer's agent
3. Dual agent.

Seller Agent

Seller's agent represents sellers only. Prior to 1985, every agent represented the seller, since the seller paid the commission at the completion of the sale. Most buyers did not know that their agent represented only the seller. The broker represents the seller and owes undivided loyalty, confidentiality and accountability to the seller. In negotiating for the best price and terms, the agent must put the sellers interests first.

Buyer Agent

With the increase in the practice of buyer brokerage in most states have been able to represent buyers in the transaction with a written "buyer agency agreement" not unlike the "listing agreement" for sellers. In this case, buyers are clients of the buyer agency.

Exclusive Buyers Agent (EBA)

Some brokerages represent buyers only and are know as Exclusive Buyer Agents, (EBAs). Consumer Report's states "you can find a true buyer's agent only at a firm that does not accept listings." The advantages of using an exclusive buyer agent is that they avoid conflicts of interest by working in the best interests of the buyer and not the seller, avoid homes and neighborhoods likely to fare poorly in the marketplace, ensure the buyer does not unknowingly overpay for a property, fully inform the buyer of the adverse conditions, encourages the buyer make offers based on true value instead of the listed price which sometimes can be overstated, and works to save the buyer money. A buyer agency firm that commissioned a study found EBA purchased homes were seventeen times less likely to go into foreclosure.

A buyer's agent represents buyers only. A real estate broker can exclusively represent the buyer of real property. The agent represents the buyer and is accountable to the buyer. The agent must obey the buyer's instructions and keep confidential anything the buyer tells the agent that may affect the purchase of real property. In negotiating prices and terms the agent must put the buyers interest first. Please refer to the following "Greater Las Vegas Association of Realtors© Exclusive Right to Represent Buyer and Agency Agreement."

GREATER LAS VEGAS ASSOCIATION OF REALTORS®
EXCLUSIVE RIGHT TO REPRESENT BUYER
AND AGENCY AGREEMENT

THE PRINTED PORTION OF THIS AGREEMENT HAS BEEN APPROVED BY THE GREATER LAS VEGAS ASSOCIATION OF REALTORS®. NO REPRESENTATION IS MADE AS THE LEGAL VALIDITY OR ADEQUACY OF ANY PROVISION OR THE TAX CONSEQUENCES THEREOF FOR LEGAL OR TAX ADVICE, CONSULT YOUR ATTORNEY OR TAX ADVISOR.

I/We, _____ ("Buyer") hereby exclusively employs and grants to _____ ("Broker")

(Company Name)

the irrevocable right, commencing on _____ , _____ , and expiring at midnight on _____ , _____ , to locate property and negotiate terms and conditions acceptable to Buyer for purchase, exchange, option, or lease as follows:

1. General Nature of Property: Buyer represents that he intends to acquire an interest in one or more properties meeting the following general description:
Type: _____ Residential _____ Land _____ Commercial _____ Other: _____

2. Broker Compensation: Broker's compensation shall be paid at the time of and as a condition of closing: as follows.
    a. The amount of compensation shall be _____ % of the selling price of the Property or the set amount of $ _____ .
    b. Buyer agrees to compensate Broker if the Buyer or any other person acting on the Buyer's behalf enters into an agreement to purchase, exchange, option, or lease any property of the general nature described herein.
    c. Buyer authorizes Broker to accept compensation from seller or seller's broker, which compensation shall be credited against any compensation owed by Buyer to Broker under this Agreement.
    d. If completion of any transaction is prevented by Buyer's default or with the consent of Buyer, the total compensation due under this Agreement shall be immediately due and payable by Buyer.
    e. Buyer agrees to pay such compensation if Buyer within _____ calendar days after the termination of this Agreement enters into an agreement to purchase, exchange, option or lease any property shown to or negotiated on behalf of the Buyer by Broker during the term of this Agreement, unless Buyer enters into a subsequent buyer-broker exclusive employment agreement with another Broker.

3. Retainer Fee: Buyer agrees to pay and Broker acknowledges receipt of a non-refundable retainer fee in the amount of $ _____ payable to Broker for initial counseling, consultation and research, which retainer fee _____ (shall) _____ (shall not be) credited against any other compensation owed by Buyer to Broker as provided above.

4. New Home/Lot Sales: Buyer acknowledges that some sellers (particularly new home subdivisions, open houses and for-sale-by-owner) will compensate Broker only if Broker accompanies Buyer on the first home/lot visit. Buyer agrees that if Buyer makes a first visit without Broker, resulting in a seller's refusal to compensate Broker, that Buyer will compensate Broker as provided above.

Revised 03/03

Copyright by:
GREATER LAS VEGAS ASSOCIATION OF REALTORS®
Exclusive Authorization to Represent Buyer and Agency Agreement
Page 1 of 3

Dual Agency

Dual agency occurs when the same brokerage represents both the seller and the buyer under written agreements. Individual state laws interpret dual agency rather differently.

Many states discourage dual agency. Instead "transaction brokerage" provides the buyer and seller with a limited form of representation, but without any fiduciary obligations. Buyer and sellers are advised to consult a licensed real estate professional for a written definition of the state's laws regarding agency, and many states require written disclosures to be signed by all parties outlining their duties and obligations.

In some states dual agency can be practiced in situations where the same brokerage (but not agent) represents both the buyer and the seller. If one agent from the brokerage has a home listed and another agent from that brokerage has a buyer-brokerage agreement with a buyer who wishes to buy the listed property, dual agency occurs by allowing each agent to be designated as "intra-company" agent. Only the broker is the dual agent.

The agent must reveal in writing his role as an agent representing more than one party. Dual agency is legal in most states, but can become difficult when deciding what statements made by buyers and sellers are confidential.

Disclosed Dual Agency

Disclosed Dual Agency is when the agent represents both buyer and seller of the same property. Dual agency can only be done with written permission of both clients. This type of agency relationship was previously known as dual agency, and is referred to as an agent representing more than one party. In this case the agent owes both the seller and buyer a duty to deal with them fairly and honestly. The agent does not represent either the seller or the buyer exclusively. Neither party can expect the agent's undivided loyalty. Undisclosed dual agency is illegal. Please refer to the following "Confirmation Regarding Real Estate Agent Relationship" and the "Consent to Act" forms that are used concurrently to show written confirmation of a dual agency situation.

CONSENT TO ACT

This form does not constitute a contract for services nor an agreement to pay compensation.

DESCRIPTION OF TRANSACTION: The real estate transaction is the ☐ sale and purchase *or* ☐ lease of

Property Address: _____

_____

In Nevada, a real estate licensee may act for more than one party in a real estate transaction; however, before the licensee does so, he or she must obtain the written consent of each party. This form is that consent. Before you consent to having a licensee represent both yourself and the other party, you should read this form and understand it.

Licensee: The licensee in this real estate transaction is _____ ("Licensee") whose

license number is _____ and who is affiliated with _____ ("Brokerage").

Seller/Landlord _____
                        Print Name

Buyer/Tenant _____
                        Print Name

CONFLICT OF INTEREST: A licensee in a real estate transaction may legally act for two or more parties who have interests adverse to each other. In acting for these parties, the licensee has a conflict of interest.

DISCLOSURE OF CONFIDENTIAL INFORMATION: Licensee will not disclose any confidential information for one year after the revocation or termination of any brokerage agreement entered into with a party to this transaction, unless Licensee is required to do so by a court of competent jurisdiction or is given written permission to do so by that party. Confidential information includes, but is not limited to, the client's motivation to purchase, trade or sell, which if disclosed, could harm one party's bargaining position or benefit the other.

DUTIES OF LICENSEE: Licensee shall provide you with a "Duties Owed by a Nevada Real Estate Licensee" disclosure form which lists the duties a licensee owes to all parties of a real estate transaction, and those owed to the licensee's client. When representing both parties, the licensee owes the same duties to both seller and buyer. Licensee shall disclose to both Seller and Buyer all known defects in the property, any matter that must be disclosed by law, and any information the licensee believes may be material or might affect Seller's/Landlord's or Buyer's/Tenant's decisions with respect to this transaction.

NO REQUIREMENT TO CONSENT: You are not required to consent to this licensee acting on your behalf. You may
- Reject this consent and obtain your own agent,
- Represent yourself,
- Request that the licensee's broker assign you your own licensee.

CONFIRMATION OF DISCLOSURE AND INFORMATION CONSENT

BY MY SIGNATURE BELOW, I UNDERSTAND AND CONSENT: I am giving my consent to have the above identified licensee act for both the other party and me. By signing below, I acknowledge that I understand the ramifications of this consent, and that I acknowledge that I am giving this consent without coercion.

I/We acknowledge receipt of a copy of this list of licensee duties, and have read and understand this disclosure.					
Seller/Landlord	*Date*	*Time*	*Buyer/Tenant*	*Date*	*Time*
Seller/Landlord	*Date*	*Time*	*Buyer/Tenant*	*Date*	*Time*

Approved Nevada Real Estate Division
Replaces all previous editions

Page 1 of 1

524
Revised 05/01/05

CONFIRMATION REGARDING REAL ESTATE AGENT RELATIONSHIP

This form does not constitute a contract for services

Property Address

In the event any party to the real estate transaction is also represented by another licensee who is affiliated with the same Company, the Broker may assign a licensee to act for each party, respectively. As set forth within the *Duties Owed* form, no confidential information will be disclosed. **This is** ☐ **is not** ☐ **such a transaction.**

I/We confirm the duties of a real estate licensee of which has been presented and explained to me/us. My/Our representative's relationship is:

_____ is the AGENT of   _____ is the AGENT of

☐ Seller/Landlord Exclusively ② ☐ Buyer/Tenant Exclusively ③   ☐ Buyer/Tenant Exclusively ③ ☐ Seller/Landlord Exclusively ②
☐ Both Buyer/Tenant & Seller/Landlord ①   ☐ Both Buyer/Tenant & Seller/Landlord ①

① IF LICENSEE IS ACTING FOR MORE THAN ONE PARTY IN THIS TRANSACTION, you will be provided a **Consent to Act form for your review, consideration and approval or rejection. A licensee can legally represent both the Seller/Landlord and Buyer/Tenant in a transaction, but ONLY with the knowledge and written consent of BOTH the Seller/Landlord and Buyer/Tenant.**

② A licensee who is acting for the Seller/Landlord exclusively, is not representing the Buyer/Tenant and has no duty to advocate or negotiate for the Buyer/Tenant.

③ A licensee who is acting for the Buyer/Tenant exclusively, is not representing the Seller/Landlord and has no duty to advocate or negotiate for the Seller/Landlord.

by _____   by _____
Seller's/Landlord's Company   *Buyer's/Tenant's Company*
Licensed Real Estate Agent   *Licensed Real Estate Agent*

_____ _____   _____ _____
Date   *Time*   *Date*   *Time*

Seller/Landlord _____ Date _____ Time _____   Buyer/Tenant _____ Date _____ Time _____

Seller/Landlord _____ Date _____ Time _____   Buyer/Tenant _____ Date _____ Time _____

Approved Nevada Real Estate Division
Replaces all previous editions
Greentree Realty 6364 W Sahara Ave Las Vegas, NV 89146
Phone: (702) 897 - 0522   Fax: (702) 896 - 1069   John Rosich

560
Revised 4/1/99

john rosich

Produced with ZipForm™ by RE FormsNet, LLC 18025 Fifteen Mile Road, Clinton Township, Michigan 48035   www.zipform.com

Transaction Brokerage

The transaction broker crafts a transaction by bringing a willing buyer and a willing seller together and assists with the closing of details. The transaction broker is not a fiduciary of any party, but must abide by law as well as professional ethical standards.

Requirements for a Commission

Only licensed real estate brokers and salespersons can receive a commission in the purchase, sale, lease or exchange of real property. The license must be current and in an active status. The assistance of a licensed real estate agent includes a number of services, such as examining property for basic valuations. This is not to be confused with the services of a licensed appraiser.

Brokers

A real estate broker negotiates agreements to sell, exchange purchase, rent or lease interests in real property for a fee. A broker is responsible for accepting and escrowing all funds, such as a deposit placed on the purchase of a home, and for finalizing transactions. A real estate broker must supervise a transaction conducted by a salesperson.

Subagents

A subagent is an agent of the broker and may be hired without the permission of the principal. States laws relieve brokers of the liability of subagents by eliminating the "common law" areas of agency in real estate licensing legislation,

Salespersons

A real estate a sales person (in some states salespersons are referred to as a broker) engages in the same activities as a broker, except completing the negotiation of any agreement or transaction. A salesperson also, has no authority or control over escrow funds. A salesperson must be affiliated with a broker, either as an employee or as an independent contractor, and work under the supervision of the broker, (in some states referred to as the managing broker).

Master/servant Relationship

The master/servant relationship is the typical employer/employee relationship. The general rule, as to whether a master/servant relationship exists, is based on the extent of control the employer has over the servant. When the employer closely supervises the activities of the employee and controls the means by which the employee's work is accomplished is defined as a servant or employee.

Independent Contractor

In an employer/independent contractor situation the employer has much less control over the acts of the agent. The employer is generally concerned with the end result and not with the means employed by the agent to accomplish those results. In effect, the employer is generally not concerned where the employee is, or what, the employee is doing at any given time. In most cases the real estate agent is an independent contractor.

Earnest Money Deposits

All parties need to be clear about who will hold any earnest money deposit funds and what will happen in the event of a dispute between the parties. All agreements should be in writing and no party should sign an agreement or pay any money until they are comfortable in their understanding of the terms. If a broker accepts money, he must deposit the payment into the broker's trust account or deposit the payment in an escrow account. The broker is *not* required to have a trust account for the purchase or sale of real estate.

Purchase and Sale Agreement

A purchase and sale agreement is the contract between buyer and seller. The purchase and sale agreement controls the sale of the real property from sellers to buyers. It includes information about what is being sold, the sale price and financing, the type of title, the closing date, the amount of deposit and the amount of financing.

Parties to an Agency Relations

Principal	The principal is the one who employs another to act on his behalf.
Agent	The agent with fiduciary responsibilities is the one who is employed to represent a principal.
Sub-Agent	The subagent is, by common law, defined as the one who is employed to represent an agent representing a principal. A third party to a transaction is one who is not a party to the particular agency agreement. A consumer third party is a "customer."

Laws of Agency

Laws of agency specify the agent's fiduciary responsibilities, ("COALD")

- Care

- Obedience

- Accounting

- Loyalty

- Disclosure

Disclosure

Disclosure of representation is done by using a *Duties Owed Form.* Please refer to the form titled "Duties Owned By A Nevada Real Estate Licensee" which is required by agents responsible to clients. The disclosure includes:

1. Disclosure representation, either orally or in writing, prior to showing.
2. If representation changes, a new disclosure is required at once.
3. Must disclose if representing a relative.
4. When representing buyer and seller (dual agency), agent must get consent of both parties in writing.
5. Disclosure must state the source of any expected compensation to the broker.

Mandatory Disclosures

Seller and agent must reveal all known material facts. Licensee who withholds or lies about material facts may be guilty of misrepresentation, or fraud.

A listing agent has a duty to present all offers to the client, unless otherwise specified in writing. Multiple offers should be presented simultaneously, and in the order they are received.

States also have a requirement for a Seller's Real Property Disclosure Form. Please refer to the "Seller's Real Property Disclosure Form."

Liability for Another's Acts

Brokers are responsible for all professional acts they perform and the performance of salespersons associated with them. Unless a party knowingly misrepresented or concealed, neither the party to a transaction nor any licensee is responsible for a misrepresentation nor a concealment of a material fact made by someone else.

Failure to Present All Offers

The agent must make the principal fully aware of all offers, regardless of the unacceptability of the offer. The rejection of the offer must be made writing. The principal, not the agent, makes the decision as to which offer is acceptable, rejected, or counter offered.

Failure to Inform the Client of the True Value of the Property

The broker must inform the principal of the true value of the subject property. This is a fuzzy area because of the concept that the broker may not know but should have known.

Failure to Disclose the Agent as the Purchaser

If the broker attempts to purchase the subject property through a "straw buyer," the broker is violating regulatory statutes.

Types of Agency

Special Agency

Real estate agents are special agents. Special agency is created when an agent is authorized to perform a particular act without the ability to bind the principal. The special agent has limited authority to do a specific thing or conduct a specific task. Real estate agents are special agents because they have limited authority. The agent is hired for a specific purpose, to find a ready, willing and able buyer for the principal/seller.

General Agency

A general agent is authorized to handle all the matters of a principal in one area or in specific areas, such as the responsibility to run the business affair of the principal. General agents have authority to conduct a wide range of activities on a continuous basis on behalf of the principal.

Universal Agency

Universal agents are authorized by the principal to do all things that can be lawfully delegated to an agent.
Universal agents have the greatest degree of authority. The universal agency is created when an agent is authorized to perform in place of the principal. This is accomplished through a *power of attorney*, which is appointed as an Attorney-in-Fact.

Creation of an Agency

Agency relationship are consensual, (by verbal agreement), rather than contractual. Attorneys will not usually have a written agency agreement with their client. Agency may be formed expressly, by ratification or by estoppel.

Express agency created through an oral or written agreement.
Implied agency created through the actions of the parties.
Agency by ratification created "after the fact" when a previously unauthorized action is confirmed by a
Ostensible agency or **agency by estoppel** – created when a third party is led to believe an agency relationship exists.

134

The Listing Agreement

Brokers present sellers with a standard listing agreement containing standard language. The client may negotiate different terms that are usually acceptable to the client and the broker. The typical items that are included in a listing agreement are the length of the listing term, the commission that will be paid and any type of advertising that will be done.

Types of Listing Agreements

Exclusive Right to Sell

- Exclusive right to sell agreements clearly state that the agent is paid regardless of who obtains the buyer.
- It gives maximum broker protection by eliminating procuring cause disagreements.
  Please refer to the following "Exclusive Authorization and Right to Sell, Exchange or Lease Brokerage Listing Agreement."

GREATER LAS VEGAS ASSOCIATION OF REALTORS®
MULTIPLE LISTING SERVICE
Exclusive Authorization and Right to Sell, Exchange or Lease
Brokerage Listing Agreement

THE PRINTED PORTION OF THIS AGREEMENT HAS BEEN APPROVED BY THE GREATER LAS VEGAS ASSOCIATION OF REALTORS®.
NO REPRESENTATION IS MADE AS THE LEGAL VALIDITY OR ADEQUACY OF ANY PROVISION OR THE TAX CONSEQUENCES THEREOF.
FOR LEGAL OR TAX ADVICE, CONSULT YOUR ATTORNEY OR TAX ADVISOR.

1. **EXCLUSIVE RIGHT TO SELL:** I/We, _____
(hereinafter referred to as "Seller") hereby employs and grants _____ (hereinafter referred to as
_____(Company Name)_____
"Broker") the exclusive and irrevocable right, commencing on _____, and expiring on _____ ,
to sell, lease or exchange the Real Property located in the City of _____ , County of _____ ,
Nevada, APN #: _____ commonly known as: _____ (hereinafter
referred to as "The Property").

2. **TERMS OF SALE:** The listing price shall be $ _____ , terms available: Cash ____ CONV ____ FHA ____ Lease ____
VA ____ Lease Option ____ Owner Will Carry ____ Other _____ .

3. **PERSONAL PROPERTY:** The following items of Personal Property are included in the above price and shall be conveyed unencumbered in
escrow by a valid bill of sale: _____
_____
_____

4. **MULTIPLE LISTING SERVICE (MLS):** Broker is a participant of THE GREATER LAS VEGAS ASSOCIATION OF REALTORS®
(GLVAR) Multiple Listing Service, and the listing information will be provided to the MLS to be published and disseminated to its Participants and
Subscribers in accordance with its Rules and Regulations. Broker is authorized to cooperate with other real estate Brokers, and to report the sale, its
price, terms and financing for the publication, dissemination information and use by authorized Association members, MLS Participants and
Subscribers.

5. **TITLE INSURANCE:** Seller agrees to provide Buyer with a policy of title insurance in the amount of the selling price.

6. **COMPENSATION TO BROKER:** Seller agrees to pay Broker as compensation for services _____ % of selling price of the Property or
$ _____ amount. If leased _____ % of the total rental agreed to be paid by lessee or $ _____ .
The amount or rate of real estate commission is not set by law; it is determined by each Broker individually and may be negotiated between Seller and
Broker.

Compensation shall be due:

a. if the Property is sold or leased by Broker, or through any other person including Seller, on the above terms or any other price and terms acceptable
to Seller during the above time period or any extension of said time period;

b. if the Property is transferred, conveyed, leased, rented, or made unmarketable by a voluntary act of Seller without the consent of Broker, during the
time period or any extension of said time period.

c. if within _____ calendar days of the final termination, including extensions, of this Agreement, the Property is sold, conveyed, or otherwise
transferred to anyone with whom the Broker has had negotiations or to whom the Property was shown prior to the final termination. This section
(c) shall not apply if Seller enters into a valid Brokerage Listing Agreement with another licensed real estate Broker after the final termination of
this Exclusive Brokerage Listing Agreement.

In the event of an exchange, permission is hereby given to the Broker to represent such parties as Broker may deem appropriate and collect
compensation from them provided that there is full disclosure to all parties. If completion of sale is prevented by default of Seller, or the refusal Seller
to accept an offer in accordance with the price and terms of this Agreement, then upon event, Broker is authorized to take any action reasonably
necessary to collect said commission. If completion of sale is prevented by a party to the transaction other than Seller, Broker may collect it's
commission only if and when Seller collects damages by suit or otherwise, and then in an amount not less than one-half of the damages recovered, but
not to exceed the above compensation after first deducting title expenses, escrow expenses and the expenses of collection if any. Broker is authorized
to cooperate and divide with other brokers the above compensation in any manner acceptable to Broker. Seller hereby irrevocably assigns to Broker the
funds and proceeds of Seller in escrow equal to the above compensation. In the event any sum of money due under this Agreement remains unpaid for
a period of thirty (30) days, such sum shall bear interest at the rate of (_____) percent per annum from the due date until paid.

7. **DEPOSIT:** Broker is authorized to accept on Seller's behalf a deposit to be applied toward purchase price or lease.

8. **AGENCY RELATIONSHIP:**

a. Broker shall act as the agent of the Seller and may also assign or designate a licensee of the Broker who shall act as the representative of the Seller
in any resulting transaction.

b. Depending upon the circumstances, it may be necessary or appropriate for the assigned or designated licensee to act as agent for both Seller and
Buyer, exchange parties, or one or more additional parties. If applicable, Broker and the assigned or designated licensee shall disclose to Seller
any election to act as a dual agent representing both Seller and Buyer and obtain the written **Consent To Act Form** signed by all parties to the
transaction.

c. Broker may also have licensees in its company who are agents of the Buyer who may show and negotiate an offer to purchase Seller's Property. In
this event the licensees that represent the Buyer will only represent the Buyer in the transaction with all fiduciary duties owed to the Buyer and not
the Seller this, therefore, does not create a dual agency.

9. **SELLER'S REAL PROPERTY DISCLOSURE STATEMENT:** Unless exempt under NRS chapter 113, Seller shall truthfully complete and
sign a Seller's Real Property Disclosure Statement concerning the condition of the Property.

10. **SELLER'S INDEMNIFICATION:** Seller agrees to save, defend, and hold Broker harmless from all claims, disputes, litigation, and/or
judgments arising from any incorrect information supplied by Seller or from any material facts which Seller fails to disclose.

By Initialing below, Seller acknowledges that they have read, understood, and agreed to each and every provision of this page.

Sellers Initials

Revised 07/02
Copyright© 2001 GLVAR

Page 1 of 2 Brokerage Listing Agreement

11. FAIR HOUSING: Broker shall offer the Property for sale or lease without regard to race, color, sex, creed, religion, national origin, handicap, or familial status in compliance with federal, state, and local anti-discrimination laws.

12. LEAD-BASED PAINT: Seller shall complete the Disclosure of Information on Lead-Based Paint Hazards if the property was built prior to 1978 in accordance with Federal Regulations.

13. SIGN: Seller authorizes Broker to install a FOR SALE/LEASE sign on the Property.

14. KEYBOX: Seller [____] (does) [____] (does not) authorize Broker to install a keybox in connection with the showing of the Property. Seller acknowledges that they have been advised that:

a. the purpose and function of the keybox is to permit access to the interior of the Property by all members of the Multiple Listing Service (MLS) of the GLVAR;

b. Seller should safeguard Personal Property and valuables located within the Property;

c. it is not a requirement of the GLVAR's MLS for a Seller to allow the use of a keybox;

d. where a tenant/lessee occupies the Property, the tenant/lessee's consent is also required;

e. neither the listing nor selling Broker nor the GLVAR is an insurer against the loss of Personal Property. Seller hereby releases Broker and the GLVAR from any responsibility relating to the keybox.

15. TAX WITHHOLDING: Seller agrees to perform any act reasonably necessary to carry out the provisions of FIRPTA (Internal Revenue Code 1445).

16. MEDIATION/ARBITRATION: The Broker and Seller hereby agree that any dispute concerning the terms and conditions of this contract shall be resolved through mediation and arbitration proceedings at the GLVAR in accordance with the standards of practice of the National Association of REALTORS®. If a lawsuit if filed by either party, that lawsuit shall be stayed until the dispute is resolved or terminated in accordance with this paragraph.

17. ATTORNEYS FEES: In the event suit is brought by either party to enforce this Agreement, the prevailing party is entitled to court costs and reasonable attorneys fees.

18. ADVERTISING: Seller acknowledges that a photo of the Property may be taken by an authorized representative for publication in the MLS computer system. Seller agrees that the Property may be advertised in all formats of media including but not limited to electronic and print advertising.

19. ADDITIONAL TERMS: _____

_____

_____

_____

_____

_____

20. NEVADA LAW APPLIES: This Agreement is executed and intended to be performed in the State of Nevada, and the laws of Nevada shall govern its interpretation and effect. The parties agree that the State of Nevada, and the county in which the Property is located, is the appropriate judicial forum for any litigation, arbitration or mediation related to this Agreement.

21. ENTIRE CONTRACT: All prior negotiations and agreements between the parties are incorporated in this Agreement, which constitutes the entire contact. Its terms are intended by the parties as a final, complete, and exclusive expression of their agreement with respect to its subject matter and may not be contradicted by evidence of any prior agreement or contemporaneous oral agreement. This Agreement and any supplement, addendum, or modification, including any photocopy or facsimile, may be executed in two or more counterparts, all of which shall constitute one and the same writing. The terms of this Agreement may not be amended, modified or altered except through a written agreement signed by all of the parties hereto.

22. PARTIAL INVALIDITY: In the event that any provision of this Agreement shall be held to be invalid or unenforceable, such ruling shall not affect the validity or enforceability of the remainder of the Agreement in any respect whatsoever.

23. WARRANTY OF OWNERSHIP: Seller warrants that Seller is the sole Owner of the Property or has the authority to execute this Agreement. By signing below Seller acknowledges that Seller has read and understands this Agreement, agrees to the terms thereof, and has received a copy.

SELLER:

Date _____ , _____ Telephone _____ FAX _____ E-Mail _____

Seller _____ Address _____

Seller _____ City _____ State _____ Zip _____

BROKER:

Date _____ , _____ Telephone _____ FAX _____ E-Mail: _____

Company _____ Address _____

Broker's Signature _____ City _____ State _____ Zip _____

Designated Licensee _____

Exclusive Agency

An exclusive agency agreement contains the following conditions:

- Owner retains right to sell the real estate himself without paying a commission.
- If anyone other than the owner obtains the buyer, agent gets paid.
  Please refer to the Exclusive Agency form on the following page.

GREATER LAS VEGAS ASSOCIATION OF REALTORS®
MULTIPLE LISTING SERVICE
EXCLUSIVE AGENCY LISTING AGREEMENT

THE PRINTED PORTION OF THIS AGREEMENT HAS BEEN APPROVED BY THE GREATER LAS VEGAS ASSOCIATION OF REALTORS®
NO REPRESENTATION IS MADE AS THE LEGAL VALIDITY OR ADEQUACY OF ANY OF ANY PROVISION OR THE TAX CONSEQUENCES THEREOF.
FOR LEGAL OR TAX ADVICE, CONSULT YOUR ATTORNEY OR TAX ADVISOR.

1. EXCLUSIVE RIGHT TO SELL: I/We, _____
(hereinafter referred to as "Seller") hereby employs and grants _____ (hereinafter referred to as
(Company Name)
"Broker") the exclusive and irrevocable right, commencing on _____, and expiring on _____,
to sell, lease or exchange the Real Property located in the City of _____, County of _____,
Nevada, APN #: _____ commonly known as: _____
(hereinafter referred to as "The Property").

2. TERMS OF SALE: The listing price shall be $ _____, terms available: Cash ____ CONV ____ FHA ____ Lease ____
VA ____ Lease Option ____ Owner Will Carry ____ Other _____.

3. PERSONAL PROPERTY: The following items of Personal Property are included in the above price and shall be conveyed unencumbered in
escrow by a valid bill of sale: _____
_____

4. MULTIPLE LISTING SERVICE (MLS): Broker is a participant of THE GREATER LAS VEGAS ASSOCIATION OF REALTORS®
(GLVAR) Multiple Listing Service, and the listing information will be provided to the MLS to be published and disseminated to its Participants and
Subscribers in accordance with its Rules and Regulations. Broker is authorized to cooperate with other real estate Brokers, and to report the sale, its
price, terms and financing for the publication, dissemination information and use by authorized Association members, MLS Participants and
Subscribers.

5. TITLE INSURANCE: Seller agrees to provide Buyer with a policy of title insurance in the amount of the selling price.

6. COMPENSATION TO BROKER: Seller agrees to pay Broker as compensation for services _____ % of selling price of the Property or
$ _____ amount. If leased _____ % of the total rental agreed to be paid by lessee or $ _____ .
The amount or rate of real estate commission is not set by law; it is determined by each Broker individually and may be negotiated between Seller and
Broker.

Compensation shall be due:
(a) if the Property is sold or leased by Broker, or through any other person excluding Seller, on the above terms or any other price and terms
acceptable to Seller during the above time period or any extension of said time period;
(b) if the Property is transferred, conveyed, leased, rented, or made unmarketable by a voluntary act of Seller, without the consent of Broker,
during the time period or any extension of said time period;
(c) if within _____ calendar days of the final termination, including extensions, of this Agreement, the Property is sold, conveyed, or
otherwise transferred to anyone with whom the Broker has had negotiations or to whom the Property was shown prior to the final termination. This
section (c) shall not apply if Seller enters into a valid Brokerage Listing Agreement with another licensed real estate Broker after the final
termination of this Exclusive Agency Listing Agreement;
in the event of an exchange, permission is hereby given to the Broker to represent such parties as Broker may deem appropriate and collect
compensation from them provided that there is full disclosure to all parties. If completion of sale is prevented by default of Seller, or the refusal Seller
to accept on offer in accordance with the price and terms of this Agreement, then upon event, Broker is authorized to take any action reasonably
necessary to collect said commission. If completion of sale is prevented by a party to the transaction other than Seller, Broker may collect it's
commission only if and when Seller collects damages by suit or otherwise, and then in an amount not less than one-half of the damages recovered, but
not to exceed the above compensation after first deducting title expenses, escrow expenses and the expenses of collection if any. Broker is authorized
to cooperate and divide with other brokers the above compensation in any manner acceptable to Broker. Seller hereby irrevocably assigns to Broker the
funds and proceeds of Seller in escrow equal to the above compensation. In the event any sum of money due under this Agreement remains unpaid for
a period of thirty (30) days, such sum shall bear interest at the rate of (_____) percent per annum from the due date until paid.

7. DEPOSIT: Broker is authorized to accept on Seller's behalf a deposit to be applied toward purchase price or lease.

8. AGENCY RELATIONSHIP:
(a) Broker shall act as the agent of the Seller and may also assign or designate a licensee of the Broker who shall act as the representative of the
Seller in any resulting transaction.
(b) Depending upon the circumstances, it may be necessary or appropriate for the assigned or designated licensee to act as agent for both Seller and
Buyer, exchange parties, or one or more additional parties. If applicable, Broker and the assigned or designated licensee shall disclose to Seller any
election to act as a dual agent representing both Seller and Buyer and obtain the written **Consent To Act Form** signed by all parties to the
transaction.
(c) Broker may also have licensees in its company who are agents of the Buyer who may show and negotiate an offer to purchase Seller's Property.
In this event the licensees that represent the Buyer will only represent the Buyer in the transaction with all fiduciary duties owed to the Buyer and
not the Seller this, therefore, does not create a dual agency.

9. SELLER'S REAL PROPERTY DISCLOSURE STATEMENT: Unless exempt under NRS chapter 113, Seller shall truthfully complete and
sign a Seller's Real Property Disclosure Statement concerning the condition of the Property.

By Initialing below, Seller acknowledges that they have read, understood, and agreed to each and every provision of this page.

Sellers Initials

Revised 07/02

Page 1 of 2 Exclusive Agency
Copyright© 2001 GLVAR

Greentree Realty 6364 W Sahara Ave Las Vegas, NV 89146
Phone: (702) 897 - 0522   Fax: (702) 896 - 1069   John Rosich   139   john rosich

10. SELLER'S INDEMNIFICATION: Seller agrees to save, defend, and hold Broker harmless from all claims, disputes, litigation, and/or judgments arising from any incorrect information supplied by Seller or from any material facts which Seller fails to disclose.

11. FAIR HOUSING: Broker shall offer the Property for sale or lease without regard to race, color, sex, creed, religion, national origin, handicap, or familial status in compliance with federal, state, and local anti-discrimination laws.

LEAD-BASED PAINT: Seller shall complete the Disclosure of Information on Lead-Based Paint Hazards if the property was built prior to 1978 in accordance with Federal Regulations.

13. SIGN: Seller authorizes Broker to install a FOR SALE/LEASE sign on the Property.

14. KEYBOX: Seller [____] (does) [____] (does not) authorize Broker to install a keybox in connection with the showing of the Property. Seller acknowledges that they have been advised that:

    (a) the purpose and function of the keybox is to permit access to the interior of the Property by all members of the Multiple Listing Service (MLS) of the GLVAR;

    (b) Seller should safeguard Personal Property and valuables located within the Property;

    (c) it is not a requirement of the GLVAR's MLS for a Seller to allow the use of a keybox;

    (d) where a tenant/lessee occupies the Property, the tenant/lessee's consent is also required;

    (e) neither the listing nor selling Broker nor the GLVAR is an insurer against the loss of Personal Property. Seller hereby releases Broker and the GLVAR from any responsibility relating to the keybox.

15. TAX WITHHOLDING: Seller agrees to perform any act reasonably necessary to carry out the provisions of FIRPTA (Internal Revenue Code 1445).

16. MEDIATION/ARBITRATION: The Broker and Seller hereby agree that any dispute concerning the terms and conditions of this contract shall be resolved through mediation and arbitration proceedings at the GLVAR in accordance with the standards of practice of the National Association of REALTORS®. If a lawsuit if filed by either party, that lawsuit shall be stayed until the dispute is resolved or terminated in accordance with this paragraph.

17. ATTORNEYS FEES: In the event suit is brought by either party to enforce this Agreement, the prevailing party is entitled to court costs and reasonable attorneys fees.

18. ADVERTISING: Seller acknowledges that a photo of the Property may be taken by an authorized representative for publication in the MLS computer system. Seller agrees that the Property may be advertised in all formats of media including but not limited to electronic and print advertising.

19. ADDITIONAL TERMS: _____
_____
_____
_____
_____
_____

20. NEVADA LAW APPLIES: This Agreement is executed and intended to be performed in the State of Nevada, and the laws of Nevada shall govern its interpretation and effect. The parties agree that the State of Nevada, and the county in which the Property is located, is the appropriate judicial forum for any litigation, arbitration or mediation related to this Agreement.

21. ENTIRE CONTRACT: All prior negotiations and agreements between the parties are incorporated in this Agreement, which constitutes the entire contact. Its terms are intended by the parties as a final, complete, and exclusive expression of their agreement with respect to its subject matter and may not be contradicted by evidence of any prior agreement or contemporaneous oral agreement. This Agreement and any supplement, addendum, or modification, including any photocopy or facsimile, may be executed in two or more counterparts, all of which shall constitute one and the same writing. The terms of this Agreement may not be amended, modified or altered except through a written agreement signed by all of the parties hereto.

22. PARTIAL INVALIDITY: In the event that any provision of this Agreement shall be held to be invalid or unenforceable, such ruling shall not affect the validity or enforceability of the remainder of the Agreement in any respect whatsoever.

23. WARRANTY OF OWNERSHIP: Seller warrants that Seller is the sole Owner of the Property or has the authority to execute this Agreement. By signing below Seller acknowledges that Seller has read and understands this Agreement, agrees to the terms thereof, and has received a copy.

24. NOTIFICATION: Seller agrees to notify Agent in writing within 24 hours of acceptance of any offer of sale, lease or exchange including identity of parties, price and terms.

25. LIST PRICE: Seller agrees that his offer of the property for sale or exchange shall not be a lower price than stated above or as amended with Agent.

SELLER:

Date _____ , _____ . Telephone _____ FAX _____ E-Mail _____

Seller _____ Address _____

Seller _____ City _____ State _____ Zip _____

BROKER:

Date _____ , _____ . Telephone _____ FAX _____ E-Mail _____

Company _____ Address _____

Broker's Signature _____ City _____ State _____ Zip _____

Designated Licensee _____

Revised 07/02

Open/Non-Exclusive

Open listings allow owners to list with more than one broker, and the listing broker is paid only if he obtains the buyer which can cause possible procuring cause disagreements, and it may be terminated at any time prior to performance.

Net Listing

Net listings state that broker receives as commission all money above a minimum guaranteed sales price. Net listings are illegal or not recommended in most states.

Essential Elements of a Listing

- The listing must be in writing and signed.
- *Commission* amounts are clearly stated and/or methods of compensation paid to the listing broker are *negotiable.* As a result the listing agreement commission is not price fixing and is not a violation of Sherman Anti-trust Act.
- The sale price and terms of commission are clearly stated.
- Listings must have a definite beginning and termination date.

A Listing May Be Terminated By:

- Performance by both parties (closing the sale).
- Expiration.
- Mutual rescission.
- Death or incapacity of either broker or seller (NOTE: death of salesperson does not terminate a listing).
- Destruction of premises.
- Bankruptcy of either broker or seller.

Carryover Clause
Override Clause
Safety Clause
Protection Clause
Extender Clause

A carryover clause provides for a broker to collect a commission for a certain length of time after the termination of the listing. If a buyer was exposed to the property during the time of the listing and the subject property was procured after the listing expired. Many states have laws that terminate this clause once seller signs new listing. Otherwise, seller could potentially become liable for two commissions.

Buyer Agency Agreement

Buyer representation agreements require purchasers to compensate the broker when purchasing property through any source. The agency agreement must have a beginning and ending date.

Compensation

Compensation has traditionally been based on a percentage of the sales price, split between the buying and selling brokers, and then between the agent(s) and his/her real estate agency. While a split based on the percentage received by the broker is generally normal, in some brokerages agents may pay a monthly desk fee for office costs, etc. and then retain one hundred percent of the commission received.

National Association of Realtors (NAR)

Several notable groups exist to promote the real estate industry and to assist members who are in it. The National Association of Realtors (NAR) is the largest real estate organization by far and one of the largest trade groups anywhere. Their membership exceeds one million. NAR also has state chapter in each state as well as thousands of local chapters. Upon joining the local chapter, the new member is automatically enrolled into the state and national organizations.

Multiple Listing Service (MLS)

A large advantage of membership in the National Association of Realtors is access to the Multiple Listing Services (MLS) maintained by the organization for the benefit of members. Access to the MLS usually requires payment of additional dues by the member. MLS shows every listing taken by a Realtor in the jurisdiction.

AGENCY QUIZ

1. The responsibility of a real estate sales agent in a listing agreement relationship include all of the following except:

   (A) Exercise of due care

   (B) Accountability

   (C) Obedience

   (D) Repair of defects

2. The listing broker owes a direct fiduciary relationship to whom?

   (A) The listing salesperson

   (B) The buyer

   (C) The buyer's broker

   (D) The seller

3. The best description of a special agent would be a person who/is:

   (A) An attorney

   (B) A broker

   (C) Has limited authority

   (D) Has contractual authority

4. An agency agreement to sell a specific piece of real property will be terminated by all of the following except:

   (A) Death of the broker

   (B) Bankruptcy of the seller

   (C) Insanity of the broker

   (D) Revocation of the listing salesperson's license

5. The position of trust assumed by the broker as an agent for the principal is described most accurately as:

   (A) Trustee relationship

   (B) Trustor relationship

   (C) Confidential relationship

   (D) Fiduciary Relationship

6. In handling a real estate transaction, a broker should:

    (A) Not reveal building code violations

    (B) Reveal only things that are part of the public record

    (C) Reveal items requested by the seller

    (D) Provide the client with a statement of the receipts and disbursements from the client's earnest money deposit.

7. Most likely the real estate broker has an agency relationship with:

    (A) Buyer

    (B) Seller

    (C) Escrow

    (D) Attorney

8. The relationship between property owner and broker is that of:

    (A) Seller and purchaser

    (B) Principal and agent

    (C) Principal and sales agent

    (D) Optionor and optionee

9. The cooperating broker in a real estate transaction may be any of the following except:

    (A) Listing broker

    (B) Subagent

    (C) Selling agent

    (D) Buyer's agent

10. Salespeople may accept compensation of their pre-determined share of the commission:

    (A) From the multiple listing service

    (B) From the owner of the property

    (C) From their employing broker

    (D) From a cooperating broker

11. A licensee acting on behalf of a property owner is best described as:

(A) A dual agent

(B) An implied agency

(C) A fiduciary

(D) Ratified

12. The amount of commission a broker must pay a salesperson from a real estate sales transaction is determined by:

(A) The listing agreement

(B) Local agreement of brokers

(C) Mutual agreement between the salesperson and the broker

(D) The earnest money agreement

13. As an agent of the seller, a real estate broker is usually authorized to do all of the following except

(A) Bind the principal under a sales contract

(B) Advertise the listed salesperson

(C) Place a "for sale" sign on the listed property

(D) Cooperate with other brokers

14. Broker Ross has been sued for conversion. This means that Ross allegedly

(A) Failed to disclose material facts

(B) Misappropriated his principal's funds

(C) Commingled the principals' money with his own

(D) All of the above

15. Commingling is the opposite of

(A) Subrogation

(B) Mixing

(C) Subordination

(D) Separation

16. The prime obligation of an agent to the principal is

   (A) Loyalty

   (B) Deference

   (C) Mutual trust

   (D) Respect

17. Real estate license law prohibits real estate brokers from acting as principals on their own account without

   (A) The approval of the state regulatory agency

   (B) The approval of the local real estate board

   (C) Full disclosure of their license status

   (D) Reservations

18. A real estate broker

   (A) Must only act for one party in a transaction

   (B) May act for both parties if licensed for a minimum of one year

   (C) A fiduciary and has the duty to remain neutral

   (D) May act for both parties with the knowledge and written permission of both parties.

19. If a broker deposits his own funds into his trust account a situation is created called

   (A) Prepayment

   (B) Advance commission

   (C) Commingling

   (D) Escheat

20. An owner of a property gave a listing to a broker. Shortly thereafter the owner died. In this case the

   (A) Agency is immediately terminated

   (B) Broker is entitled to his full commission from the estate

   (C) Listing agreement is binding on the heirs of the deceased owner

   (D) Broker is entitled to a reasonable time thereafter to procure a buyer during which time the listing will remain if force.

CHAPTER 8 PROPERTY DISCLOSURES AND ENVIRONMENTAL ISSUES

Learning Objectives

- Property Condition Disclosure Forms
  - Agents Role in Preparation
  - When Seller's Disclosure Misrepresents Property Condition
- Warranties
  - Types of Available Warranties
  - Coverage Provided
- Need for Inspection and Obtaining/Verifying Information
  - Agent Responsibility to Verify Statements Included Marketing Information
  - Agent Responsibility to inquire about "Red Flag" issues
  - Responding to Non-Client Inquiries
- Material Facts Related to Property Condition or Location
  - Land/Soil Conditions
  - Accuracy of Representation of Lot or Improvement Size, Encroachments or Easements Affecting Use
  - Pest Infestation, Toxic Mold and Other Interior Environmental Hazards
  - Structural Issues, Including Roof, Gutters, Downspouts, Doors, Windows Foundation
  - Condition of Electrical and Plumbing Systems, and of Equipment, or Appliances that are Fixtures
  - Location with in Natural Hazard or Specially Regulated Area, Potentially Uninsurable Property
  - Known Alterations or Additions
    - Material Facts Related to Public Controls, Statutes or Public Utilities
    - Local Zoning and Planning Information
    - Boundaries of School/Utility, Taxation Districts, Flight Paths
    - Local Tax and Special Assessments, other
    - Liens
    - External Environmental Hazards (Lead, Radon, Asbestos, Formaldehyde foam Insulation, High-Voltage Power Lines, Water Deposal Sites, Underground Storage Tanks, Soil or Groundwater Contamination, Hazardous Waste
- Stigmatized/Psychologically Impacted Property/ Megan's Law Issues

Required Disclosures When Selling Real Estate

Any real estate licensee must follow state and local laws in regard to disclosure of material facts regarding the property being sold. These laws require informing the buyer about specific hazards or problems affecting the property before the sale is completed. Most state laws require that disclosers be on special forms that the seller must sign and date, and to be sure that the buyer acknowledges receipt of the disclosure by signing the form as well.

Home sellers may be obligated to disclose problems that could affect the property's value or desirability. In most states, it is illegal to fraudulently conceal major physical defects in the seller's property. Many states now require sellers to take a proactive role by making written disclosures about the condition of the property.

When a buyer and seller enter into a real estate sales contract the seller has certain obligations to disclose any known defects, needed repairs, and violations of law, which the home may manifest. The contract also provides the buyer with the opportunity to inspect the property thoroughly, and hire a professional inspector and/or engineer inspect the property.

Most state laws follow a doctrine of "implied habitability" rather than "caveat emptor – buyer beware." This means that the home seller is presumed to be selling a home that is habitable, structurally sound and functional unless the seller otherwise informs the buyer. Home sellers must disclose any significant problems they have experienced with their home and what they may have done to remedy the problem.

In most states brokers and property sellers are not responsible for problems of which they have no knowledge, but in some states brokers are responsible to disclose any defect about which they should have had knowledge.

Seller's Real Property Disclosure Form

Most states require the seller to complete a real property disclosure form before entering into a contract. The seller must complete a form approve the particular state that asks the seller about the appliances, electrical/plumbing /heating systems, roof, site conditions and known easements and encumbrances. The buyer receives a copy of the form and may rely on the seller's representations in determining whether the property condition is satisfactory.

Federal Disclosures

Every state has its own laws regarding disclosures, so the forms may vary depending state where the real estate transaction is located. A federal disclosure such as lead based paint for all transactions if the home was built before 1978. The disclosure the buyer 10-days to conduct inspections for lead based paint, unless that time period contingency is waived in writing.

Material Facts

Material facts are commonly referred to as anything that would affect the buyer's decision to purchase or the price and terms the buyers offers. If there is a defect or if the seller or the seller's agent has knowledge about a defect, it should be disclosed. In California, sellers are to notify buyers if a death has occurred on the property in the last 3 years. Some buyers do not want a home where someone has died in the house.

Causes of Death

Many homebuyers are fine with news of a death occurring in the house as long as it wasn't gruesome or violent. There are also buyers who believe homes that are haunted by former occupants who died in the house. If the agent has specific details, he might want to consider sharing it with the buyer, or buyer's agent unless it pertains to AIDS. The agent should check with local laws and a real estate attorney for advice about deaths surrounding AIDS because in some states, AIDS falls into a protected class and could be subject to discrimination claims as well.

What Must Be Disclosed

By law, real estate agents cannot fill out any seller's home disclosure unless the agent is the seller or a party to the transaction. Generally, the seller must disclose only information within the general knowledge of the seller. However, some states law's identify certain problems that the seller is responsible to search for, whether the seller sees signs of the problem or not. In these cases, or where the seller could have seen a particular defect but turned a blind eye, the seller could ultimately end up in court compensating the buyer for the costs plus legal fees.

State Legislation

More than half the states now require some sort of disclosure when real property containing one to four dwelling units is sold. Some states publish a booklet for consumers called Disclosures in Real Property Transactions, which give detailed current information about all the required disclosures. Some of the required disclosures include:

- Real estate transfer disclosure statement
- Bonds and taxes (special assessment districts)
- Natural hazard disclosure statement
- Ordinance location (ordinance refers to military weapons and ammunition
- Earthquake guides
- Smoke detector statement of compliance
- Disclosure regarding lead based paint hazards
- Notice regarding the advisability of title insurance
- Certification regarding water heater's security against earthquake
- Locations of registered sex offenders (Megan's law)
- Visual inspection by agents
- Agency relationship disclosures
- Disclosure about the negotiability of real estate commissions
- Association disclosures to common interest owners

Many of these mandatory disclosures simply require that the sellers reveal what they already know. Both the buyer and seller's agent must conduct a reasonably competent and diligent visual inspection of the accessible areas of the property and disclose what they find.

151

The seller does not have to conduct any expert investigations for the buyer's benefit. However, if the seller has hired an expert they need to give a copy of the expert's report to the buyer. Also, the seller is not obliged to repair or correct any problems or defects, except by mutual agreement with the buyer.

The mandatory disclosure makes it clear that sellers and their agents must disclose what they know and make the property available for inspections. Buyers have the right and duty to hire experts and conduct their own investigations.

Most real estate purchases are financed by lenders that may require other types of investigations and reports. The most common lender requirements are a pest report, real estate appraisal and a preliminary title report. Lenders may also require environmental assessments, floodplain investigations and letters from planning and building departments.

It is customary for the seller to pay for the termite inspection and the buyer to pay for the appraisal, the home inspection and other reports as needed.

The following is a list of the most common investigations that the buyers and sellers use to negotiate a sale and/or get a loan for residential property:

- Pest report
- Title report
- Home inspection
- CC&Rs (covenants, conditions and restrictions)
- Planning and zoning reports
- School locations
- Crime statistics
- Energy audits

The following reports apply to rural properties and bare land

- Septic site reports
- Septic system inspections
- Well inspections
- Land survey
- Road maintenance agreements
- Easements

152

The following reports apply to properties with potential environmental hazards

- Asbestos
- Lead paint
- Environmental assessment (underground storage tanks)
- Structural geology report (hillside and ocean front lots)
- Volatile organic compounds (VOC) formaldehyde, etc.
- Electromagnetic field (EMF)
- Radon

The following reports apply to income property

- Traffic report
- Market analysis
- Rent survey
- Americans with Disabilities Act (ADA)
- Fire safety

Real estate agents should be aware of the factors that affect the value, desirability and intended use of real estate.

Property Condition Disclosure Forms

Residential property sellers must provide a "Seller's Property Disclosure Form" to each buyer who makes a written offer. State law mandates the form used by the seller. The seller's representations regarding the property are based upon the seller's knowledge at the time of the disclosure. An example of a Seller's Real Property Disclosure Statement follows this page.

Broker Forms Checklist

Many real estate brokers are concerned that their salespeople are aware of all of the disclosure forms that they are required to have filled out prior to any residential real estate closing. Broker Antonio Correia requires that his salespeople become familiar with the attached checklist and use it to assure they have completed every required form.

The individual states are revising their disclosure requirements regularly; as a result it is the responsibility of every licensed real estate agent to be mindful of updates and changes to these disclosures requirements.

NATIONAL PROPERTIES REALTY
SALES FILE * CHECKLIST (REV. 04.30.10)
Fax: (702)263-3929; _e-mail_: **nationalprorealty@yahoo.com***

Property Address: _____ MLS#: _____

Buyer's Name: _____ Phone #: _____

Buyer's Agent's Name: _____ Phone#: _____

Co-Op Agent's Name: _____ Phone #: _____

Escrow #: _____ COE Date: _____

Attention Agents: These documents are required in the Broker's Office OR *_E-MAILED_ within **five (5) calendar days** of the **Purchase** Agreement being signed. Documents must be in order according to this check list. Please be sure that all documents are signed, initialed and dated by all parties, as needed. Include all original documents generated by you in addition to fully executed copies. ALWAYS USE _"ZIP FORMS"_.

1. _____ **TAX STAR** (Ownership Confirmation)
2. _____ **MLS STATUS** SHEETS: **C/P & S**
3. _____ **DUTIES OWED**
4. _____ **RESIDENTIAL DISCLOSURE GUIDE** (pg. **29** only)
5. _____ CONFIRMATION (If it's a New Home, or a different contract than Zip Forms)
6. _____ CONSENT TO ACT (If dual agency transaction). **Broker's approval needed.**
7. _____ Residential **PURCHASE AGREEMENT**
8. _____ Short Sale Addendum, if property sold as **"SHORT SALE"**.
9. _____ REO Addendum, if property sold as **"REO"**.
10. _____ Copy of any other documents/Counters pertinent to this transaction **generated either by you or the Other Agent.**
11. _____ COPY OF EARNEST MONEY (Posted & dated by Title Co.)
12. _____ LOAN PRE-QUALIFICATION OR PRE-APPROVAL LETTER. If CASH, **POF**
13. _____ ESTIMATED COSTS & NET PROCEEDS **OR** good faith estimate from lender
14. _____ **SELLER'S REAL PROPERTY DISCLOSURE OR**
15. _____ **BUYER'S** WAIVER OF NRS-113, chapter 113 Rights (**signed and notarized**)
16. _____ DISCLOSURES, TO INCLUDE: _CONSTUCTION DEFECT_ _____; _MOLD_ _____ _PEST_ _____; _LEAD_ _____ (built before **1978**); _BELTWAY_ _____; _AIRPORT_ _____.
17. _____ **INFO. STATEMENT**- Disclosure of **Homeowner's Rights** (pg. 4 only.)
18. _____ PURCHASER'S RECEIPT OF THE CIC OF **"Resale Package"**.
19. _____ RECEIPT **"For Your Protection"** Notice Home Inspection.
20. _____ COPY OF **HOME INSPECTION/Certifications or WAIVER**
21. _____ **WALK THROUGH** INSPECTION AND RELEASE
22. _____ COPY OF **HOME WARRANTY** or signed **Decline.**
23. _____ ESCROW INSTRUCTIONS
24. _____ PRELIMINARY TITLE REPORT
25. _____ **HUD-1 Final** Settlement Statement from Title Co.

Waiver of Property Condition Rights

States have passed legislation to allow sellers to avoid completing disclosure forms. Nevada has developed a "Waiver of NRS Chapter 113 Rights" form for those agreements that do not require a condition of the property

Introduction

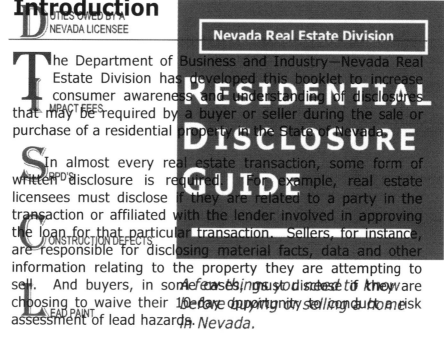

The Department of Business and Industry—Nevada Real Estate Division has developed this booklet to increase consumer awareness and understanding of disclosures that may be required by a buyer or seller during the sale or purchase of a residential property in the State of Nevada.

In almost every real estate transaction, some form of written disclosure is required. For example, real estate licensees must disclose if they are related to a party in the transaction or affiliated with the lender involved in approving the loan for that particular transaction. Sellers, for instance, are responsible for disclosing material facts, data and other information relating to the property they are attempting to sell. And buyers, in some cases, must disclose if they are choosing to waive their 10-day opportunity to conduct a risk assessment of lead hazards.

These are only a few examples of what must be disclosed during a real estate transaction. While it is impossible to outline which disclosures are needed in every situation (as each real estate transaction is unique), this booklet contains discussions on the most commonly-required state, federal and local disclosures.

References to real estate licensees and the sale of residential properties in this booklet apply only to the state of Nevada. This guide, however, does not specifically address vacant land or commercial properties.

We hope that you will find this booklet helpful and that it becomes a valuable resource during your real estate transaction. For more information, please visit our website at **www.red.state.nv.us** or contact us at:

LAS VEGAS OFFICE
2501 E. Sahara Ave.
Suite 101
Phone: (702) 486-4033
Fax: (702) 486-4275

CARSON CITY OFFICE
1179 Fairview Dr.
Suite E
Phone: (775) 687-4280
Fax: (775) 687-4868

State of Nevada
Department of Business & Industry
Real Estate Division

155

Table of Contents

State & Federal Disclosures

    Common-Interest Communities 6

    Condominium Hotels 8

    Consent to Act 10

    Construction Defects 11

    Duties Owed By a Nevada Real Estate Licensee 12

    Energy Consumption Evaluation 14

    Impact Fees 15

    Lead-Based Paint* 16

    Lien for Deferred Taxes 17

    Manufactured Housing—
        Used Manufactured/Mobile Homes 18
        Manufactured Home Parks 19

    Open Range Disclosure 20

    Seller's Real Property Disclosure 22

    Water & Sewer Rates 23

Local/Miscellaneous Disclosures

    Pool Safety & Drowning Prevention 25

    Airport Noise 26

    Building & Zoning Codes 26

    Environmental Hazards 26

    Home Inspections 27

    Gaming (Initial Purchaser in New Construction Only) ... 27

    Licensee Disclosures 28

    Road Maintenance District 28

    Soil Report (New Construction Only) 28

Acknowledgement Form 29

Contact Information 31

Federal Disclosure

Common-Interest Communities

⇒ **Purpose of Disclosure**

The purpose of the information statement required when purchasing a home or unit in a common-interest community is to make the buyer aware of all rights, obligations and other aspects related to owning a unit within a common-interest community (also known as a homeowner's association).

⇒ **Who must provide the disclosure?**

The seller must, at seller's expense, provide an information statement with the sale of any unit belonging to a common-interest community. The statement is entitled *"BEFORE YOU PURCHASE PROPERTY IN A COMMON-INTEREST COMMUNITY DID YOU KNOW..."*

⇒ **When is it due?**

The statement must be delivered to the buyer not later than the date the offer becomes binding on the purchaser.

⇒ **Additional Information**

Resale Package
In addition to the information statement, the seller must provide the prospective buyer with a **resale package** which includes the following: declarations, bylaws, rules and regulations, monthly assessments, unpaid assessments of any kind, current operating budget, financial statement, reserve summary, unsatisfied judgments, status of any pending legal actions, and a statement of any transfer fees, transaction fees or any other fees associated with the resale of a unit.

For more information:

Form: Before You Purchase Property in a Common-Interest Community Did You Know...

Website: http://red.state.nv.us/forms/584.pdf

NRS: 116.4101—116.41095

6   State

Common-Interest Communities

The resale package must be delivered as soon as practicable or before conveyance of the unit. Unless the buyer has accepted conveyance of the unit, the buyer may cancel the contract to purchase, by written notice, until midnight of the fifth calendar day following receipt of the resale package. This provision must be stated in the contract.

Public Offering Statement

If the property is a new unit in a common-interest community or if the community is subject to any developmental rights, or contains converted buildings or contains units which may be in a time share, or is registered with the Securities and Exchange Commission, the buyer must also be provided with a **Public Offering Statement** disclosing applicable information, including:

- development rights of contractors
- construction schedule
- description of proposed improvements
- mechanical & electrical installations
- initial or special fees
- number & identity of units in timeshare

Unless the buyer has personally inspected the unit, the buyer may cancel the contract to purchase, by written notice, until midnight of the fifth calendar day following the date of execution of the contract. This provision must be stated in the contract.

For more information:

Form: Before You Purchase Property in a Common-Interest Community Did You Know...

Website: http://red.state.nv.us/forms/584.pdf

NRS: 116.4101—116.41095

State   7

159

Condominium Hotels

⇒ **Purpose of Disclosure**

The purpose of the information statement required when purchasing a home or unit in a condominium hotel is to make the buyer aware of all rights, obligations and other aspects related to owning a unit within a condominium hotel.

⇒ **Who must provide the disclosure?**

The seller must provide an information statement with the sale of any unit belonging to a condominium hotel. The statement is entitled *"BEFORE YOU PURCHASE PROPERTY IN A CONDOMINIUM HOTEL DID YOU KNOW..."*

⇒ **When is it due?**

The statement must be delivered to the buyer not later than the date the offer becomes binding on the purchaser.

⇒ **Additional Information**

Resale Package
In addition to the information statement, the seller must provide the prospective buyer with a **resale package** which includes the following: declarations, bylaws, rules and regulations, monthly assessments, unpaid assessments of any kind, current operating budget, financial statement, reserve summary, unsatisfied judgments and status of any pending legal actions.

For more information:

Form: Before You Purchase Property in a Condominium Hotel Did You Know...

Website: http://red.state.nv.us/forms/584a.pdf

NRS: 116B.740—116B.765

Construction Defects

⇒ **Purpose of Disclosure**

The purpose of disclosures relating to construction defects is to make the buyer aware of any construction defects in the property.

⇒ **Who must provide the disclosure?**

If there is a construction defect, the contractor must disclose the information in understandable language that is underlined and in bold-faced type with capital letters. If the property is or has been the subject of a construction defect claim or lawsuit, the seller must provide the following information to the buyer:

- copies of all notices given to contractor
- expert opinions obtained by claimant
- terms of settlement or order of judgment
- detailed report of all repairs

⇒ **When is it due?**

Construction defects must be disclosed to the buyer before purchase of the residence. If the property is or has been the subject of a defect claim or lawsuit, the information must be disclosed 30 days before close of escrow, or if escrow is less than 30 days, then immediately upon signing the sales agreement. If a claim is made while in escrow, the disclosure must be made within 24 hours of notice of complaint.

⇒ **Additional Information**

If the property is located within a common-interest community and is the subject of a defect claim or lawsuit, this information must be disclosed in the buyer's **resale package** (see Common-Interest Communities).

For more information:

NRS: 40.640, 40.688

Duties Owed By a
Nevada Real Estate Licensee

⇒ **Purpose of Disclosure**

The purpose of the Duties Owed form is to make the buyer or seller aware of obligations owed by a real estate licensee to all parties involved in the transaction.

⇒ **Who must provide the disclosure?**

A licensee who acts as an agent in a real estate transaction must disclose to each party for whom the licensee is acting as an agent and any unrepresented party all duties owed to the parties and the licensee's relationship as an agent to each party in the transaction.

⇒ **When is it due?**

The disclosure form must be presented to the client before any documents are signed by the client.

⇒ **Additional Information**

A Nevada licensee who has entered into a brokerage agreement to represent a client in a real estate transaction shall:

1. Exercise reasonable skill and care to carry out the terms of the brokerage agreement and the licensee's duties in the brokerage agreement;
2. Not disclose, except to the licensee's broker, confidential information relating to a client for 1 year after the revocation or termination of the brokerage agreement, unless licensee is required to do so by court order or the client gives written permission;

For more information:

Form: Duties Owed By a Nevada Real Estate Licensee
NRS: 645.193; 645.252—645.254

Duties Owed By a
Nevada Real Estate Licensee

3. Seek a sale, purchase, option, rental or lease of real property at the price and terms stated in the brokerage agreement or at a price acceptable to the client;
4. Present all offers made to, or by the client as soon as practicable, unless the client chooses to waive the duty of the licensee to present all offers and signs a waiver of the duty on a form prescribed by the Division;
5. Disclose to the client material facts of which the licensee has knowledge concerning the real estate transaction;
6. Advise the client to obtain advice from an expert relating to matters which are beyond the expertise of the licensee; and
7. Account to the client for all money and property the licensee receives in which the client may have an interest.

Waiver of Duty to Present All Offers
Authorization to Negotiate Directly with Seller

A client may choose to waive the broker's duty to present all offers by signing a waiver on a form, the "Waiver Form", prescribed by the Division. Concurrent with the option of a client to waive the duty of his/her broker to present all offers is the form "Authorization to Negotiate Directly with Seller", which gives permission in writing to authorize a licensee to negotiate a sale or lease directly with a seller. Both forms must be utilized and signed by a client who waives the duty to present all offers. Otherwise, a licensee for a buyer does not have the permission of the seller's broker to present offers or negotiate with the sellers directly.

For more information:

Form: Duties Owed By a Nevada Real Estate Licensee
NRS: 645.193; 645.252—645.254

Energy Consumption Evaluation

⇒ **Purpose of Disclosure**

The purpose of the energy consumption evaluation disclosure is to provide the buyer of a residential property with an evaluation of the energy consumption of the property based on State-prescribed standards. The disclosure form, prescribed by the Nevada Energy Commissioner, shall inform the buyer about State programs for improving energy conservation and energy efficiency in residential properties.

⇒ **Who must provide the disclosure?**

The seller of a residential property is required to provide this information on a form prescribed by the Nevada Energy Commissioner.

⇒ **When is it due?**

The disclosure must be made by the seller to the buyer before closing a transaction for the conveyance of residential property.

⇒ **Additional Information**

The disclosure requirement will take effect on January 1, 2011.

For more information:

NRS 113.115

Website Nevada Energy Commissioner

14 State

Impact Fees

⇒ **Purpose of Disclosure**

The seller of any property must give notice of any impact fees that may be imposed upon the buyer.

An impact fee is a charge imposed by a local government on new development (i.e., the construction, reconstruction, redevelopment, conversion, alteration, relocation or enlargement of any structure which increases the number of service units) to finance some of the costs attributable to the new development.

⇒ **Who must provide the disclosure?**

A seller who has knowledge of the impact fee must give written notice to the buyer, including the amount of the impact fee and the name of the local government imposing the fee.

⇒ **When is it due?**

The notice must be provided to the buyer before the property is conveyed.

⇒ **Additional Information**

If the seller fails to give this notice, the seller is liable to the buyer for the amount of the impact fee.

For more information:

NRS: 278B.320

Lien for Deferred Taxes

⇒ **Purpose of Disclosure**

If there are deferred taxes that have not been paid at the time the property is sold or transferred, the buyer must be notified in writing that there is a lien for deferred taxes on the property.

⇒ **Who must provide the disclosure?**

The seller must notify the buyer of the lien.

⇒ **When is it due?**

The lien must be disclosed at the time the property is sold or transferred.

⇒ **Additional Information**

The owner of the property on the date the deferred taxes become due is liable for the deferred taxes.

For more information:

NRS: 361A.290

Manufactured Housing— Used Manufactured/Mobile Homes

⇒ **Purpose of Disclosure**

The purpose of the Used Manufactured/Mobile Home disclosure is to make the buyer aware that a used manufactured or mobile home that has not been converted to real property is personal property and subject to personal property taxes.

⇒ **Who must provide the disclosure?**

The real estate licensee shall provide the form to the purchaser as soon as practicable, but before title is transferred.

⇒ **Additional Information**

This disclosure also informs the purchaser that title will not pass unless the county assessor's endorsement is placed on the face of the title, verifying that taxes have been paid in full.

The disclosure also instructs the consumer to submit certain documents to Nevada's Manufactured Housing Division and the county assessor within 45 days after the sale is complete and before a certificate of ownership will be issued.

For more information:

Form: Used Manufactured/Mobile Home Disclosure
Website: Manufactured Housing Division
NRS: 645.258, 489.521, 489.531, 489.541

---

18 State

Open Range Disclosure

⇒ **Purpose of Disclosure**

⇒ **Purpose of Disclosure**

The purpose of the Open Range Disclosure is to inform the prospective buyer of a disclosure relating to placing or buying a manufactured or mobile home in a manufactured home park to make the buyer aware that the range may be subject to cattle, sheep or other domestic animals by custom, license, lease or permit are grazed or permitted to roam. It also warns the prospective buyer that the parcel may be subject to county or State claims of right of way, (commonly referred to as R.S. 2477 rights-of-way) including rights-of-way that may be unrecorded, undocumented or unsurveyed, and used by miners, ranchers, hunters or others, for access or recreational use, in a manner which interferes with the use and enjoyment of the parcel.

⇒ **Who must provide the disclosure?**

If the landlord requires approval of a prospective buyer and tenant, the landlord must post a sign, which is clearly readable at the entrance of the park, which advises consumers that before a manufactured home in the park is sold, the buyer and tenant must be approved by the landlord.

⇒ **Additional information**

If the property will remain in the manufactured home park, make sure you have a lease agreement with the park manager and that you know the park's rules and regulations.

Remember: the seller or a manufactured home dealer cannot promise that you'll be accepted as a tenant in a particular manufactured home park. You must apply for the lease yourself and should do so before finalizing the purchase of your home. The landlord must approve or deny a completed application from a prospective buyer and tenant within 10 days after the date the application is submitted.

⇒ **When is it due?**

The disclosure must be provided to the potential buyer, with the requirement that the buyer sign the disclosure

(continued on next page...)

For more information:

Form: Open Range Disclosure Form 551

NRS: 489.170

Real Estate Division Position Statement, dated July 1, 2010

Website: Manufactured Housing Division—Placing or Buying Your Home in a Rental Community

NRS State 168.170

Open Range Disclosure

(Cont'd)

form acknowledging the date of receipt of the original disclosure document, before the sales agreement is signed.

⇒ **Additional Information**

The disclosure acknowledges fencing the property to keep livestock out and recognizes the property owner's entitlement to damages if livestock enter a fenced property but warns against harming roaming livestock even on a fenced property.

The law requires that the seller retain a copy of the disclosure document that has been signed by the buyer acknowledging the date of receipt of the document, provide a copy to the buyer, and record the original disclosure document containing the buyer's signature and the seller's notarized signature in the office of the county recorder in the county where the property is located.

For more information:

Form: Open Range Disclosure Form 551

NRS: 113.065; 568.355

Real Estate Division Position Statement, dated July 1, 2010

Seller's Real Property Disclosure

⇒ **Purpose of Disclosure**

The purpose of the Seller's Real Property Disclosure form is to make the buyer aware of the overall condition of the property before it is transferred. This disclosure is not a guarantee nor does it take the place of an inspection. This form is not required for new home sales.

⇒ **Who must provide the disclosure?**

The seller must complete the "Seller's Real Property Disclosure" form, detailing the condition of the property, known defects, and any other aspects of the property which may affect its use or value.

⇒ **When is it due?**

The disclosure must be delivered to the buyer at least 10 days prior to conveyance of the property.

⇒ **Additional Information**

The content of the disclosure is based on what the seller is aware of at the time. If, after completion of the disclosure form, the seller discovers a new defect or notices that a previously disclosed condition has worsened, the seller must inform the purchaser, in writing, as soon as practicable after discovery of the condition, or before conveyance of the property.

The buyer may waive this form in writing, signed and notarized, or rescind the sales agreement for non-disclosure.

For more information:

Form: Seller's Real Property Disclosure
NRS: 113.130; 113.140; 113.150

22 State

Water & Sewer Rates

⇒ **Purpose of Disclosure**

The purpose of the disclosure relating to water and sewer rates is to inform the buyer of a previously unsold home or improved lot of public utility rates when service is for more than 25 but fewer than 2,000 customers.

⇒ **Who must provide the disclosure?**

The seller must post a notice, which shows the current or projected rates, in a conspicuous place on the property.

⇒ **When is it due?**

The notice must be posted and a copy provided to the buyer before the home is sold.

⇒ **Additional Information**

The notice must contain the name, address and telephone number of the public utility and the Division of Consumer Complaint Resolution of the Public Utilities Commission of Nevada.

For more information:

NRS: 113.060

Pool Safety and Drowning Prevention Disclosure

⇒ **Purpose of Disclosure**

The purpose of the Southern Nevada Health District's pool safety and drowning prevention disclosure is to make the buyer aware of the risk of death by drowning in private and public pools particularly for children 4 years or younger.

⇒ **Who must provide the disclosure?**

The information is provided by the Nevada Real Estate Division (NRED) in agreement with the Southern Nevada Health District (SNHD) to promote SNHD's efforts to inform the public on drowning prevention.

⇒ **When is it due?**

The disclosure will be provided to the buyer before the sales agreement is signed by way of the Residential Disclosure Guide in which it is contained. The buyer is advised to visit SNHD's website http://www.southernnevadahealthdistrict.org/drowning_prevention.htm for information.

⇒ **Additional Information**

Drowning is the leading cause of unintentional injury death in Clark County for children four years of age and under. The majority of drowning deaths occur in the family pool. Preventable mistakes include leaving a child unattended near a body of water in which a child's nose and mouth can be submerged.

More information on drowning facts, preventable mistakes, how to be prepared to prevent a drowning, pool security, drowning statistics, adult supervision and more can be obtained at SNHD's website at http://www.southernnevadahealthdistrict.org/drowning_prevention.htm and http://www.gethealthyclarkcounty.org/injury_prev/drowning.html.

Website: http://www.southernnevadahealthdistrict.org/drowning_prevention.htm

Miscellaneous Disclosures

Depending upon the transaction, the following disclosures may also be required from a buyer, seller or licensee:

⇒ **AIRPORT NOISE**

Buyers should investigate the impact of airport flight paths and the noise levels at different times of the day over that property.

⇒ **BUILDING & ZONING CODES**

The purpose of the building and zoning disclosure is to inform the buyer of transportation beltways and/or planned or anticipated land use within proximity of the subject property of which the seller has knowledge.

For more information on building and zoning codes, contact your local jurisdiction.

⇒ **ENVIRONMENTAL HAZARDS**

Although the seller is required to disclose the presence of environmental hazards, a statement that the seller is not aware of a defect or hazard does not mean that it does not exist. **It is the buyer's responsibility to be informed and take additional steps to further investigate.** Some potential hazards that may be found in Nevada include:

- **Radon** (www.epa.gov/radon)
- **Floods** (http://www.epa.gov/ebtpages/ emernaturaldisastefloods.html)
- **Methamphetamine Labs** (NRS 40.770 & 489.776)
- **Wood-Burning Devices** (http://www.epa.gov/iaq/pubs/ combust.html)
- **Underground Storage Tanks** (http://www.epa.gov/ ebtpages/industoragetanksundergroundstorage tanks.html)
- **Well & Septic Systems** (http://www.epa.gov/ebtpages/ wategroundwaterwells.html)

Miscellaneous Disclosures

⇒ **ENVIRONMENTAL HAZARDS , cont'd.**

- **Contaminated Soils** (http://www.epa.gov/ebtpages/pollsoilcontaminants.html)
- **Groundwater** (www.epa.gov/safewater/protect/citguide.html)
- **Public Pools & Spas** (http://www.poolsafety.gov/vgb.html)

For more information on environmental hazards, visit: www.epa.gov.

⇒ **HOME INSPECTIONS**

When obtaining an FHA-insured loan, this disclosure informs the buyer about the limits of the Federal Housing Administration appraisal inspection and suggests the buyer obtain a home inspection to evaluate the physical condition of the property prior to purchase.
The form is entitled, "For Your Protection: Get a Home Inspection."

For more information on FHA home inspections, visit: www.epa.gov.

⇒ **GAMING (Initial Purchaser in New Construction Only)**

If there is a gaming district near the property, the seller must disclose information which includes a copy of the most recent gaming enterprise district map, the location of the nearest gaming enterprise district, and notice that the map is subject to change. This disclosure is required for Nevada counties with population over 400,000.

The information must be provided at least 24 hours before the seller signs the sales agreement. The buyer may waive the 24-hour period.

The seller must retain a copy of the disclosure.

For more information on gaming, see: NRS 113.080

Miscellaneous Disclosures

⇒ **LICENSEE DISCLOSURES**

In addition to the "Consent to Act" and the "Duties Owed by a Nevada Real Estate Licensee" forms (see pages 10 & 12), a real estate licensee is required to disclose other information such as his relationship to one or more parties in the transaction and/or having a personal interest in the property.

For more information regarding duties and disclosures owed by a licensee, see: NRS 645.252-645.254, NAC 645.637 and NAC 645.640.

⇒ **ROAD MAINTENANCE DISTRICT**

The sale of residential property within a road maintenance district is prohibited unless the seller provides notice to the purchaser, including the amount of assessments for the last two years.

For more information, see: NRS 320.130.

⇒ **SOIL REPORT (New Construction Only)**

If the property has not been occupied by the buyer more than 120 days before completion, the seller must give notice of any soil report prepared for the property or for the subdivision in which the property is located.

The seller must provide such notice upon signing the sales agreement.

Upon receiving the notice, the buyer must submit a written request within 5 days for a copy of the actual report. The seller must provide a free report to the buyer within 5 days of receiving such request.

Upon receiving the soil report, the buyer has 20 days to rescind the sales agreement. This rescission right may be waived, in writing, by the buyer.

For more information, see: NRS 113.135.

Nevada Real Estate Division

RESIDENTIAL DISCLOSURE GUIDE

**State of Nevada
Department of
Business & Industry
Real Estate Division**

I/We acknowledge that I/we have received a copy of the Residential Disclosure Guide.

DATE _____

_____
Client—Print Name

_____
Client—Signature

_____
Client—Print Name

_____
Client—Signature

Make copy of page for additional signatures.

Retain original or copy in each transaction file.

Contact Information

Nevada Real Estate Division (LV) 2501 East Sahara, Suite 101 Las Vegas, NV 89104 Phone: (702) 486-4033 Fax: (702) 486-4275 Email: realest@red.state.nv.us Website: www.red.state.nv.us	**Nevada Real Estate Division (CC)** 788 Fairview Drive, Suite 200 Carson City, NV 89701 Phone: (775) 687-4280 Fax: (775) 687-4868 Email: realest@red.state.nv.us Website: www.red.state.nv.us
Manufactured Housing Division (LV) 2501 East Sahara, Suite 204 Las Vegas, NV 89104 Phone: (702) 486-4135 Fax: (702) 486-4309 Email: nmhd@mhd.state.nv.us Website: http://mhd.state.nv.us	**Manufactured Housing Division (CC)** 788 Fairview Drive, Suite 100 Carson City, NV 89701 Phone: (775) 687-5500 Fax: (775) 687-5521 Email: nmhd@mhd.state.nv.us Website: http://mhd.state.nv.us
Ombudsman Office (Common-Interest Communities) 2501 East Sahara, Suite 202 Las Vegas, NV 89104 Phone: (702) 486-4480 Toll Free: (877) 829-9907 Fax: (702) 486-5137 Email: CICOmbudsman@red.state.nv.us Website: www.red.state.nv.us/CIC/cic_home.htm	**U.S. Environmental Protection Agency** Ariel Rios Building 1200 Pennsylvania Avenue, N.W. Washington, DC 20460 Phone: (202) 272-0167 Website: www.epa.gov
National Lead Information Center 8601 Georgia Avenue, Suite 503 Silver Spring, MD 20910 Phone: (800) 424-LEAD Fax: (301) 585-7976 Email: hotline.lead@epa.gov Website: www.epa.gov/lead	**Department of Health and Human Services – Center for Disease Control & Prevention** 1600 Clifton Road Atlanta, GA 30333 Phone: (404) 639-3311 Public Inquiries: (800) 311-3435 Website: www.cdc.gov
U.S. Consumer Product Safety Commission 4330 East West Highway Bethesda, MD 20814 Phone: (301) 504-7923 Fax: (301) 504-0124 Website: www.cpsc.gov	

Megan's Law

Perhaps one of the most important legislative actions took place in regard to "Megan's Law."1994, 7-year-old Megan Kanka was raped and murdered in a New Jersey suburb. Her attacker was a

178

convicted sex offender and was a nearby neighbor. Law enforcement personal were not allowed to disclose the presence of a sex offender in the neighborhood at time. This prompted New Jersey congressman Dick Zimmer to draft a bill that became Megan's Law. All states have passed variations of Megan's Law. A state's Criminal History Repository shall maintain a website containing information about serious and high-risk sex offenders with photographs if they are available.

QUIZ MANDATED DISCLOSURES

1. The standard policy of fire insurance protects an owner for all except:

A. Fire loss
B. Lightning damage
C. Hail damage
D. Loss suffered in removal of property that suffered a fire

2. Fidelity bonds provide protection against:

A. Employees leaving for other employment
B. Employee theft
C. Inflation because of rising interest rates
D. Mysterious disappearance

3. Ownership of what type of property would make an owner strictly liable for injury to a tenant?
A. Residential property
B. Commercial property
C. Industrial property
D. None of the above.

4. An owner's liability as to acts of a tenant would be based on:

A. Foresee ability
B. Agency law
C. Strict liability
D. An insurable interest

5. Obtaining insurance protection prior to the issuance of a policy would be know as a:
A. Option
B. Binder
C. Bond
D. Right of first refusal

6. The Civil Rights Act applies only to race is the Civil Rights Act of:

A. 1866
B. 1964
C. 1968
D. 1988

7. Directing a prospective tenant away from a property because you did not feel that they would be comfortable there based on the race of the current residents would be:
A. Blockbusting

B. Steering
C. Redlining
D. Legal

8. Which of the following would NOT be a member of a protected group under the 1988 Fair Housing Amendment Act?
A. A blind person
B. A person with AIDS
C. A drug addict
D. An alcoholic

9. A tenant has a Seeing Eye dog. The lessor can:
A. Charge an increased rent because of the pet
B. Increase the security deposit to cover possible damage by the dog
C. Refuse to rent to the person if there is a no-pet policy that in uniformly enforced
D. Do none of the above

10. An exception to the prohibition against discrimination as to familial status would be:
A. Children under the age of 18
B. A prospective tenant who is pregnant
C. Housing for the elderly
D. An unmarried mother

11. Which of the following advertising language would be acceptable?
A. "Mother in Law suite"
B. "Walk up
C. "Family room"
D. All of the above

11. The best test to determine if an action is ethical would be to consider the:

A. Cost
B. Legality
C. Golden rule
D. Benefits

CHAPTER 9 –REAL ESTATE PRACTICE

Learning Objectives

- Trust Accounts
    - Purpose and Definition of Trust Accounts
    - Responsibilities for Trust Monies
    - Commingling/Conversion
    - Monies Held in Trust Accounts
  - Fair Housing Laws
    - Protected Classes
    - Covered Transactions
    - Specific Laws and Their Effects
    - Exceptions
    - Compliance
    - Types of Violations and Enforcement
    - Fair Housing Issues in Advertising
- Advertising
    - Incorrect "Factual" Statements vs. "Puffing"
    - Uninformed Misrepresentation vs. Deliberate Misrepresentation (Fraud)
    - Truth in Advertising
- Agent Supervision
    - Liability/Responsibility to Train and Supervise
    - Independent Contractors
    - Employees
- Commission and Fees
    - Procuring Cause/Protection Clauses
    - Referrals and Finder Fees
- General Ethics
    - Practicing Within an Area of Competence
    - Avoiding Unauthorized Practice of Law
- Technology
- Antitrust Violations in Real Estate

Trust Funds

Each state has developed a set of guidelines in regard to trust funds. The following is the guidelines adopted by the State of Nevada. Its contents are similar to the rules adopted by other states.

Proper accounting for trust funds and adequate record keeping are basic to the management of a brokerage office and the legal responsibility of the broker. This booklet will assist real estate brokers to understand the statutory and regulatory requirements of Nevada's license law for the handling of trust funds.

Failure of a real estate broker to manage properly or account for "funds belonging to others" can result in license revocation whether that failure is one of ignorance or negligence, whether intentional or unintentional. A broker's fiduciary responsibility makes the maintenance of adequate records necessary. The broker is personally responsible for the supervision and maintenance of the trust fund accounts and records. Neither delegation of duties, ignorance of daily brokerage or management activities, nor failure to establish internal control relieves the broker of the responsibility and potential liability that can result from a failure to account adequately for money or maintain records. Inadequate records or failure to maintain control of the trust funds can result in internal theft, commingling of funds, misuse of trust funds, litigation and/or disciplinary action. The use of an outside record keeping or accounting service does not eliminate the need for broker supervision or substitute for the broker's fiduciary responsibility.

WHAT CONSTITUTES TRUST FUNDS?

Provisions of Chapter 645 of Nevada Revised Statutes, (NRS 645) and Chapter 645 of Nevada Administrative Code (NAC 645) set forth the responsibilities of real estate brokers with regard to record keeping and the handling of trust funds. Trust funds are money or things of value that are received by the broker or salesperson on behalf of a principal or client or other person in the performance of duties for which a real estate license is required, which are not the property of the broker but are being held for the benefit of others.

Trust funds do not include money relating to any property in which the broker or his personnel have an ownership interest. No matter how small the percentage of ownership, the intermingling of these funds with those of clients would constitute commingling. A separate bank account, not a trust account, may be established

WHO HOLDS TRUST FUNDS?

A broker may hold money or things of value for the benefit of others for many reasons. For example, earnest money deposits are funds held pending consummation of a sale transaction. Funds are held as payment of final settlement costs. In the property management field, a broker may keep security and maintenance deposits on rental properties, may hold mortgage payments for a client/principal, or may hold rents collected but not yet disbursed to the property owner. The money or things of value may include a check written to a title company or a mortgage company, a personal note made payable to the seller, title to a motor vehicle, jewelry or other personal property. The handling and safe keeping of all of these must be accounted for in a broker=s internal records and to a broker=s principal.

WRITTEN CONTRACT GOVERNS

Proper accounting for money in a transaction begins with the written contract between the seller and buyer, between the lessor/landlord and lessee/tenant, and the broker and client. The broker must specify in the contract how trust funds are to be held and where they are to be deposited. Law to maintain a bank trust account does not mandate Nevada brokers, however, they must account for all funds. A broker may instead deposit money directly to escrow, if the contract so specifies. He may also pay funds

directly to the seller or landlord in a transaction if all persons having an interest in the money agree in writing to that arrangement. Under any circumstance, the broker is personally responsible and liable for the deposit at all times, even if the funds were delivered directly to the seller or landlord to hold. When depositing funds directly to an escrow account, the licensee may not deposit to any escrow company in which he or anyone associated with him in the real estate business has an interest unless proper disclosures are made. A proper disclosure must be made in writing and state the interest the broker or member of his staff has in that escrow company. Further, the parties to the transaction must acknowledge the disclosure.

BROKER HAS OWNERSHIP INTEREST

In the event that any type of trust funds are received from a cooperating broker or other third party regarding a property in which the broker/company has an ownership interest, full disclosure of the interest held must be made, and one of the following procedures should be followed:

1. Place the funds in the cooperating broker's trust account;
2. Obtain the informed consent from the other principal in the transaction thereby permitting the funds to be held by the broker/company acting as a principal and not held "in trust"; or
3. Deposit the funds with an escrow or title company.

Even though the broker may deposit directly to escrow, without a deposit to the trust account, he must maintain a record of what happened to those funds while in his custody. Minimum documentation for that record is a copy of the check and a receipt from the escrow agent, which must be held in the transaction file. It is suggested that the Cash Receipts Journal also have a notation that the funds were received and delivered to escrow rather than deposited into the broker's trust account. The client ledger for the transaction should record the disposition of the funds.

The trust account must be established in a bank in the state of Nevada and clearly identified as a trust account. The broker must be a trustee for the funds. The only sole signatories acceptable on a trust account would be a broker or, in the instance of a property management account, a designated property manager. Dual signatories on the trust account may be employees of the broker, salespersons licensed with the broker or the designated property manager. Whenever possible, the broker should use an employer's tax identification number instead of a personal social security number to establish a trust account.

Branch offices are not required to establish a trust account separate from the home office trust account. But, if the broker does establish a trust account for the branch, the branch manager, or designated property manager of the branch office must be a signer on that trust account.

NOTIFY THE DIVISION OF LOCATION OF TRUST ACCOUNT

Whenever a broker establishes a trust account, statutes require that he notify the Division of the account number and the name and location of the depository. Whenever a broker changes a trust account, or the broker's bank changes name and/or account number, the new account information must be supplied to the Division. A form for these notices is available from the Division. The form is also an authorization for properly identified Division representatives to inspect the records of this account. NRS 645.310 and NAC 645.655.

A trust account must allow the broker to withdraw money from that account without prior notice and without penalties for such withdrawals.

SERVICE CHARGES

Because most financial institutions levy a service charge on a checking account, the Nevada Real Estate Commission permits a broker to deposit adequate personal funds to cover this charge. This minimal amount a broker is permitted to deposit must be accounted for in the journals and ledgers in the same manner as client funds but clearly identified as broker's funds. Following this procedure will not be considered commingling by the Division. The maximum dollar amount of broker funds should not exceed
$100.00.

INTEREST AND OTHER ECONOMIC BENEFITS

Nevada law does not specifically address the establishment of interest bearing trust accounts to hold trust funds. Such accounts must be handled with extreme caution because of prohibitions against commingling, conversion, breach of fiduciary duty, and practical considerations.

Federal law generally prohibits financial institutions from paying interest on commercial demand accounts. Interest may be paid on such accounts if the entire beneficial interest in the account As held by one or more individuals or by an organization which is operated primarily for religious, philanthropic, charitable, educational, political, or similar purposes and which is not operated for profit or on deposits of public funds. Authorizes the payment of

Interest on real estate trust accounts to certain non- profit charitable organizations. Such authorization is typically limited to client funds, which are nominal in amount or held for a short period of time. Nevada has **not** enacted such legislation.

Since brokers are required to account for and remit client's money on demand, federal law will preclude the establishment of an interest-bearing trust account in most situations. A discussion of the limited circumstances in which an interest- bearing checking account may be established under federal law is beyond the scope of this booklet. Assuming one's ability under federal banking law to establish an interest-bearing trust account, additional considerations will limit or, as a practical matter, preclude their use. There must be full disclosure and consent of the parties to the transaction as to the disposition of any interest earned. This requires an agreement between the broker and the parties as to who will receive interest and how it will be remitted to the parties. If the broker is to benefit from any of the interest earned, that money must be withdrawn from the account and separately accounted for to prevent commingling. Such an arrangement may result in income tax liability to the client under assignment of income rules. A tax expert should therefore be consulted if the broker is to benefit from interest on trust funds. Accounting for and payment of interest must be done in accordance with the broker/client agreement, and done in a timely manner.

Any time that a real estate broker handles funds in his office there is a need to identify the nature of the funds. All staff that handles funds in the office should be adequately trained regarding how to distinguish the nature of the funds. Funds can be of two types and can be placed in any of three types of bank accounts. The two types of funds are company funds and client funds. The three types of bank accounts are company (proprietary) operating accounts, broker trust accounts and custodial client accounts.

COMPANY OPERATING FUNDS

Company funds are received for services rendered, such as

brokerage commissions, lease fees, property management fees, etc. These funds belong to the company/broker and must always be maintained separately from client funds.

COMPANY (PROPRIETARY) OPERATING ACCOUNTS

Company operating accounts are established in the name of the broker or company and should be used to hold only broker or company funds. No client funds should ever be deposited into these accounts. The bank records should indicate that the account is owned by the broker or company and the records should reflect that entity's federal tax identification number.

CLIENT FUNDS

Client funds are any funds received that are to be held for the benefit of a client. Examples of client funds are earnest money deposits, security deposits, rent receipts from management account tenants, etc. These funds ***MUST ALWAYS*** be kept separate from company funds. Clerical or unlicensed staff may not be aware of the distinction between the types of funds and so must be properly supervised by the broker to avoid accidental commingling of company and client funds, thereby placing the broker=s license in jeopardy.

BROKER TRUST ACCOUNT

Broker=s trust accounts are established in the name of the company/broker but must have the words A trust account on the bank statement and on the printed checks. The bank must clearly understand that funds in these accounts do not belong to your company or broker in order to eliminate the possibility of attachment in the case of a judgment, IRS action or other liability, which may arise to the company or broker. These accounts are used
to hold client funds only.

OUT OF STATE BROKERS

A broker licensed in another state and performing brokerage

functions in the state of Nevada under a Cooperative Broker Agreement will look to the cooperating Nevada broker for an accounting of all money. Only the Nevada broker shall handle any money received in the transaction.

CUSTODIAL CLIENT ACCOUNTS

Custodial client accounts are bank accounts, which are opened in the name of a client and are primarily used for property management accounts. The name and ownership of the account with the bank should be that of the client and should show the broker only as the mailing address for statements and communications.

The client as well as the broker must be a signer on this type of account. If an account holds client funds and does not have the client as a signer on the account, it is by definition a trust account and must be treated as such.

When funds are received for a client, for whom the broker is using a custodial account, the funds are considered a trust fund until they are actually deposited into the custodial account at the bank. The broker has the same level of responsibility for these funds before depositing as for any other trust funds. Once they are deposited, they are considered *delivered* to the client because the client has access to the funds by his signature. Handling disbursements from this type of account holds similar fiduciary responsibilities for the broker and care must always be exercised.

There is some risk for a broker who uses a custodial account rather than a trust account because the broker does not have exclusive control over the funds. Since the client may withdraw funds without consent of the broker, the broker may write checks on the account and discover that the client has withdrawn the funds necessary to cover the checks, resulting in returned checks on the account. For this reason brokers are urged to exercise great caution when using a custodial account.

Handling client funds or Trust funds is one of the most important responsibilities that a real estate broker has. The broker=s attention to detail, his commitment to

189

professionalism, his personal and professional integrity and ethical conduct are all reflected in how trust funds are handled. Although the actual processing of the administrative procedures may be delegated to staff or other licensed broker/salesmen within the firm, the ultimate responsibility always lies with the broker of record.

TIMELY DEPOSITS

All trust funds are to be deposited in a timely manner, whether the funds were received as part of a sale or lease negotiation or as a property management function. Before the funds are actually deposited into a bank trust account, they should be adequately secured in a locked cash box, locked filing cabinet, or other secure location from where they are not likely to disappear. A broker should have a clear office policy regarding the care of   the trust funds from the time they are received to the time they reach the bank. This policy should be carefully monitored within the office.

Unless specifically stipulated otherwise in the written contract between the parties to a transaction, a licensee who receives any type of trust funds on behalf of a broker shall pay over those funds to that broker, or to the escrow company designated in the contract, within one business day after receiving those funds. NAC 645.657. When an offer to purchase ripens into a contract or when the broker receives funds related to a property management account, the broker should deposit the trust funds into the broker=s trust account or deliver the funds to the authorized escrow agent before the end of the next banking day. Holding the trust funds beyond these deadlines is a violation of NRS 645 and NAC 645.

ACCURATE ACCOUNTING

The real estate broker must maintain a sufficient Paper trail regarding the trust funds within his files so that at any future time, a client, an auditor or other investigator can reconstruct what happened to the trust funds and   when. Copies of deposit receipts, along with a copy of the check, money order, or even a photocopy of the cash if payment was made in cash, should be maintained in the appropriate file. Accurate references on check book registers and trust account

ACCOUNT RECORDS

All trust account checks should be imprinted with sequential numbers and deposit slips should be printed in duplicate with the name of the real estate brokerage imprinted on them.

REQUIRED RECORDS

The minimum records required for a broker=s trust account are Cash receipts journal; - Cash disbursements journal, or an itemized check stub; - Client ledger, or sub-ledgers if using a consolidated trust account; - Transaction files, numbered or indexed; - Bank account statements and checks.

The broker must keep a record of all of the money that is received by him whether for deposit to the trust account or for deposit directly to escrow. This record must show: The date and amount of money that was received; - The date and amount of money that was deposited; - The dates and amounts of all withdrawals; -Parties for whom the deposit or withdrawal was made; - To whom the money belongs.

A **cash receipts journal** is the diary or daily chronological record of trust funds (things of value) received for the benefit of another. This journal is used to record the date of receipt, the amount of money or value received, and the form of funds received (i.e., cash, check, note, etc.). It also records from whom If the funds were not deposited to the broker=s trust account, the cash receipts journal should record the location of the funds or assets.

A **cash disbursement journal**, like the check stubs or check register, is used to keep track of all disbursements. It must show the date and amount of disbursement, to whom the money was paid, on whose behalf it was paid, the transaction file number, and the resulting balance. Depending upon the bookkeeping used, the cash receipts and cash disbursements journals may be combined into one journal (exhibit #1).

CLOSING AN OFFICE

When a broker closes his office, a few simple steps are required to comply with Division regulations. Broker's license must be inactivated and surrendered to the Division. All salesman and broker-salesman licensees associated with that broker must be terminated at the same time and their licenses surrendered to the Division. Broker must file a notice with the Division stating the location of the office records. Location must be within the state of Nevada in a storage facility, home, office or other facility. Records must be accessible during normal business hours. Records must be maintained by the broker for a minimum of five years Any trust or custodial account monies must be accounted for and properly disbursed. The accounts must then be closed.

Mrs. Murphy Rule

One of the first attempts to regulate fair housing was in New York in 1957, which served as a model for several of the subsequent state laws and was itself based on existing fair-employment statutes. While granting exceptions for the rental of rooms in or attached to owner-occupied homes ("Mrs. Murphy rule"), the ordinance (as amended in 1962) stated that:

"No owner … real estate broker… or other person having the right to sell, rent, lease … or otherwise deny or withhold from any person or group of persons such housing accommodations, or represent that such housing accommodations' are not available for inspection, when I fact they are so available, because of the race, color, religion, national origin or ancestry of such persons" it also barred discrimination by banks and lending institutions. Finally, it outlined a procedure handling complaints and enforcing the policy. Housing discrimination is a pervasive problem in this country. It is severely under reported. The U.S. Department of Housing and Urban Development (HUD) estimates that more than two million instances of discrimination occur each year, and less than one percent are reported.

Fair Housing Act

The 1968 Fair Housing Act specifically deals with discrimination based on race, national origin, color, or religion. In 1974 an amendment was added that also includes any discrimination on the basis of sex. On the following pages is a copy of the U.S. Department of Housing and Urban Development, U.S. Office of Fair Housing and Equal Opportunity Pamphlet that explains the Fair Housing Law.

The Fair Housing Act prohibits discrimination in housing on the basis or:

- Race or color
- National origin
- Religion
- Sex
- Familial status (families with children)
- Disability

Under the Fair Housing Act, the following activities are illegal:

- Refuse to rent or sell housing

- Refuse to negotiate for housing

- Make housing unavailable

- Set different terms, conditions, or privileges for sale or rental

- Provide different housing services or facilities

- Falsely, deny that housing is available for inspection, sale or rental

- For profit, persuade owners to sell or rent (blockbusting)

- Deny any access to or for membership in a facility or service (such as multiple listing service) related to the sale of housing

- Refuse to make reasonable accommodations in rules or services if necessary for a disabled person to use of housing

- Threaten or interfere with anyone making a fair housing complaint

- Refuse to provide municipal services, property insurance or hazard insurance for dwellings, or providing such services or insurance differently

-

Civil Rights Act of 1866 and 1964

This section explains federal legislation dealing with fair housing including the Civil Rights Acts of 1866 and 1964, the Federal Fair Housing Act of 1969, the Fair Housing Amendments Act of 1988, and the Americans with Disabilities Act of 1990. Advertising practices are also included in this category.

The Fair Housing Act of 1968 is a federal law prohibiting discrimination in housing. The law has a wide spread effect on homeowner, renter, apartment managers and anyone working in the real estate industry.

U.S. Department of Housing and Urban Development
Office of Fair Housing and Equal Opportunity

Fair Housing

Equal Opportunity for All

Please visit our website: www.hud.gov/fairhousing

Fair Housing – Equal Opportunity for All

The rich diversity of our people, coupled with the unity of spirit upon which this nation was founded, is America's true strength. We are a nation that celebrates equality of opportunity, which makes it all the more disturbing when new immigrants, minorities, families with children, and people with disabilities are denied housing because of unfair housing discrimination.

The Department of Housing and Urban Development enforces the Fair Housing Act and the other federal laws that prohibit discrimination and the intimidation of people in their homes. These laws cover virtually all housing in the United States – private homes, apartment buildings, and condominium developments – and nearly all housing transactions, including the rental and sale of housing and the provision of mortgage loans.

Equal access to rental housing and homeownership opportunities is the cornerstone of this nation's federal housing policy. Landlords who refuse to rent or sell homes to people based on race, color, national origin, religion, sex, familial status, or disability are violating federal law, and HUD will vigorously pursue them.

Housing discrimination is not only illegal; it contradicts in every way the principles of freedom and opportunity we treasure as Americans. The Department of Housing and Urban Development is committed to ensuring that for everyone seeking a place to live, *all* housing is Fair Housing.

Mel Martinez

Mel Martinez
Secretary

Contents

The Fair Housing Act 1

What Housing Is Covered? 1

What Is Prohibited? 1

Additional Protection If You Have A Disability 3

Housing Opportunities for Families 5

If You Think Your Rights Have Been Violated 6

What Happens When You File A Complaint? 10

Does the U.S. Department of Justice
Play A Role? 11

What Happens After A Complaint Investigation? 12

In Addition 13

U.S. Department of Housing and Urban Development
Secretary Mel Martinez
451 7th Street, S.W.
Washington, DC 20410-2000

196

The Fair Housing Act

The Fair Housing Act prohibits discrimination in housing because of:

- Race or color
- National origin
- Religion
- Sex
- Familial status (including children under the age of 18 living with parents or legal custodians; pregnant women and people securing custody of children under 18)
- Handicap (Disability)

What Housing Is Covered?

The Fair Housing Act covers most housing. In some circumstances, the Act exempts owner-occupied buildings with no more than four units, single-family housing sold or rented without the use of a broker and housing operated by organizations and private clubs that limit occupancy to members.

What Is Prohibited?

In the Sale and Rental of Housing: No one may take any of the following actions based on race, color, national origin, religion, sex, familial status or handicap (disability):

- Refuse to rent or sell housing
- Refuse to negotiate for housing
- Make housing unavailable
- Deny a dwelling
- Set different terms, conditions or privileges for sale or rental of a dwelling
- Provide different housing services or facilities
- Falsely deny that housing is available for inspection, sale or rental
- For profit, persuade owners to sell or rent (blockbusting) or
- Deny anyone access to or membership in a facility or service (such as a multiple listing service) related to the sale or

1

rental of housing.

In Mortgage Lending: No one may take any of the following actions based on race, color, national origin, religion, sex, familial status or handicap (disability):

- Refuse to make a mortgage loan

- Refuse to provide information regarding loans

- Impose different terms or conditions on a loan, such as different interest rates, points, or fees

- Discriminate in appraising property

- Refuse to purchase a loan or

- Set different terms or conditions for purchasing a loan

In Addition: It is illegal for anyone to:

- Threaten, coerce, intimidate or interfere with anyone exercising a fair housing right or assisting others who exercise that right

- Advertise or make any statement that indicates a limitation or preference based on race, color, national origin, religion, sex, familial status or handicap (disability). This prohibition against discriminatory advertising applies to single-family and owner-occupied housing that is otherwise exempt from the Fair Housing Act.

2

Additional Protection If You Have A Disability

If you or someone associated with you:

- Have a physical or mental disability (including hearing, mobility and visual impairments, chronic alcoholism, chronic mental illness, AIDS, AIDS Related Complex and mental retardation) that substantially limits one or more major life activities

- Have a record of such a disability or

- Are regarded as having such a disability

your landlord may not:

- Refuse to let you make reasonable modifications to your dwelling or common use areas, at your expense, if necessary for the disabled person to use the housing. (Where reasonable, the landlord may permit changes only if you agree to restore the property to its original condition when you move.)

- Refuse to make reasonable accommodations in rules, policies, practices or services if necessary for the disabled person to use the housing

Example: A building with a "no pets" policy must allow a visually impaired tenant to keep a guide dog.

Example: An apartment complex that offers tenants ample, unassigned parking must honor a request from a mobility-impaired tenant for a reserved space near her apartment if necessary to assure that she can have access to her apartment.

However, housing need not be made available to a person who is a direct threat to the health or safety of others or who currently uses illegal drugs.

3

199

Requirements for New Buildings: In buildings that are ready for first occupancy **after** March 13, 1991, and have an elevator or four or more units:

- Public and common areas must be accessible to persons with disabilities
- Doors and hallways must be wide enough for wheelchairs
- All units must have:
  - An accessible route into and through the unit
  - Accessible light switches, electrical outlets, thermostats and other environmental controls
  - Reinforced bathroom walls to allow later installation of grab bars and
  - Kitchen and bathrooms that can be used by people in wheelchairs

If a building with four or more units has no elevator and will be ready for first occupancy after March 13, 1991, these standards apply to ground floor units.

These requirements for new buildings do not replace any more stringent standards in State or local law.

4

Housing Opportunities for Families

Unless a building or community qualifies as housing for older persons, it may not discriminate based on familial status. That is, it may not discriminate against families in which one or more children under 18 live with:

- A parent

- A person who has legal custody of the child or children or

- The designee of the parent or legal custodian, with the parent or custodian's written permission.

Familial status protection also applies to pregnant women and anyone securing legal custody of a child under 18.

Exemption: Housing for older persons is exempt from the prohibition against familial status discrimination if:

- The HUD Secretary has determined that it is specifically designed for and occupied by elderly persons under a Federal, State or local government program or

- It is occupied solely by persons who are 62 or older or

- It houses at least one person who is 55 or older in at least 80 percent of the occupied units, and adheres to a policy that demonstrates an intent to house persons who are 55 or older.

A transition period permits residents on or before September 13, 1988 to continue living in the housing, regardless of their age, without interfering with the exemption.

Discrimination in Advertising

The Fair Housing Act is violated regularly in newspaper-classified advertising. The act states that it is illegal " to make, print, or publish and notice, statement, or advertisement with respect to sale or rental of a dwelling that indicates any preference limitation or discrimination based on race, color, religion, national origin or an intention make any such preference."

For example an apartment owner cannot advertise that he prefers to rent to "male" college students, or for a sign to specify that "Christian" renter is wanted. Exemptions are given to religious organizations and private clubs that provide lodging to members and not for commercial purposes. Exemptions are given to apartment buildings containing not more than four apartments provided the owner occupies one of the apartments as a personal residence.

Steering and Blockbusting

The Fair Housing Act states that there will be fines for illegally blockbusting and/or steering. Steering is when a real estate representative directs or "steers" prospective minority purchasers to specific areas of the city where their ethnic or racial color is primarily living. Blockbusting is similar in that it is illegal to induce property owners to sell their property by saying or implying that other people of a specific race, color sex, religion or national origin are moving into other areas.

Redlining

Lending institutions must abide by the Fair Housing Act. Prior to the Fair Housing Law some lending institutions would red-line specific areas mapped out in cities and refuse to loan to those high risk area's based on where the minorities lived. The Fair Housing Act also states that it is also illegal "to discriminate by fixing the amount, interest rate, duration or other terms or conditions of such loan or other financial assistance."

Sale or Rental

The Fair Housing Act also states that you cannot refuse to sell, rent, offer for inspection a home, or even refuse to negotiate the sale of real estate on the basis of color, religion, race, sex or nation origin.

Exceptions to the Law

There are no exceptions in regard to racial discrimination. It is not a violation to discriminate against other protected classifications in the following situations: Rental or sale of a single-family home with no broker involvement and no discriminatory advertising. Rental of units as large as a four-plex, but owners must occupy one of the units.

Units owned by religious organizations may be restricted to people of the same religion if membership in the organization is not restricted on the basis of race, color, or national origin. Non-profit organizations may restrict to members only.

Rental of units based on familial status involving buildings with at least 80% of occupants 55+.

Complaints

Complaints can be filed with HUD within one year of a discriminatory act.

HUD will file a complaint on behalf of the victim.

Penalties include injunction, damages, court costs, and attorney fees.

Aggrieved party can file civil suit directly in federal court within two years.

HUD Equal Opportunity Poster

The HUD Equal Housing Opportunity Poster must be prominently exhibited in the broker's office. Failure to display the poster can be considered evidence of discrimination.

Equal Credit Opportunity Act (ECOA)

The Equal Credit Opportunity Act (ECOA) prohibits discrimination in all consumer credit transactions based upon the same protected classes as the Fair Housing Act. It includes familial status, race, sex, handicap, color, religion and national origin. It also includes age, marital status, and receipt of public assistance.

Americans with Disabilities Act (ADA)

The purpose of the American with Disabilities Act (ADA) is to ensure equal access to public accommodations for disabled people. The act prohibits employment discrimination if the business employs fifteen or more.

Disabilities are defined as any physical or mental impairment that substantially limits one or more major life activities. ADA includes those suffering from AIDS, HIV, and alcoholism. The law specifically excludes those convicted of dealing drugs. Both current and recovered mental patients are protected.

Included in the requirements of the ADA is the removal of architectural and communication barriers and provide auxiliary aids when "readily achievable." The Act allows disabled tenants to make changes at their expense, and the owner may require tenant to return property to original condition at lease termination.

Advertising

The real estate brokerage firm always bears the responsibility for an advertisement's compliance with the license as regardless of whether the firm or one of its affiliated licensees places the advertisement. Some licensees want to believe that the person who pays for the advertisement bears the responsibility. This may not be the case.

Any licensee or any size brokerage form has only limited funds for advertising. In order to maximize the benefits from advertising dollars, each licensee and every firm must plan for advertising carefully in order to assure effective advertising.

To accomplish advertising goal, the broker (or the broker's licensee) should review each advertisement prepared for the firm by licensees or professionals. The review should seek to determine that all advertising:

- Is consistent with company policy or content. For example, company policy may prohibit any inclusion of financing terms in any advertisement permit discussion of amenities and price

- Property addresses are the focus market. For example, an advertisement on a property in county A might not reach the desired audience. If it to run in a local newspaper in county B

- Does not lead the publicity believe that it is being made by a private party not licensed by the real estate commission

- Complies with the requirements of the fair housing laws

- Does not misrepresent any material facts about the property advertised. For example, statements about zoning must be accurate

- Does not misrepresent any terms, values, policies or services of the firm's business

- It is consistent with the trade name and franchise name requirements, if the firm

The public will accept (and perhaps even expects) a certain level of exaggeration in advertising they do not accept misrepresentations and inaccuracies. Thus a program of advertising consistent with the law is really a prescription for effective advertising.

Misrepresentation

Misrepresentation is a contract law concept. It means a false statement of fact made by one party to another party, which has the effect of inducing that party into the contract. For example, under certain circumstances, false statements or promises of a real estate agent regarding the quality or nature of the real estate that the seller has may constitute misrepresentation.

A misrepresentation need not be intentionally false to create liability. A statement made with conscious ignorance or reckless disregard for the truth can create liability. Non-disclosure of material or important facts by a fiduciary such as a real estate agent can result in liability.

If the statement concerns the character or quality of a home, etc., any statement, no matter how innocent may create liability if the statement concerns the character of quality of a piece of real estate and the statement is not true. In such a case, the statement must be one of fact. This does not include so called puffing, or the glowing opinions of seller in the course of a sale pitch, (such statements as "you will love this house," or "it's a great deal."

Generally statements of opinion or intention are not statements of fact in the context of misrepresentation.

BROKER/SALESPERSONS AGREEMENTS

There is no standard agreement between salespersons and brokers.

Most agreements spell out the broker responsibilities such as being continually licensed; provide office space, furniture, telephone, etc. Further the broker is to make all current listings available to the salesperson, provide educational training, and counseling as necessary.

Salespersons shall abide by all local, state, and federal rules, regulations, and ordinances relating to or affecting the real estate profession.

Salespersons must have pre-approval for any advertising, and a policy of errors and omissions insurance.

The commission and fee schedule should also be included in the agreement, with the salesman's percentage of the broker's commission specified.

For example, a broker salesperson agreement may be a "contract addendum split platform" which could be a 50/50 split, 55/45 split, 60/40 split, 65/35 split, 70/30 split, 75/25split, or an 80-/20 split. Which means the salesperson may receive anywhere from a 50% of the broker's commission, or all the way up to a 100% share of the broker's commission.

Some high performing salespersons prefer to have an agreement whereby the salesperson receives one hundred percent of the broker's commission.

Regardless of the commission agreement there will probably be some fees that the sales person will have to pay out of their share of the commission they earn including:
- A franchise fee if applicable
- A transaction fee

- A one time start up fee
- Office participating fee paid per month and a furniture rental fee
- Relocation lead fee
- Should there be a termination the salesperson may be able to take their listings with them for a fee per listing and if the listing is sold there may be a selling commission percentage fee.
- Any contract renegotiation will probably require a 30 notice before the change takes effect.

Ethical Issues

Ethics, in the medical field is based on the Latin phase "primum non nocere", translated as "first do no harm." Real estate professions should probably start their procedures with the "primum non nocere' philosophy in mind.

Real estate professionals should also keep in mind the "Golden Rule" which suggests that we should treat people in the same way that we would like to be treated.

Much has been written about real estate ethics. The best is found in the Board of Realtors© Code of Ethics.

Code of Ethics and Standards of Practice
of the NATIONAL ASSOCIATION OF REALTORS ®

Effective January 1, 2006

Duties to Clients and Customers
Duties to the Public
Duties to REALTORS®

Where the word REALTORS® is used in this Code and Preamble, it shall be deemed to include REALTOR-ASSOCIATE®s.

While the Code of Ethics establishes obligations that may be higher than those mandated by law, in any instance where the Code of Ethics and the law conflict, the obligations of the law must take precedence.

Preamble

Under all is the land. Upon its wise utilization and widely allocated ownership depend the survival and growth of free institutions and of our civilization.

REALTORS® should recognize that the interests of the nation and its citizens require the highest and best use of the land and the widest distribution of land ownership. They require the creation of adequate housing, the building of functioning cities, the development of productive industries and farms, and the preservation of a healthful environment.

Such interests impose obligations beyond those of ordinary commerce. They impose grave social responsibility and a patriotic duty to which REALTORS® should dedicate themselves, and for which they should be diligent in preparing themselves. REALTORS®, therefore, are zealous to maintain and improve the standards of their calling and share with their fellow REALTORS® a common responsibility for its integrity and honor.

In recognition and appreciation of their obligations to clients, customers, the public, and each other, REALTORS® continuously strive to become and remain informed on issues affecting real estate and, as knowledgeable professionals, they willingly share the fruit of their experience and study with others. They identify and take steps, through enforcement of this Code of Ethics and by assisting appropriate regulatory bodies, to eliminate practices which may damage the public or which might discredit or bring dishonor to the real estate profession. REALTORS® having direct personal knowledge of conduct that may violate the Code of Ethics involving misappropriation of client or customer funds or property, willful discrimination, or fraud resulting in substantial economic harm, bring such matters to the attention of the appropriate Board or Association of REALTORS®. (Amended 1/00)

Realizing that cooperation with other real estate professionals promotes the best interests of those who utilize their services, REALTORS® urge exclusive representation of clients; do not attempt to gain any unfair advantage over their competitors; and they refrain from making unsolicited comments about other practitioners. In instances where their opinion is sought, or where REALTORS® believe that comment is necessary, their opinion is offered in an objective, professional manner, uninfluenced by any personal motivation or potential advantage or gain.

The term REALTOR® has come to connote competency, fairness, and high integrity resulting from adherence to a lofty ideal of moral conduct in business relations. No inducement of profit and no instruction from clients ever can justify departure from this ideal.

In the interpretation of this obligation, REALTORS® can take no safer guide than that which has been handed down through the centuries, embodied in the Golden Rule, "Whatsoever ye would that others should do to you, do ye even so to them."

Accepting this standard as their own, REALTORS® pledge to observe its spirit in all of their activities and to conduct their business in accordance with the tenets set forth below.

Duties to Clients and Customers

Article 1
When representing a buyer, seller, landlord, tenant, or other client as an agent, REALTORS® pledge themselves to protect and promote the interests of their client. This obligation to the client is primary, but it does not relieve REALTORS® of their obligation to treat all parties honestly. When serving a buyer, seller, landlord, tenant or other party in a non-agency capacity, REALTORS® remain obligated to treat all parties honestly. (Amended 1/01)

- Standard of Practice 1-1

    REALTORS®, when acting as principals in a real estate transaction, remain obligated by the duties imposed by the Code of Ethics. (Amended 1/93)

- Standard of Practice 1-2

    The duties the Code of Ethics imposes are applicable whether REALTORS® are acting as agents or in legally recognized non-agency capacities except that any duty imposed exclusively on agents by law or regulation shall not be imposed by this Code of Ethics on REALTORS® acting in non-agency capacities.

    As used in this Code of Ethics, "client" means the person(s) or entity(ies) with whom a REALTOR® or a REALTOR®'s firm has an agency or legally recognized non-agency relationship; "customer" means a party to a real estate transaction who receives information, services, or benefits but has no contractual relationship with the REALTOR® or the REALTOR®'s firm; "prospect" means a purchaser, seller, tenant, or landlord who is not subject to a representation relationship with the REALTOR® or REALTOR®'s firm; "agent" means a real estate licensee (including brokers and sales associates) acting in an agency relationship as defined by state law or regulation; and "broker" means a real estate licensee (including brokers and sales associates) acting as an agent or in a legally recognized non-agency capacity. (Adopted 1/95, Amended 1/04)

- Standard of Practice 1-3

    REALTORS®, in attempting to secure a listing, shall not deliberately mislead the owner as to market value.

- Standard of Practice 1-4

    REALTORS®, when seeking to become a buyer/tenant representative, shall not mislead buyers or tenants as to savings or other benefits that might be realized through use of the REALTOR®'s services. (Amended 1/93)

- Standard of Practice 1-5

    REALTORS® may represent the seller/landlord and buyer/tenant in the same transaction only after full disclosure to and with informed consent of both parties. (Adopted 1/93)

- Standard of Practice 1-6

    REALTORS® shall submit offers and counter-offers objectively and as quickly as possible. (Adopted 1/93, Amended 1/95)

- Standard of Practice 1-7

    When acting as listing brokers, REALTORS® shall continue to submit to the seller/landlord all offers and counter-offers until closing or execution of a lease unless the seller/landlord has waived this obligation in writing. REALTORS® shall not be obligated to continue to market the property after an offer has been accepted by the seller/landlord. REALTORS® shall recommend that sellers/landlords obtain the advice of legal counsel prior to acceptance of a subsequent offer except where the acceptance is contingent on the termination of the pre-existing purchase contract or lease. (Amended 1/93)

- Standard of Practice 1-8

    REALTORS®, acting as agents or brokers of buyers/tenants, shall submit to buyers/tenants all offers and counter-offers until acceptance but have no obligation to continue to show properties to their clients after an offer has been accepted unless otherwise agreed in writing. REALTORS®, acting as agents or brokers of buyers/tenants, shall recommend that buyers/tenants obtain the advice of legal counsel if there is a question as to whether a pre-existing contract has been terminated. (Adopted 1/93, Amended 1/99)

- Standard of Practice 1-9

    The obligation of REALTORS® to preserve confidential information (as defined by state law) provided by their clients in the course of any agency relationship or non-agency relationship recognized by law continues after termination of agency relationships or any non-agency relationships recognized by law. REALTORS® shall not knowingly, during or following the termination of professional relationships with their clients:

    1. reveal confidential information of clients; or

    2. use confidential information of clients to the disadvantage of clients; or

    3. use confidential information of clients for the REALTOR®'s advantage or the advantage of third parties unless:

        a. clients consent after full disclosure; or
        b. REALTORS® are required by court order; or
        c. it is the intention of a client to commit a crime and the information is necessary to prevent the crime; or
        d. it is necessary to defend a REALTOR® or the REALTOR®'s employees or associates against an accusation of wrongful conduct.

    Information concerning latent material defects is not considered confidential information under this Code of Ethics. (Adopted 1/93, Amended 1/01)

- Standard of Practice 1-10

    REALTORS® shall, consistent with the terms and conditions of their real estate licensure and their property management agreement, competently manage the property of clients with due regard for the rights, safety and health of tenants and others lawfully on the premises. (Adopted 1/95, Amended 1/00)

- Standard of Practice 1-11

    REALTORS® who are employed to maintain or manage a client's property shall exercise due diligence and make reasonable efforts to protect it against reasonably foreseeable contingencies and losses. (Adopted 1/95)

- Standard of Practice 1-12

When entering into listing contracts, REALTORS® must advise sellers/landlords of:

1. the REALTOR®'s company policies regarding cooperation and the amount(s) of any compensation that will be offered to subagents, buyer/tenant agents, and/or brokers acting in legally recognized non-agency capacities;

2. the fact that buyer/tenant agents or brokers, even if compensated by listing brokers, or by sellers/landlords may represent the interests of buyers/tenants; and

3. any potential for listing brokers to act as disclosed dual agents, e.g. buyer/tenant agents. (Adopted 1/93, Renumbered 1/98, Amended 1/03)

- Standard of Practice 1-13

When entering into buyer/tenant agreements, REALTORS® must advise potential clients of:

1. the REALTOR®'s company policies regarding cooperation;

2. the amount of compensation to be paid by the client;

3. the potential for additional or offsetting compensation from other brokers, from the seller or landlord, or from other parties;

4. any potential for the buyer/tenant representative to act as a disclosed dual agent, e.g. listing broker, subagent, landlord's agent, etc., and

5. the possibility that sellers or sellers' representatives may not treat the existence, terms, or conditions of offers as confidential unless confidentiality is required by law, regulation, or by any confidentiality agreement between the parties. (Adopted 1/93, Renumbered 1/98, Amended 1/06)

- Standard of Practice 1-14

Fees for preparing appraisals or other valuations shall not be contingent upon the amount of the appraisal or valuation. (Adopted 1/02)

- Standard of Practice 1-15

REALTORS®, in response to inquiries from buyers or cooperating brokers shall, with the sellers' approval, disclose the existence of offers on the property. Where disclosure is authorized, REALTORS® shall also disclose whether offers were obtained by the listing licensee, another licensee in the listing firm, or by a cooperating broker. (Adopted 1/03, Amended 1/06))

Article 2

REALTORS® shall avoid exaggeration, misrepresentation, or concealment of pertinent facts relating to the property or the transaction. REALTORS® shall not,

PRACTICE OF REAL ESTATE QUIZ

1. If a lending institution avoids making loans on real estate in certain neighborhoods, it is most likely practicing
   (A) Steering
   (B) Blockbusting
   (C) Filtering
   (D) Redlining

2. The federal Fair Housing Law provides for
   (A) Low income housing projects
   (B) Low down payment on government loans
   (C) Equal housing opportunity
   (D) Minimum construction standards

3. What type of discrimination is not covered by Federal Fair Housing Laws?
   (A) Marital status
   (B) Religion
   (C) Race
   (D) Sex

4. It is unlawful for a landlord in an apartment building to refuse to rent real property
   (A) On the basis the tenant was not born in the United States
   (B) To an unmarried person
   (C) To a person who has a poor credit rating
   (D) Both A & B

5. Which of the following statements concerning discrimination is true?
   (A) The sale of a home may be limited to married couples only
   (B) A broker can accept a listing with the understanding that the owner will only sell to an unmarried man.
   (C) Real estate licensees are bound by the laws of discrimination
   (D) Discrimination is not presently covered under the laws of discrimination

6. Blockbusting occurs when
   (A) A broker uses racial fears to prompt people in a changing neighborhood to sell their homes
   (B) A broker shows prospective buyers houses only in certain areas
   (C) One lending institution buys all the houses on the block
   (D) A lending institution does not make loans in a certain part of the city

7. After broker Jones takes a listing from homeowner Brown, Brown indicates that he will not sell to a minority person
   (A) Make verbal acknowledgement of the fact
   (B) Explain to Brown that this violates federal law and he cannot do it
   (C) Report the incident to the local housing agency
   (D) Not this on the listing agreement

8. Ruth Malone believes that she has been kept from being shown a desirable property because of her sex. In order to seek redress for her grievances. Ms. Malone's course of action should be:
   (A) File a civil suit for lis pendens in court
   (B) File criminal charges in a state court
   (C) Institute a civil suit in either state or federal court
   (D) File criminal charges in a federal court

9. First Federal Thrift would violate the Federal Fair Housing Act by denying a loan to Jones because of which of the following:
   (A) Minority background
   (B) Low earnings
   (C) Poor credit history
   (D) Sporadic job history

10. A particular savings and loan association has blocked out certain regions of the community where it will not place loans because of ghetto conditions. Such a proactive is called
    (A) Redlining
    (B) Steering
    (C) Warehousing
    (D) Relocating

11. A parcel of real estate has subdivision restrictions placed against it in 1950. These deed restrictions prohibit the sale of the property to anyone other than members of the Caucasian race. By the term of these deed restrictions they are to expire in 1999. These deed restrictions are
    (A) Invalid, even if the owner agrees
    (B) Valid until 1999
    (C) Invalid, because they were filed prior to 1964.
    (D) Valid because they were filed prior to 1964

214

12. When you are taking a listing on an owner-occupied single-family residence. If the owner states that you are not to show the property to anyone of the Irish nationality, you should
    (A) Ignore what he requires and proceed with the listing
    (B) Comply with your principal's request
    (C) Make note of the fact in the listing and continue to list hoping that no Irish want to see the property.
    (D) Refuse to take the listing

13. Title VIII of the Civil Rights Act, the Fair Housing Act, applies to
    (A) A single family home owned and sold by private individuals who own more than three such dwellings at one time.
    (B) Multiple-family units containing six apartments, with an owner that occupies one of the residences.
    (C) A single-family unit that is individually owned by a broker selling it.
    (D) All of the above.

14. Joe Lee, an African-American, came into a broker's office in search of a parcel of real property. The broker should show him
    (A) Properties in white neighborhoods only.
    (B) Properties in African-American neighborhoods only.
    (C) The same selection as the broker would show any other person seeking similar properties.
    (D) An equal amount of white and African American owned properties.

15. Who enforces the Truth-In-Lending Law?
    (A) Fair Employment Practices Commission
    (B) Federal Trade Commission
    (C) Real Estate Commissioner
    (D) Secretary of Sate

Property Management

A property management firm operates on the landlord's behalf and tenant. Duties of a property manager including accepting rent, responding to and addressing maintenance issues, advertising vacancies for landlords, and doing credit and background checks on tenants. In exchange for the service they provide, the property management company charge the landlord a percentage of the gross rent collected each month.

Property managers may manage construction, development, and repair and maintenance on a property. Property manager relations with tenants give a face to the landlord and provide a buffer for those landlords desiring to distance themselves from their tenant.

There are many facets to this profession, including participating in or initiating litigation with tenants, contractors and insurance agencies. Litigation is at times considered a separate function, set aside for trained attorneys. Although a person will be responsible for this in his/her job description, there may be an attorney working under the property manager. Special attention is given to landlord/tenant law and most commonly evictions, non-payment, harassment, reduction of pre-arranged services, and public nuisance are legal subjects that gain the most amount of attention from property managers. Therefore, it is a necessity that a property manger be current with applicable municipal, county and d state laws and practices.

Property management include accepting rent, responding to and addressing maintenance issues, advertising vacancies for landlords, and doing credit and background checks on tenants. In exchange for the services they provide, They charges landlords a percentage of the gross rent collected each month, in addition to any lease origination commissions. Property management companies also manage the homeowner associations - HOAs.

In addition to managing income and expense related activity, property managers may also manage construction, development, repair and maintenance on a property. The direction/choreography of repair/maintenance is quite large part of a property manager's function. Property manager relations with tenants give a face to the landlord and provide them the necessary buffer to accomplish their desire to profit and distance themselves from their tenants.

There are many facets to the property management profession, including participating in and/or initiating litigation with tenants, contractors, and insurance agencies. Special attention is given to Landlord/Tenant law. In particular evictions, non-payment, harassment, reduction of pre-arranged services, and public nuisance are legal subjects that gain the most amount of attention from property managers. They must be current with new laws and practices in their localities, cities and states.

National and local property management associations serve as a valuable resource. They provide assistance on current trends in property management. Property managers act as a fiduciary and strive to maximize the landlord's investments.

Licensing

Most states require property management companies to be licensed real estate brokers if they are collecting rent, listing properties for rent or help negotiated leases.

Most states have a public license check system on-line for anyone holding real estate salesperson or real estate broker's license. A few states such as Washington, Idaho and Maine do not require property managers to real estate licenses.

Generally, property manager who engage in only association management need not be a licensed real estate broker. Some states, when not requiring a real estate license, do require association managers to register with the state.

RESIDENTIAL PROPERTY MANAGEMENT AGREEMENT

This PROPERTY MANAGEMENT AGREEMENT (hereinafter referred to as the "Agreement"), entered into this _____ day of _____, _____ by and between _____ (hereinafter referred to as "Owner") of the property or properties described below (hereinafter referred to as the "Property") and _____ (hereinafter referred to as the "Broker") which is duly licensed to manage the Property. In consideration of the mutual terms of this Agreement the parties agree as follows:

1. NOTICES. Any notices, demands, consents and reports necessary or provided for under this Agreement shall be in writing and shall be addressed as follows:

TO OWNER: TO BROKER:

Name: _____   Name: _____
Address: _____   Address: _____
_____   _____
Phone: _____   Phone: _____
Fax: _____   Fax: _____
Email: _____   Email: _____

All notices shall be faxed <u>and</u> sent by regular mail. Notices shall be effective as of the date the notice is faxed and mailed (whichever is later).

2. EMPLOYMENT OF MANAGING BROKER

(A) Employment and Acceptance. Owner employs Broker as the sole exclusive Agent of Owner to manage the Property upon the terms and conditions provided herein. Broker accepts the employment and shall furnish the services of the organization for the management of the Property. Owner shall pay all of the expenses in connection with this service described herein.

(B) Relationship of Broker to Owner. The relationship of the parties to this Agreement shall be that of principal and Agent, and all duties to be performed by Broker under this Agreement shall be on behalf of Owner, in Owner's name and for Owner's account. In taking any action under this Agreement, Broker shall be acting only as Agent for Owner, and nothing in this Agreement shall be construed as creating a partnership, joint venture or any other relationship between the parties or as requiring Broker to bear any portion of losses arising out of or connected with the ownership or operation of the Property. Broker shall not at any time during the period of this Agreement be considered a direct employee of Owner. Neither party shall have the power to bind or obligate the other except as expressly set forth in this Agreement, except that Broker is authorized to act with such additional power as may be necessary to carry out the spirit and intent of this Agreement. Broker, under this Agreement, shall not be responsible for delays in the performance of any obligation unless there is an intentional delay caused by Broker or it's employees.

(C) Description of the Property. The properties to be managed by Broker under this Agreement are described on Exhibits _____ through _____ attached hereto (hereinafter jointly referred to as "the Property.").

(D) Term. The term of this Agreement shall be for an initial period of _____ years (the "initial term") beginning on _____, _____ and ending _____, _____; and thereafter shall then renew for a like term unless terminated by either party.

3. BROKER COMPENSATION AND EXPENSES. As compensation for the services rendered by Broker under this Agreement (and exclusive of reimbursement of the expenses to which Broker is entitled hereunder), Owner shall pay Broker as follows:

(A) Management Services. Broker shall be paid the greater of $ _____ per month or _____ % of the monthly gross collected rents. Payments due Broker for periods of less than the scheduled rental periods shall be prorated.

(B)   Leasing. For the procurement of a Tenant(s) for whom a lease is signed, Broker shall be paid a leasing fee as follows: $ _____ - OR - _____ % of the monthly rent – OR- _____ % of the annual rent. Owner also authorizes payment of an MLS referral commission to the referring broker not to exceed $ _____ .

(C)   Lease Renewals. For Lease renewals, Broker shall be paid a leasing fee of $ _____ - OR - _____ % of the monthly rent – OR- _____ % of the annual scheduled rent.

(D)   Advertising. Owner agrees to pay in advance for all newspaper classified advertisements placed on Owner's behalf and to pay the Multiple Listing Service real estate commission to any real estate Broker including Broker's leasing staff, who brings a qualified tenant that results in a signed lease.

(E)   Selling Commission. If, within the term of this Agreement or within 180 days thereafter, a tenant shall enter into a purchase agreement or lease/option to purchase the Property, Broker shall be deemed the procuring cause of the sale, and Owner shall pay Broker a fee of _____ %. If within the term of this Agreement, Owner shall decide to sell the Property on the market, Owner shall list the Property with Broker for a fee of _____ %.

(F)   Interest on Unpaid Sums. Any sums due Broker under the terms of this Agreement, and not paid within 30 days after such sums have become due, shall bear interest at the rate of 12% per annum.

(G)   Extraordinary Services. An hourly fee of $ _____ per hour shall be paid to Broker for all necessary or requested tasks not considered normal management duties.

4. BANK ACCOUNTS

(A)   Trust Accounts. Broker shall establish a separate Trust Account, apart from any company or corporate account, for the deposit of collected receipts in an institution whose deposits are insured by the federal government. Such depository shall be selected by Broker. Designated funds relating to the Property in the Trust Account remain the property of Owner subject to disbursement of expenses by Broker as described in this Agreement. Any interest accrued on this account will be retained by Broker. Broker shall notify Owner if a new reserve amount is required.

(B)   Initial Deposit and Reserve. Immediately upon commencement of this Agreement, Owner shall remit to Broker the sum of $ _____ as a reserve. Owner shall maintain the reserve stated above at all times in the Trust Account to enable Broker to pay the obligations of Owner under this Agreement as they become due. Broker shall notify Owner if additional funds are required.

(C)   Security Deposit Trust Account. Broker ☐ shall ☐ shall not maintain a separate Security Deposit Trust Account for security deposits, cleaning, pet, and key and other deposits.

5. COLLECTION OF RENTS AND OTHER RECEIPTS

(A)   Broker's Authority. Broker shall collect all rents, charges and other amounts receivable on Owner's account in connection with the management and operation of the Property. Such receipts shall be deposited in the Trust Account maintained by Broker for the Property.

(B)   Special Charges. If permitted by applicable law, Broker may collect from the tenants and retain any and or all, but not limited to the following: an administrative charge for late payment of rent, a charge for returned or non-negotiated checks, interest and a rental application fee.

(C)   Security Deposits. Broker shall collect a security deposit and deposit it into the Trust Account and disburse it in accordance with NRS Chapter 118A. Any interest earned on tenant security deposits shall be retained by Broker.

6. DISBURSEMENTS OF RENTS AND OTHER RECEIPTS

(A)   Operating Expenses. From the Trust Account, Broker is hereby authorized to pay or reimburse itself for all expenses and costs of operating the Property and for all other sums due Broker under this Agreement, including Broker's compensation.

Broker _____
Owner _____

john rosich

(B) Debt Service. Owner shall give Broker advance written notice of at least 30 days to make any additional monthly or recurring payments (such as mortgage indebtedness, general taxes, special assessments or insurance premiums) out of Owner's proceeds from the Property. If Owner notifies Broker to make such payments after the beginning of the term of this Agreement, Broker shall have the authority to name a new contingency reserve amount, and Owner shall maintain this new contingency reserve amount at all time in the Trust Account.

(C) Net Proceeds. To the extent that funds are available and after maintaining the cash contingency reserve amount as specified in Paragraph 3(b), Broker shall transmit the cash balances to Owner monthly.

7. BROKER IS NOT REQUIRED TO ADVANCE FUNDS. If the balance of the Trust Account is at any time insufficient to pay disbursements due and payable, Owner shall, not later than 10 days after notice, remit to Broker sufficient funds to cover the deficiency and replenish the contingency reserve. In no event shall Broker be required to use its own funds to pay such disbursements, nor shall Broker be required to advance any monies to Owner or to the Trust Account. If Broker advances any monies in connection with the Property to pay any Owner expense, Owner shall reimburse Broker, including interest at a rate of 12% per annum, and Broker may deduct such amounts from any monies due Owner.

8. FINANCIAL AND OTHER REPORTS

(A) Owner/IRS Relationship. Owner is required to file all required Internal Revenue Service (IRS) forms and meet all IRS requirements.

(B) Reports. Broker shall furnish Owner with a statement of cash receipts and disbursements from the operation of the Property monthly. In addition, Broker shall, on a mutually acceptable schedule, prepare and submit to Owner such other reports as are agreed on by both parties. Broker shall submit as required by the IRS at the conclusion of each calendar year a Form 1099 indicating the total income received from the Property.

9. LEASING AND RENTING

(A) Broker's Authority. Broker is authorized to negotiate, prepare and sign all leases, including all renewals and extensions of leases and to cancel and modify existing leases for Owner. All costs of leasing shall be paid out of the Property Trust Account. Leases are to be written on Broker's standard lease form.

(B) Enforcement of the Leases. Broker is authorized to institute, in Owner's name, all legal actions or proceedings for the enforcement of any lease term, for the collection of rent or other income from the Property, or for the eviction or dispossession of the tenants or other persons from the Property. Broker is authorized to sign and serve such notices as Broker deems necessary for lease enforcement, including the collection of rent or other income. If Broker deems it necessary, Broker may retain an attorney of Broker's choice (unless Owner supplies Broker with the name of Owner's attorney). Owner shall pay all attorneys fees and court costs.

(C) Management/Maintenance Review. Broker shall make management/maintenance reviews of the Property at the time of occupancy, when the tenant vacates and at such other times as Broker feels necessary or advisable and report matters concerning the condition of the Property to Owner. In the event of vacancy, Broker will take reasonable precautions to secure the Property.

10. REASONABLE MAINTENANCE AND REPAIR

(A) Ordinary/Emergency Maintenance Repair. Broker shall make or cause to be made, through contracted services, employees or otherwise, all ordinary repairs and replacements reasonably necessary to preserve the Property in a habitable condition and for the operating efficiency of the Property, and all alterations required to comply with lease requirements, governmental regulations or insurance requirements. Any cost exceeding $ _____ must be approved by Owner in advance except that in an emergency where repairs are immediately necessary for the preservation and safety of the Property, to avoid the suspension of any essential service to the Property, to avoid danger or life of property, or to comply with federal, state or local law; such emergency repairs shall be made by Broker at Owner's expense without prior approval.

(B) Smoke Detectors. At Owner's expense, smoke detectors will be installed on the Property in working condition in accordance with the law prior to the tenant's occupancy. During the occupancy, it shall be the tenant's responsibility to maintain all smoke detectors.

Broker _____

Owner _____

john rosich

11. UTILITIES AND SERVICES. Broker shall, in Owner's name and at Owner's expense, make contracts for electricity, gas or water and such other services as necessary or prudent for the operation of the Property. All utility charges and deposits shall be Owner's responsibility.

12. INSURANCE.

(A) Owner's Insurance. Owner shall obtain and keep in force adequate insurance against damage and against liability for loss, damage or injury to property or persons which might arise out of the occupancy, management, operation or maintenance of the Property. The deductible required under such insurance policies shall be Owner's expense. Broker shall be covered as an additional insured on all liability insurance maintained with respect to the Property. Liability insurance shall be adequate to protect the interests of both Owner and Broker and in form, substance and amounts reasonably satisfactory to Broker, but not less than $500,000 (five hundred thousand dollars). Owner shall provide Broker with proof of fire insurance policies in force and shall obtain adequate vandalism coverage for the Property. Owner shall furnish Broker with certificate evidencing fire and liability insurance or with duplicate copies of such policies within 15 days after the date of this Agreement. Such policies shall provide that notice of default or cancellation shall be sent to Broker as well as Owner and shall require a minimum of 30 days written notice to Broker before any cancellation of or changes to such policies.

(B) Tenant's Insurance. Tenants ☐ shall ☐ shall not be required to obtain renter's insurance.

13. SAVE HARMLESS. Owner shall indemnify, defend and save Broker harmless from all loss, investigation, suits, damage, cost, expense (including attorneys fees) liability or claims for personal injury or property damage incurred or occurring in, on or about the Property.

14. BROKER ASSUMES NO LIABILITY. Broker assumes no liability for any damages, losses, or acts of omission by the Tenant. Broker assumes no liability for any acts or omissions of Owner or previous Owners or previous brokers. Broker assumes no liability for default by any tenant. Broker assumes no liability for violations of environmental or other regulations which may become known during the term of this Agreement. Any such regulatory violations or hazards discovered by Broker shall be brought to the attention of Owner, and Owner shall promptly cure them. Broker shall not be liable in the event of bankruptcy or failure of the depository bank where Owner's funds are deposited.

15. OWNER'S RESPONSIBILITY FOR EXPENSES OF LITIGATION.

(A) Litigation and Compliance Expenses. Owner shall pay all fines, penalties, or other expenses in connection with any claim, proceeding or suit involving an alleged violation of any law pertaining to fair employment, fair credit reporting, environmental protection, rent control taxes or fair housing, including illegal discrimination on the basis of race, sex, color, religion, national origin, physical handicap, familial status, elderliness or all other protected classes; provided, however, that Owner shall not be responsible to Broker for any such expenses if Broker is finally adjudged in a court of law to have personally, and not in a representative capacity, violated any such law. Nothing contained in this Agreement shall obligate Broker to employ legal counsel to represent Owner in any such proceeding or suit.

(B) Fees for Legal Advice. Owner shall pay reasonable expenses incurred by Broker in obtaining legal advice regarding compliance with any law affecting the Property. If such expenditure also benefits other principals of Broker, Owner shall pay an apportioned amount of such expense.

16. REPRESENTATIONS

(A) Owner Representations. Owner represents and warrants: that Owner has full power and authority to enter into this Agreement; that there are no written or oral agreements affecting the Property other than disclosed tenant leases, copies of which have been furnished to Broker; that there are no recorded easements, restrictions, reservations or rights of way which adversely affect the use of the Property for the purposes intended under this Agreement; that the Property is zoned for the intended use; that all permits for the operation of the Property have been secured and are current; that the building and its construction and operation do not violate any applicable statutes, laws, ordinances, rules, regulations, orders or the like; that the information supplied by Owner is dependable and accurate; and that any loans, notes, mortgages, dues or trust deeds are fully paid and are current without defaults.

(B) Multiple Listing Service. No Multiple Listing Service or Association of REALTORS® is a party to this Agreement and no Multiple Listing Service or Association of REALTORS® sets, controls, recommends or suggests the amount of compensation for any service rendered pursuant to this Agreement.

17. TERMINATION

(A) Early Termination. This Agreement may be terminated by Owner before the termination date specified in Paragraph 1(d) by written notice to Broker not less than 30 days prior to the termination date specified in such notice, together with a cancellation fee in the amount equal to the management fee that would accrue over the remainder of the stated term of any existing lease agreement. For this purpose, the monthly management fee for the remainder of the stated term of the existing lease agreement shall be presumed to be the same as that of the last full calendar month prior to service of the notice of cancellation. In the event Owner directs Broker to transfer files and documents to a succeeding management company, Owner will pay Broker a transfer fee of $ _____ , This Agreement may be terminated by Broker before the termination date specified in Paragraph 1(d) upon 30 days written notice to Owner. Within ten days of termination, Owner will pay Broker all monies due under this Agreement.

(B) Owner Responsible for Payments. Upon termination of this Agreement, Owner shall assume the obligations of any contract or outstanding bill incurred by Broker under this Agreement. Broker may withhold funds for 30 days after the end of the month in which this Agreement is terminated in order to pay bills previously incurred but not yet invoiced and to close accounts. Broker shall deliver to Owner, within 30 days after the end of the month in which this Agreement is terminated, any balance of monies due Owner or tenant security deposits, or both, which were held by the Broker with respect to the Property, as well as a final accounting reflecting the balance of income and expenses with respect to the Property as of the date of termination or withdrawal. The security deposit will not be released unless all parties agree in writing to the transfer of the security deposit from the Broker's trust account to Owner.

18. INDEMNIFICATION SURVIVES TERMINATION. All representations and warranties of the parties contained herein shall survive the termination of this Agreement. All provisions of this Agreement that require Owner to have insured or to defend, reimburse or indemnify Broker shall survive any termination. If Broker becomes involved in any proceeding or litigation by reason of having been Owner's Broker, such provisions shall apply as if this Agreement were still in effect.

19. MISCELLANEOUS

(A) Rights Cumulative; No Waiver. The exercise of any right or remedy provided in this Agreement shall not be an election of remedies, and each right and remedy shall be cumulative. The failure of either party to this Agreement to insist at any time upon the strict observance or performance of any of the provisions of this Agreement, or to exercise any right or remedy provided in this Agreement, shall not be construed as a waiver of such right or remedy with respect to subsequent defaults. Every right and remedy provided in this Agreement may be exercised from time to time and as often as may be deemed expedient by the party exercising such right or remedy.

(B) Agreement to Mediate. All parties agree to engage in mediation through the Greater Las Vegas Association of REALTORS® prior to commencing any legal action. In any action or proceeding involving a dispute between the parties arising out of this Agreement, the prevailing party shall be entitled to receive from the other party court costs and reasonable attorneys fees to be determined by the court or arbitrator.

(C) Headings. All headings and subheadings in this Agreement and in the accompanying List of Provisions are inserted only for convenience and ease of reference and are not to be considered in the construction or interpretation of any provision of this Agreement.

20. APPLICABLE LAW AND PARTIAL INVALIDITY. The interpretation of this Agreement shall be governed by the laws of the State of Nevada. Any action arising under this Agreement shall be brought in state court in Clark County, Nevada. If any part of this Agreement shall be declared invalid or unenforceable, either party shall have the option to terminate this Agreement by written notice to the other party.

21. COMPLETE AGREEMENT. This Agreement shall be binding upon the parties, and each of their respective heirs, executors, administrators, successors and assigns. No amendment is valid unless in writing and signed by the parties. There are no warranties or representations not herein contained.

Broker _____
Owner _____

john rosich

22. FOREIGN INVESTMENTS IN REAL PROPERTY TAX ACT (FIRPTA). Pursuant to the Internal Revenue Code Section 1441, the deduction of a withholding tax on all fixed or determinable gross income shall be required of any non-resident alien individual, fiduciary, foreign partnership or foreign corporation unless exempt under provisions provided under said IRS Section. If Owner is a non-resident alien individual, fiduciary, foreign partnership or foreign corporation, Broker will require a written statement from either a CPA or U.S. Tax Attorney. Owner ☐ is ☐ is not a non-resident alien individual, fiduciary, foreign partnership or foreign corporation.

23. ADDITIONAL TERMS: _____

_____

_____

_____

_____

_____

_____

BROKER: OWNER:

By _____   _____
   Authorized Agent for Broker   Signature

By _____   _____
   Broker   Signature

Copyright© by: Greater Las Vegas Association of REALTORS®
Residential Property Management Agreement
Revised 10/03
Page 6 of 7

Broker _____
Owner _____

Produced with ZipForm™ by RE FormsNet, LLC 18025 Fifteen Mile Road, Clinton Township, Michigan 48035   www.zipform.com

john rosich

PROPERTY INFORMATION

Owner Name: _____

Property Address: _____

_____

APN: _____

Existing Tenant (if any):

Name: _____

Home Phone: _____

Work Phone: _____

Acceptable Rental Rate/Month: Minimum: $ _____   Maximum: $ _____

Acceptable Lease Term: Minimum _____ Years / Maximum: _____ Years

EXHIBIT " _____ "

Broker _____
Owner _____

john rosich

Common Interest Ownership Properties, (Condominium/Cooperatives)

Condominiums

Condominiums are buildings in which individuals separately own the *air space* inside the interior walls, floor, and ceilings of their unit, but they jointly own an interest in the common areas that they share including land, lobbys, hallways, swimming pools, and parking lots.

In addition to making their own mortgage payments, each owner is responsible for a monthly fee to the condominium association. The association is made up of the unit owners. The fee covers maintenance, repair, and building insurance. Most housing condominiums are really apartments, although there are mobile home condominiums as well.

Cooperatives

The main distinction between housing cooperatives and other forms of homeownership is a housing cooperative is *not* the direct ownership of real estate. A cooperative owner buys shares, or a membership in a cooperative housing corporation. The corporation owns or leases all real estate. As a shareholder the member in a cooperative has the exclusive right to live in a specific unit, (this is established thorough an occupancy agreement or a lease), for as long as the member does not break any of the rules or regulations of the cooperative. The shareholder membership allows a vote in the affairs of the corporation.

Shareholders can sell their shares or membership however the purchase price will vary depending the size of the unit, and whether the cooperative limits resale prices..

In effect a cooperative is ownership by a corporation, which in turn leases space to shareholders. The buyer receives corporate by-laws, shares of stock, and a propriety lease. Since there is no ownership of the unit, the buyer does not receive a deed. The cooperative owner pays assessments/association fees.

Townhouses

While most condominiums are apartments, a townhouse is attached to one or more houses, and can be part of a duplex, triplex, or communities with hundreds of homes. Buyers have a *fee simple ownership* of their homes and the land upon which the house sit. With a condominium, the unit owners jointly own the land and the common interest areas cannot be separated from others.

Townhouses can be structured in many ways. Some, particularly huge communities, have common areas, such as swimming pools – that are similar to condominiums. Some states require some disclosure and recession rights as condominiums and cooperatives.

Timeshares

Timeshare ownership is very similar to condominium ownership. The main distinction is the purchaser may buy one or more weeks of ownership. Timeshare ownership becomes a bit dicey in the way a buyer takes ownership. The purchaser has the most protection in fee ownership, however ownership in some timeshares is referred to as "right to use." A buyer under the "right to use" contract has nothing more than a business contract and has no real estate ownership. Usually any timeshares sold outside of the continental U.S. will be a "right to use" type of arrangement and the buyer is not very well protected in these situations.

Commercial Property

Commercial property is a classification of real estate that includes non-residential income producing property. Examples are: office building, gas station, restaurant, shopping center, hotel/motel, parking lot, stores, business opportunity, etc.

Subdivision (Land)

Subdivision is the act of dividing land into pieces that are easier to sell or otherwise develop, usually via plat, (blueprint). The former single piece as a whole is then known as a subdivision. If it used for housing it is known as a housing subdivision or housing development.

Subdivisions may also be for the purpose of commercial or industrial development, which could be retail malls to industrial parks. In the United States, the creation of a subdivision was often the first step toward the creation of new incorporated township or city.

In the 1920's the Coolidge administration formed the Advisory Committee on City Planning and Zoning, which undertook as its first task the creation of the Standard City Planning Enabling Act (SCPEA), which it completed in 1928. The SCPEA covered six subjects:

1. The organization and power of planning commissions, which was directed to prepare and adopt a master plan;

2. The content of the master plan;

3. Provisions for a master street plan;

4. Provisions for approval of all public improvements by the planning commission;

5. Control of private subdivision of land; and

6. Provisions of for the creation of regional planning commission.

Subdivision means the division of a lot, tract, or parcel of land into two or more lots, plats, sites, or other division of land for the purpose, whether immediate or future, of sale or of building development.

Every division of a piece of land into two or more lots, parcels or parts is a subdivision. Once a local planning board has approved a subdivision and once recorded in a recorder of deeds it is generally deemed to have created the parcels of land identified on the plat itself.

Business Opportunity Sales

A broker's license is required for charging a fee to sale a business, and in some states a separate license is required for business sales.

Bulk Sales Requirements

The Uniform Commercial Code, (UCC), requires bulk sales disclosures in the sale of goods of $500 or more. Seller must disclose creditors.

SPECIALTY AREAS QUIZ

1. The basic goal of a professional real estate manager is to

   (A) Maintain the property in as perfect condition as humanly possible
   (B) Return to the property owner in the long-term the highest possible net return
   (C) Provide financial records and accounts
   (D) All of the above

2. Which one of the following in not among the major responsibilities of a property manager?

   (A) Obtain the highest possible return for the investor
   (B) Preserve the building
   (C) Maintain high occupancy
   (D) Obtain a listing for resale

3. A property manager's duties typically include all but which one of the following

   (A) Collecting rents
   (B) Making minor repairs
   (C) Marketing space
   (D) Investing profits from client's properties

4. When a broker or property manager signs a contract to manage an owner's property he becomes a

   (A) Lesser
   (B) Trustee
   (C) Receiver
   (D) Fiduciary

5. "Security deposits" include monies paid by a tenant for a

   (A) Non-refundable cleaning fee
   (B) Conditionally refundable deposit
   (C) Payment of current rent
   (D) Non-refundable credit check fee

6. If a tenant ha an essential service repaired and deducts the cost from the rent the tenant may also

   (A) Terminate the tenancy with ten days written notice to the landlord
   (B) Terminate the tenant with fourteen days written notice to the landlord
   (C) Recover damages from the landlord
   (D) Do none of the above

7. Net leases are used least often with

(A) Apartments
(B) Rental spaces
(C) Office space
(D) Industrial space

8. A lease of land only, on which the tenant agrees to construct a residence within a certain period of time, is best called

(A) Ground lease
(B) Gross lease
(C) Net lease
(D) Percentage lease

9. A lease whereby the amount of rent is based upon the tenant's volume of business is known as

(A) Ground lease
(B) Gross lease
(C) Net lease
(D) Percentage lease

10. The willful destruction of any part of the land, which would injure or prejudice the landlord's reversionary right is called

(A) Waste
(B) Unlawful performance
(C) Obsolescence
(D) Condemnation

11. The assignment of a lease, which includes an option to purchase

(A) Is voidable by the landowner
(B) Is prohibited by the Statute of Frauds
(C) Will cause the option to become unenforceable
(D) Transfers to option to the assignee

12. When real estate is sold on which there is an existing lease containing no provisions in the event of sale, the lease

(A) Has to be renewed at expiration
(B) Expires immediately
(C) Becomes a sub-lease
(D) Is binding on the new owner

13. Smith leased a building to Brown for a period of ten years. After two years Brown abandoned the leasehold. Smith reentered the property, accepting Brown's actions as ending the lease. This termination
Is identified as

(A) Surrender
(B) Recession
(C) Release
(D) Cancellation

14. Upon the death of the lessee, the interest in leasehold rests in

(A) The lessor
(B) The state
(C) The estate of the lessee
(D) A third party trust

15. A tenant leased a heated apartment, but the landlord failed to provide heat because of a defective heating plant. The tenant vacated and refused to pay rent. This is an example of

(A) Actual eviction
(B) Abandonment
(C) Negligence
(D) Constructive eviction

16. In every lease the lessor gives the lessee an implied covenant of

(A) Further assurance
(B) Seisen
(C) Compliance
(D) Quiet enjoyment

17. A forcible entry or wrongful detainer action would usually be used by an offended

(A) Holder of a note, which is in default
(B) Lessor
(C) Grantor
(D) Lessee

18. In inflationary times, a property manager would not want a long-term lease with rents based upon

(A) Graduated amounts
(B) The consumer price index
(C) The cost of living index
(D) A fixed rate

19. The repairs of fire damage to an office building is an example of

   (A) Regular recurring costs
   (B) Periodic costs
   (C) Recurring variable cost
   (D) Non-recurring variable cost

20. A commercial property has 43,000 square feet is rented at $5 per square foot. Actual rents collected over the past year totaled only $182,750. What occupancy rate should be used in the budget forecast for the next year?

   (A) 80 %
   (B) 85%
   (C) 82%
   (D) 89%

Chapter – 10 – Financing and Settlement

Learning Objectives

A. Financing concepts and components
   1. Methods of financing
      a. Mortgage financing – conventional and non-conventional loans
      b. Seller financing – land contract/contract for deed
   2. Lien theory vs. title theory and deed of trust
   3. Sources of financing (primary and secondary mortgage markets, and seller financing)
   4. Types of loans and loan programs
   5. Mortgage clauses
B. Lender Requirements
   1. FHA requirements
   2. VA requirements
   3. Buyer qualifications and Loan to Value (LTV)
   4. Hazard and flood insurance
   5. Private Mortgage Insurance (PMI) and mortgage insurance premium MIP)
C. Federal Financing Regulations and Regulatory Bodies
   1. Truth in Lending and Regulation Z.
   2. TILA-RESPA Integrated Disclosures (TRID)
      a. Consumer Financial Protection Bureau (CFPB)
      b. Loan Estimate (LE)
      c. Closing Disclosure (CD)
   3. Real Estate Settlement and Procedures Act (RESPA)
      a. Referrals
      b. Rebates
   4. Equal Credit Opportunity Act (ECOA)
   5. Mortgage fraud and predatory lending
D. Settlement and closing the transaction

General Concepts

In the United States, mortgages first became widely used in 1934. In that year, the Federal Housing Administration, (FHA) lowered the down payment requirements when it offered 80% loan to value loans. FHA also lengthened loan terms by introducing 15year loans to supplant 3,5, and 7-year loans, which ended with balloon payments, (the amount owed at the end of loan term was all due and had to be paid). Until the 1930's only 40% of U.S. households owned homes. Today the rate is nearly 70%. More than a third of all homeowners own their homes free and clear. Of the homeowners with mortgages, 75% have fixed rate mortgages and only 25% have adjustable rate mortgages.

In 2003, total U.S. residential mortgage production reached a record level of $3.8 trillion. The mortgage industry has had record low interest rates although the interest rates continued to vary according to the individual's credit rating.

Mortgage

A mortgage is a method of using property (real or personal) as security for payment of a debt.

The term mortgage (from French Law, literally - death vow) refers to the legal device used in securing the property, but it also commonly used to refer to the debt secured by the mortgage. The debt is sometimes referred to as the *hypothecation*, which means to pledge as security

A mortgage is a contract that pledges (hypothecates) property as security for repayment, without giving up possession. A mortgage includes covenants and clauses for foreclosure including: non-payment of principal and interest, non-payment of taxes, and inadequate or no insurance.

Mortgage Lenders

Home loans are available from several types of lenders including mortgage bankers, mortgage brokers, thrift institutions (formerly savings and loans) commercial banks and credit unions. Different lenders quote slightly different prices so the consumers should shop for the best price.

Mortgage Bankers and Mortgage Brokers

Mortgage brokers act as an intermediary between borrowers and lenders but do not usually service loans. Mortgage bankers originate and service loans with deposits and their own money.

Mortgage brokers arrange transactions but do not lend money directly. A mortgage broker's access to several lenders can result in a wider selection of loan products and terms. Mortgage brokers generally contact several lenders regarding a loan, but they are under no obligation to find the best deal unless applicants have contracted with the broker to serve as their agent. It makes sense for consumers to contract with more than one broker to find the best loan.

Whether the consumers are dealing with a mortgage banker or mortgage broker isn't always clear. Some financial institutions operate as both lenders and mortgage brokers. Most mortgage brokers do not use the word broker in their advertisements. Consumers should inquire if a mortgage broker is involved in the transaction. It is important to know this since mortgage brokers are usually paid a fee for their services that is often separate from and in addition to the lender's origination and other fees.

Lender Evaluations

The lender looks at three main areas:

1. Debt to income ratio,

2. Credit

3. Down payment.

Debt to Income Ratio

In an effort to prevent homebuyers from getting a home they cannot afford, the FHA has established strict guidelines for borrower's qualifications that are based on debt to income ratios. These ratios are used to calculate whether or not the potential borrower has the financial wherewithal to meet the demands required for home ownership.

The two ratios are as follows.

1. Mortgage Payment Expense to Effective Income
Add the total mortgage payment. This sum includes: principal and interest, escrow deposits for taxes, hazard insurance, mortgage insurance premiums, homeowner's dues, etc. Then take that amount and divide it by gross monthly income. The maximum ratio to qualify is 29%.

2. Total Fixed Payment to Effective Income

Add the total mortgage payment to all recurring monthly revolving and installment debt. This debt includes any installment loans and credit card debt. Take this amount and divide it by the gross monthly income. The maximum ratio is 41%

Conventional loan qualifications are essentially the same as outlined above. However the conventional lender will evaluate the borrower based primarily on the FICO score. The lender will look at the income. For salaried persons the W-2 is used for income documentation. The gross income is compared to the amount of fixed debt, and should not to exceed a ration of 45% including the proposed mortgage payment. The fixed debt is whatever shows up on the credit report.

FICO Scores

FICO, Fair Isaac and Company is a secret rating scheme used to predict if a prospective borrower will default on a loan. Few people know exactly how FICO scores are computed. Secondary mortgage giants such as Fannie Mae and Freddie Mac use FICO scores so the mortgage industry does as well.

In the U.S three major credit bureaus obtain and store consumer credit information. They are: Experian, formerly known as TRW, Trans Union Corp and Equifax. Lenders receive more than credit reports when they access credit reporting company records. They also get the FICO score, which serves as a credit rating on the borrower. Credit bureaus use FICO software to score credit reports so these numerical scores, ranging from a 300 to more than 900; most scores are between 600 and 700. Because credit bureaus data varies at any time, borrowers are likely to have three different but similar scores. Obviously, lenders make loan decisions based on standards they deem valuable when determining borrower's credit score, overall credit history, debt to income ratios as well as other factors.

It should be pointed out that at the present time FHA and VA have no minimum FICO credit score. Fico scores also drive the interest rate and fees the homebuyer will pay.

Down Payment and Mortgage Insurance

Lenders feel safe with a 20 percent of the home's purchase price as a down payment. However, many lenders do offer loans that require less than this amount. Consumers should understand that with less than a 20 percent down payment a lender would require homebuyers to *purchase mortgage insurance*. This protects the *lender* in case the homebuyer defaults.

Financing

Financing includes the financial aspects of any real estate transaction including financing alternatives such as FHA/VA, conventional, seller financing, second mortgages, etc.

Personal loans using real estate as the security against non-repayment of the loan have been around since lending began. Originally, U.S. real estate loans made by banking institutions were for a short term only. The banking institution would renew the loan every six months similar to a revolving line of credit. If banking institutions had cash flow problems, their only remedy was to call real estate backed loans all due and payable. Since there were no other reliable financing options available to homeowners, they could expect to lose all rights to their property during hard economic times.

This volatile lending situation was further exacerbated during the great depression when people lost their real estate holding on a grand scale. In an effort to stabilize the market Congress passed legislation that created a *secondary market* where lenders could sell their long-term loans and get reimbursed. This enabled institutions to continue the lending process.

The Loan Process

The loan process begins with the homebuyer applying for a loan from a primary market lender such as mortgage banker, mortgage broker, a bank thrift (previously known as a savings and loan) credit union, or an online lender.

Primary lenders evaluate the homebuyer's ability to repay the mortgage. If the lender's criteria are met, arrangements are then made to package the loan. The transaction between the lender and the borrower culminates in what is known as the *closing*. By signing closing documents a lender agrees to fund the purchase of the home, and the homebuyer agrees to pay the mortgage as negotiated. Once the loan is closed, the funds are transferred from the primary lender to the property seller.

Mortgage Underwriting

Mortgage pre approval, loan pre qualification are based on information submitted before verification of all documentation. After documentation verification the file goes to a mortgage underwriter who again verifies the information. The underwriter can also request any other documentation they feel is justified to strengthen the file. When the underwriter is satisfied, the homebuyer will receive an approval and. the actual closing is scheduled. The lender will pull the homebuyer credit the day of the close to make sure the homebuyer has not incurred any new debt that effects the loan qualification. The lender can cancel the closing anytime before signatures and recordation.

Points

Points are used in at least two ways by the lender. Points are fees paid to the lender or mortgage broker for the loan and are often linked to interest rates. Usually, the more points borrowers pay, the lower the interest rate. The consumer should ask for the dollar amount that the points represent as well as the number of points.

A lenders' compensation may be in the form of "points" paid at closing or as an add-on to the interest rate or both. One point is the equivalent of one percent of the loan. Consumers should ask the lenders how they are compensated. Consumers should receive the following information from their lenders.

Annual Percentage Rates – APR

APR includes both the interest and any additional costs or prepaid finance charges paid such as prepaid interest, private mortgage insurance, closing fees, points, etc. It represents the total cost of credit on a yearly basis after all charges are taken into consideration.

Lenders should provide a list of their current mortgage interest rates, and the annual percentage rate, (APR); they also need to clarify if the mortgage has fixed or adjustable rates. Adjustable rate loans have rates that can go up and down, and affect payments accordingly. Lenders must state the APR in annual terms or for the year. The APR takes into account the interest rate, the points, broker fees and certain other credit charges that consumers may be required to pay (see RESPA).

Fees

Home loans often involve many fees. They include loan origination or underwriting fee and broker fees as well as transaction settlement and closing costs. Every lender must give an estimate of the fees. Many of these fees are negotiable. Some fees are paid at the time of the application such as application and appraisal fees and others are paid at closing. In most cases, consumers' fees are added to the loan amount so that the borrower does not have to come up with the cash to pay for these fees. Such borrowing increases the loan amount and total loan costs. "No cost" loans are sometimes available, but usually involve higher interest rates. Consumers should request a breakdown of each fee, since several items may be lumped into one fee.

Types of Real Estate Loans

Although lenders seem to have a number of different kinds of loans and repayment schedules, there are three basic loan packages:

1. F.H.A.
2. V.A.
3. Conventional.

FHA Mortgage Loans

Federal Housing Administration (FHA) insured financing, insures lender against loss due to foreclosure.

FHA also enables high loan-to-value ratio (lower down payments), although mutual mortgage insurance (MMI) is required for those loans that exceed an 80% loan to value.

FHA Mortgage Insurance

FHA *Mutual Mortgage Insurance (MMI)* is a policy that protects lenders from losses when homeowners default on their home mortgages. FHA loans require Mutual Mortgage Insurance primarily for borrowers who make down payments of less than 20 percent.

Mortgage insurance is charged to the homeowner at the rate of five percent per year of the total loan amount. In addition the FHA charges an upfront mortgage insurance premium of 1.5%

The premium is canceled for loans less than fifteen years when the "loan-to-value" ratio is ninety percent or greater. For loans-greater than 15 years, the annual mortgage insurance premium is canceled when the "loan-to-value " ratio is 78%, provided the mortgagor has paid the premium for at least five years.

VA Loans

The VA home loan program, was part of the 1944 GI Bill, has provided million of war and peacetime military personnel with the opportunity of home ownership.

Banks, thrifts, mortgage companies and other private lenders-package VA guaranteed loans made to eligible veterans, providing they occupy the purchased homes. The guaranty protects the lender against any losses if the homeowner fails to repay the loan. The guaranty acts as the protection a lender would normally have with a required down payment.

In lieu of mortgage insurance the VA charges an up front fee of 2.15% of the loan. The fee drops to 1.5%. when veterans put down 10% or more. Veterans must provide the following two certificates:

Certificate of eligibility/entitlement
Certificate of reasonable value (CRV), which is a VA appraisal of the home.

Miscellaneous aspects of FHA/VA

- Rules regarding assumption depend on the date of the loan. Assumable FHA/VA loans refer to loans originated prior to and including the 1980's.
- No prepayment penalty.
- Non-veterans who qualify may assume VA loans.
- Purchase agreement must contain an "escape clause" making sale contingent upon property being appraised at sales price or higher."
- Rural Development and Farm Agency, formerly Farmer's Home Administration guarantees, insures and originates loans in rural communities of 10,000 or less population.

Conventional Loans

Lenders in the primary market make conventional real estate loans. These loans have no government insurance or guarantees. Lenders have some security since the loans are insured by private mortgage insurance, (PMI), companies. Subsequently, the lenders make loan decisions based on property values and the credit scores of mortgagors. These loans are called " conventional" since they conform to some accepted standards and can be funded by institutional lenders or private parties.

Since conventional lenders do not have to adhere to the stringent regulations that FHA and VA lenders must conform to, the borrower should be more cautious of such lenders. Conventional lenders have lobbied vigorously against regulatory requirements and, as a result they can charge the borrowers many fees that federal loan programs restrict. *Obviously, conventional loans are more financially beneficial to lenders than borrowers.* Some conventional lenders tell clients that their loans are better for the consumer than VA or FHA loans. This is an exaggeration, at best. Conventional lenders are subject to some institutional regulations, but not as many when compared to VA or FHA requirements.

Other Sources of Capital for Real Estate Loans

Commercial Banks

Commercial banks prefer short-term loans for commercial business, which includes new construction loans.

Life Insurance Companies

Life insurance companies/credit unions/pension funds – prefer long-term commercial and industrial *participation loans*. With participation loan the lender receives interest plus an ownership equity position in income-producing properties.

Types of Mortgage Loans

Fixed Rate Mortgage

The most common way to repay a loan is to make regular payments of the capital (also called the principal) and interest over a set period of time. Mortgage repayments are typically made throughout the term of the mortgage. In the early years, the repayments are largely interest only and just a small portion capital. Near the end of the mortgage term, the repayments are mostly capital and small part interest. In this way, the prepayment amount that determined at the outset is calculated to ensure the loan is repaid at a specified period in the future. This gives the borrower assurance that by maintaining repayment, the loan will be cleared at a specified date.

Budget Mortgage

A budget loan is where borrowers pay (P & I), (principal and interest), plus (T) a monthly percentage of the real estate taxes and (I) a monthly percentage of the homeowner's insurance into the lender's impound account that is actually owned by the borrower. Some states require lenders to pay interest on the borrower's impounds.

244

Adjustable Rate Mortgage – ARM

The adjustable rate mortgage (ARM) is a loan where the interest rate and loan payments are subject to change based upon variations in an economic index, ARM's may include interest and/or payment caps.

Adjustable Rate Loan Disclosure Requirements

The disclosure requirements for ARM loans include:

- The booklet titled Consumer Handbook on Adjustable Rate Mortgages published by the Federal Reserve Board.
- A loan program disclosure for each variable-rate program in which the consumer expresses an interest.

The consumer applying for a mortgage may rescind the application until midnight of the third business day following consummation of the transaction. Within 20 calendar days after receipt of a notice of recession, the lender is required to return any deposit. If an advertisement states a rate of finance charge, it may state the rate as an annual percentage rate, (APR) using that term.

Option Adjustable Rate Mortgage

Option ARM's were introduced in 1981, and have been widely used by lenders as a mortgage product since then. An Option ARM allows the borrower the option to pay as little as one percent interest rate.

Negative Amortization

This results in the difference between the payment and interest on the loan becoming *negative amortization* and is added to the loan balance.

The interest rate will adjust every month, depending on the loan the index is tied to. These loans are useful to people who have a lot of equity n their home and don't want to pay higher monthly costs. The loans are also attractive to investors, since they allow them flexibility in choosing which payment to make every month.

One of the important features of these loans is that minimum payments are often fixed for each year up to an initial term of five years. The minimum payment may rise a little each year, (payment size increases of 7.5% are common), but payments remain the same for another year. The interest rate may fluctuate each month. Subsequently, one cannot predict the amount of negative amortization ahead of time.

Graduated Payment Mortgage

The graduated payment loan has lower payments in the beginning and the payments increase according to a prearranged schedule, and may have negative amortization. *Negative amortization* is the difference of the artificially lower payment and the true payment is added to the loan amount. In effect, the borrower owes more than was originally borrowed.

Straight Mortgage

A term or straight loan is an *interest only* loan until its maturity at the end of term. Then the entire principal and interest (balloon payment) is due in one lump sum.

Reverse Annuity Mortgage

A reverse annuity mortgage is one where the lenders make payments to mortgagors over specific term. The balance is due upon sale of property, death of mortgagor(s), or at the end of the term.
The borrower must be at least 62 years of age and have significant equity in their home. The borrower can take a lump sum, a line of credit, a fixed monthly payment, or a combination.

Reverse annuity mortgages are backed by the federal government, which accounts for at least 90% of the market, and are called Home Equity Conversion Mortgages, (HCEM). Private lenders market HCEM's.
Unlike traditional loans, reverse annuity mortgages don't have minimum-income requirements. Borrowers don't have to worry about built up interest that exceeds the property's value. The borrower keeps the title to their home, and their estate will pay off the loan when they die.

Shared Appreciation Mortgage

A shared appreciation mortgage is when the lender receives a portion of the profit when the property is sold, in return for a lower interest rate.

Package Mortgage

A package mortgage is one that includes personal property as security, in addition to the real property. This mortgage may be used to finance the purchase of a furnished condominium, etc.

Blanket Mortgage

A blanket mortgage is where more than one property is pledged as security. It may also contain a partial release clause so owners can sell or develop the released parcel.

Open End Mortgage

An open-end mortgage allows the borrower to obtain further advances at a later date. Such advances are limited to the difference between original loan amount and current amount owed.

Purchase Money Mortgage

A purchase money mortgage is when the seller is the lender. The seller "takes back" a mortgage, and puts a lien on the property in the amount of the purchase money mortgage.

Wrap Around Mortgage

A wraparound mortgage is a method of financing that does not let the lender know that the property has been purchased, to avoid the due on sale clause. Buyers send the mortgage payment to a title company, who then pays the first mortgage with a title company check. If the lender discovers the wrap around mortgage they will require a new loan be put in place of the "wrapped" mortgage.

Construction Loan

A construction loan is an interim financing loan that is made available in installments (obligatory advances), during the construction process. These are typically adjustable rate/short term loans, made by commercial banks. Lenders usually require a commitment for a "take out" or long term loan before funding of a construction loan.

Hard Money Loan

Hard money loans are made available through various funding sources. Hard moneylenders provide financing for entities in need of capital to start a company, expand an existing company, or to provide monies for debt consolidation and operating capital. A hard money real estate loan is usually obtained at a higher interest rate than a conventional loan with differing terms. The main advantage of hard money loans is the speed in which the loans can be funded. In some cases these loans may be the only source available for certain borrowers.

Jumbo Mortgage

Jumbo loans or non-conforming loans are made at an amount in excess of the loan limits set by FHA or VA. Typically these loans have higher interest rates than conventional loans.

Bridge Loan

A bridge loan is a temporary loan that enables the borrower to purchase a new property before the presently owned property is sold.

Option Loan

Several years ago, when home prices began to rise sharply, lenders pushed loans that let the homeowner pay interest only loans. These payments are allowed for an initial period that generally lasts five years. A pay option loan allows borrowers to pay whatever amount they choose to, during the initial period. Obviously, once this period expires, homeowners will owe more than originally borrowed because of negative amortization.

The Secondary Market

The secondary mortgage market buys mortgages from primary (local) lenders to supplement the mortgage and lending process.

After the closing, the primary lender either holds the mortgage in its portfolio, along with other loans it has made or, more frequently, sells the mortgage in the secondary mortgage market. The federal entities Freddie Mac, and its larger sister Fannie Mae, buy home loans from banks and other lenders to supply ready cash to the multi-trillion dollar home-mortgage market. Freddie Mac and Fannie Mae buy mortgages from lenders to keep in their portfolios or package loans into securities for sale on Wall Street. Investors buy the real estate backed securities.

The Secondary Market Process

The Servicer

The secondary market process works in the following manner. The homeowner sends a monthly payment to the lender through the mortgage service company that manages payments. The service company keeps a small fee for managing the borrower's payments and sends the rest of the monthly payment to a secondary agency, such as Freddie Mac. The secondary agency then releases the remainder of the mortgage payment to the investors who hold Freddie Mac mortgage securities.

The servicer is also responsible for doing the foreclosure process. So the borrower will receive notice of default from the servicer for the investor. The servicer is not required to release the name(s) of the investor, but they may do so.

Freddie Mac, Fannie Mae and the Secondary Mortgage Market

Four decades ago, Congressional charters set up Fannie Mae and Freddie Mac, as government sponsored enterprises, (GSEs) privately owned financial institutions established by the government to fulfill a public mission. The two GSEs were created to provide a stable source of funding for residential mortgages across the country, including loans on housing for low and moderate-income families. Fannie Mae and Freddie Mac carry out that mission through their operations in the secondary mortgage market. They purchase mortgages that meet certain standards from banks and other originators, pool those loans into Mortgage Backed Securities (MBS) that they guarantee against losses from defaults on the mortgages, and sell the securities to investors – a process known as *securitization*. They fund these portfolio holdings (MBS) by issuing debt obligations, known as agency securities, which are sold to investors.

In 2009, the two GSEs owned or guaranteed roughly half of all outstanding mortgages in the United States (including a significant share of sub-prime mortgages), and they financed three-quarters of new mortgages originated that year. More than 90 percent of new mortgages made in 2009 carried a federal guarantee.

When primary mortgage lenders sell loans in the secondary market, they generally sell them as loans to institutions like Freddie Mac. Lenders then use the proceeds received from Freddie Mac to make new loans to other homebuyers in their community. Freddie Mac is one of the largest mortgage investors. As a major player in the secondary mortgage market, they buy mortgages that meet its underwriting standards, and package those loans into securities, that it sells to investors on Wall Street.

The mortgages that Freddie Mac purchases are bundled or pooled together as mortgage backed securities (MBS). Freddie Mac guarantees timely payments of principal and interest to MBS investors, and finances such purchases by issuing debt and mortgage securities. Investors value Freddie Mac since it guarantees the homogeneous quality and liquidity of MBS. Because of these attributes, investors in MBS are willing to accept a slightly lower yield as the funds pass to them.

Freddie Mac uses funds from securities sales to purchase more loans from primary lenders. In this way, Freddie Mac is constantly replenishing the pool of funds available for new loans. This allows a primary lenders to use the cash they get from Freddie Mac to originate new mortgages. This makes the process fast, convenient, and affordable.

Fannie Mae

Fannie Mae is a private shareholder owned company that works to make sure mortgage money is available to people in communities throughout the United States It is similar in operation to Freddie Mac.

The Federal government established Fannie Mae in 1938 to increase the flow of mortgage money through a secondary market. Fannie Mae was authorized by the Federal Housing Administration (FHA) to purchase mortgages, which replenish the supply of loanable money to the primary market.

In 1968, Fannie Mae became a private company that operates with private capital on a self-sustaining basis. In an effort to reach out to a broader cross-section of Americans, Fannie Mae chose to expand its mortgage program by offering loans that exceeded traditional governmental limits.

Foreclosure

Foreclosure is the legal process by which an owner's right to a property is terminated, usually due to default. The mortgage lender sells at auction the property that is secured by a loan on which a borrower has defaulted. Typically, ownership of the property is transferred to the financial institution. The institution sell the property to recover the monies owned to them. In effect, mortgage foreclosure is a legal procedure whereby a property is used as security for a debt that is taken by a creditor or sold to pay off the debt.

Title Theory vs. Lien Theory States

Lien Theory States

Lien theory states have judicial foreclosures. Judicial foreclosure is initiated by lawsuit brought by mortgagee to obtain court order to sell. States that use a mortgage are required to have *a judicial foreclosure*. Judicial foreclosure is advantageous to the borrower since they have a chance to plead their case to a judge. In case of error the judge can make the correction before the borrower loses their property.

Title Theory States

The title theory states are non-judicial foreclosure. Foreclosure is done by advertisement, and no lawsuit is necessary and is used in states where a trust deed contains "power of sale" clause. The foreclosure process requires published notice of sale. The property is sold to the highest bidder at public sale. All trustee sales are final and there is *no right of redemption* such as is available in mortgage states. Trustee sales are more advantageous to the lender. However, trustee sales usually do not result in a deficiency judgment against the borrower.

Trustee foreclosures are called strict foreclosures and there is no right of redemption. Which means after foreclosure, the original owner can no longer come up with the loan amount and repurchase the home.

Foreclosure sale occur when the property is sold to the highest bidder at public sale. The high bidder receives Sheriff's Deed/Sheriff's Certificate of Sale. Proceeds from a foreclosure sale in excess of the loan amount, belongs to the mortgagor or trustor. Insufficient proceeds could not result in a deficiency judgment in a deed of trust state. A deficiency judgment is when the sale of the property is less than the loan amount, and the borrower is required to make up the difference.

Deficiency Judgment

In title theory states there is *deficiency judgment* whereby the lender can go after the foreclosed party for any difference between the foreclosed sale price and the amount of the mortgage.

Reinstatement - Redemption

Reinstatement refers to the period of time the borrower may "cure the default" by bringing payments up to date. Equitable redemption, or equity of redemption, occurs prior to the foreclosure sale. The mortgagor or trustor must pay the total balance due to stop the sale. *Statutory redemption* occurs after the foreclosure sale and continues for a period of time specified by state law. The mortgagor or trustor may redeem by paying all expenses plus balance due on mortgage. *A deed in lieu of foreclosure* is an alternative to foreclosure (mortgagor deeds to mortgagee). In effect, the borrower simply deeds the property to the lender. The *disadvantage to the mortgagee is that is does not wipe out any secondary liens.*

RESPA – Real Estate Settlement and Procedures Act

The Real Estate Settlement and Procedures Act, (RESPA), is a consumer protection statute first passed in 1974. The purposes of RESPA are to help consumers become better shoppers for settlement services and to eliminate kickbacks and referral fees from title companies to real estate brokers that unnecessarily increase the costs of settlement services.

RESPA covers loans secured with a mortgage placed on a single family home, duplex, triplex, or four-plex. These include most purchase loans, assumptions, refinances, property improvement loans, and equity lines of credit. RESPA required disclosure when a borrower applies for a mortgage loan. The mortgage brokers and/or lenders must give the borrowers:

A Special Information Booklet, which contains consumer information regarding various real estate settlement services, (required for purchase transactions, only) and

Good Faith Estimate, (GFE) of settlement costs, which lists the charges the buyer is likely to pay at settlement. This is only an estimate and the actual charges may differ. If a lender requires the borrower to use a particular settlement provider, then the lender must disclose this requirement on the GFE.

A Mortgage Servicing Disclosure Statement, which discloses to the borrower whether the lender intends to service the loan or transfer it to another lender. It also provides information about complaint resolution.

The HUD-1 Settlement Statement is a standard form that clearly shows all charges imposed on borrowers and sellers in connection with the settlement. RESPA allows borrowers to request to see the HUD-1 Settlement Statement one day before the actual settlement. The settlement agent must then provide the borrowers with a completed HUD-1 Settlement Statement based on information known to the agent at that time.

The HUD-1 Settlement Statement shows the actual settlement costs of the loan transaction. Separate forms may be prepared for the borrower and the seller. Where it is not the practice that borrower and the seller both attend the settlement, the HUD-1 should be mailed or delivered as soon as practicable after settlement.

RESPA Section 8 prohibits anyone from giving or accepting a fee, kickback or anything of value in exchange for referrals of settlement service business involving a federally related mortgage loan. In addition, RESPA prohibits fee splitting and receiving unearned fees for services not actually performed.

RESPA Section 9 prohibits a seller from requiring the homebuyer to use a particular title insurance company, either directly or indirectly, as a condition of sale. Buyers may sue a seller who violates this provision for an amount equal to three times all charges made for title insurance.

Truth in Lending – Regulation Z

The Truth in Lending Act (TILA), Title I of the Consumer Credit Protection Act, is aimed at promoting the informed use of the consumer credit by requiring disclosures about its terms and costs. In general, the law applies to credit applications primarily for personal, family or household purposes; and the loan balance equals and exceeds $25,000, or is secured by an interest in real property or a dwelling. TILA requires lenders to make certain disclosures on loans subject to the Real Estate Settlement Procedures Act (RESPA) within three business days after their receipt of a written application.

Equal Credit Opportunity Act

The Equal Credit Opportunity Act prohibits lenders from discriminating against credit applicants in any aspect of a credit transaction the basis of race, color, religion, national origin, sex, marital status, age, whether all of part of the applicants income comes from public assistance program, or whether the applicant has in good faith exercised a right under the consumer Credit Protection act.

The Fair Housing Act

The Fair Housing Act prohibits discrimination in residential real estate transactions on the basis of race, color, religion, sex, handicap, familial status or national origin. Notice that age is omitted; otherwise senior housing, etc. would be prohibited. Under these laws, a consumer cannot be refused a loan based on these characteristics nor be charged more for a loan or offered less favorable terms based on such characteristics.

Finance Terminology

Promissory Notes

A promissory note is an instrument that states a borrower's promise to repay the loan according to the terms of the loan. The borrower's signature secures the note. A negotiable instrument is considered personal property. Features include the prepayment clause (privilege to pay), and the acceleration clause (call provision).

Alienation

The alienation or due on sale clause prevents assumption without the mortgagee's consent. It also includes an acceleration clause, which allows lenders to demand immediate payment of the entire balance owed, if the mortgage is in default. When a mortgage note is paid, the mortgagee gives a *"satisfaction piece"* to release the lien.

Deed of Trust

A deed of trust is a three party instrument that some states use instead of a mortgage. In this instance, property is conveyed by the seller to a third party (trustee) as security for a loan. The trustee holds naked (bare legal) title on behalf of the lender (beneficiary). The deed of trust is a lien, and the trustee may foreclose in case of default. When the trust note is paid, the trustee gives a deed of reconveyance to release the lien.

"Assumption" versus "subject to:"

An assumption means that a new buyer takes over the existing loan on the property.

- If buyer purchases property "subject to" a mortgage, seller remains liable.
- If buyer assumes, buyer becomes liable for the debt and lender releases original borrower's liability.
- There are no loan origination fees or points when borrower assumes or purchases subject to a mortgage.

Loan to Value

Loan-to-Value (LTV) ratio/mortgage ratio – maximum percentage of value lender will loan. Based on price or appraisal, whichever is more.

Equity

Equity equals the market value today minus the total debt today.

Subordination

Subordination clause allows a change in the order/priority of a mortgage.

Defeasance Clause

Defeasance clause cancels (defeats) the mortgage when the debt is paid in full.

Escalator Clause

Escalator clause allows the lender to increase the interest rate in the event of late payment or default.

First Time Home Buyer

A first time homebuyer is one that has *not* owned a primary residence in the last three years.

Conforming Loan Limit

That loan amount that is the maximum that insured lenders will loan

Recourse Loan

Recourse loans allow the lender to go after the borrower for amounts they owe even after they have taken the collateral, (foreclosed home). *When the borrower defaults the lender can bring legal action against the borrower, even have wages garnished, to try to collect the amounts still owed.*

Non-Recourse Loan

Some collateral protects a non-recourse loan. In the case of a mortgage, the non-recourse loan is protected by the real estate itself. *In a non-recourse loan state, the borrowers are not held liable le for any amount greater than the value of the home at the time of repayment, (foreclosure).*
Below is a list of non-recourse states and anti-deficiency states. In these states the borrower is not liable for more than the home's value at the time of default. The lender can foreclose, however the lender may not sue the borrower for additional funds. If the foreclosure sale does not provide the lender with adequate funds to satisfy the loan, the lender must accept the loss.

Anti-Deficiency/Non-Recourse States

Alaska
Arizona
California
Connecticut
Florida
Idaho
Minnesota
North Carolina
North Dakota
Texas
Utah
Washington

One Action States

In the states listed below the lender is only permitted a single lawsuit to collect mortgage debt. In New York a lender must choose between the actions of foreclosing on the property or suing to collect the debt. The following states have some type of one action statute:

California
Idaho
Montana
Nevada
Utah

Default

The failure of the borrower to make the loan payments as agreed upon in the promissory note or workout plan.

Delinquency

A loan payment that is overdue but within the period allowed before actual defaults is declared.

Deficiency Judgment

A deficiency judgment is an unsecured money judgment against a borrower whose mortgage foreclosure did not provide sufficient funds to pay back the underlying or promissory note in full. The availability of a deficiency judgment depends upon whether the original note is a recourse loan.

Servicer

The entities to which the monthly mortgage payments are sent. The lender has contracted with the servicer the loan after closing. The servicer is the contact for any issues with the mortgage loan.

Forbearance

Forbearance is a situation whereby the lender allows homeowners' a period of time where no payments are made on the loan. However the principal and interest due during the forbearance time period is added to the loan amount due.

Loan Modification

Fannie Mae and Freddie Mac are key players in the Obama Administration's efforts to reduce mortgage foreclosures by modifying loans. Foreclosures are costly to both lenders and borrowers and negative on neighborhoods and home prices. More than one million foreclosures were started in 2009 on mortgages guaranteed by Fannie Mae or Freddie Mac, and another 1.6 million loans guaranteed by GSEs were at least 60 days delinquent by the end of June 2010.

HAMP

On March 4, 2009, the Treasury announced details of the Home Affordable Modification Program (HAMP) as part of the Making Home Affordable Program.
Servicers must solicit eligible borrowers who are 31 or ore days delinquent for a modification under HAMP.
The administration committed nearly $50 billion dollars to the program through the Trouble Asset Relief Program and another $25 billion through Fannie Mae and Freddie Mac. However, only a small portion of HAMP funds is likely to be spent.

Default rates on modified GSE loans are about 50 percent after nine months, but there are some signs that recent modification – which feature deeper reductions in interest and principal and declines of more than 20 percent in monthly payments – are performing better.

Financial institutions sometime re-negotiated the interest rate, the loan term and even the principal balance owed.

The banks will start by determining the 30% of the borrowers income, adjust down the interest rate to as low as 2 percent, and extend the term of the loan out as far as forty years. If this does not meet the 30% income threshold, on rare occasions principal reduction can occur.

HAFA

The Treasury announced the Home Affordable Foreclosure Alternatives Program (HAFA), which encourages short sales and deeds in lieu of foreclosure. It permits pre-approved short sale before a property is listed and releases borrowers from future liability for the mortgage debt. In addition, it provides financial incentives to borrowers, servicers, and investors while stopping loan servicers from attempting to reduce commissions established in the listing agreement as a condition for a short sale.

HARP

Home Affordable Refinance Program (HARP) gives borrowers the opportunity to refinance into more affordable loan at today's lower rates. This program is restricted to Fannie Mae or Freddie Mac loans, and the amount of the first mortgage does not exceed 125% of property's current market value. In addition, the amount owed is less than $729,750, and the mortgage was originated on or before January 1, 2009, and the mortgage payment must be greater than 31%of the borrowers gross income.

REO

Banks have an inventory of homes that have been foreclosed upon and are Real Estate Owned (REO) by the bank.

Short Sale

A short sale is a bank approved home sale for less than the amount owed to the bank. The banks may report the difference between the sale price and the loan amount as *income to the homeowner* because they received the benefit of the difference. The borrower should have the lender note the loan as "paid in full" rather than considering the difference a "charge off."

Usury

Usury originally meant the charging of interest on loans. After interest became acceptable, usury came to mean the interest above the rate allowed by law. In common usage today, usury means charging of unreasonable or relatively high rates of interest.

Usury laws have been enacted to prohibit the practice of usury. These laws regulate maximum interest rates that can be set for loans, in order to protect the borrower.

In 1978 the Supreme Court changed the rule that usury was a state mandated item. It ruled that a national bank could charge any interest rate no matter where they are located. The practical effect of the Supreme Courts ruling was to repeal every state's usury laws insofar as they deal with national banks.

Strategic Default

Strategic default occurs when the homeowner makes a calculated decision to let their home go into foreclosure. The recent housing "bubble" broke and millions of homeowners are in the position owing more than the value of their homes.

FINANCING QUIZ

1. The agreement in a junior lien permitting a first lien to be refinanced without suffering loss of priority is called

    (A) An acceleration clause
    (B) A lien waiver
    (C) A subordination clause
    (D) A release provision in the mortgage

2. Builder Jones purchased 20 lots from Brown for immediate development. Jones paid 10% down and gave trust deeds for the balance. Jones would want the trust deeds to contain

    (A) An exculpatory clause
    (B) A subordination clause
    (C) A safety clause
    (D) A lock in clause

3. Which of the following types of mortgages usually contains a partial release clause?

    (A) Blanket mortgage
    (B) Open-end mortgage
    (C) Junior lien
    (D) Purchase money mortgage

4. A properly executed promissory note establishes

    (A) The amount of debt
    (B) Who is borrower and who is lender?
    (C) The terms of repayment
    (D) All of the above

5. A mortgage that includes both real and personal property is called

    (A) Package mortgage
    (B) Chattel mortgage
    (C) Blanket mortgage

    (D) Wraparound mortgage

6. A mortgage is unusually associated with a

    (A) Deed
    (B) Land sale contract
    (C) Title policy
    (D) Promissory note

7. The gradual liquidation of a mortgage loan by regular payments to reduce principal and interest over a given period of time is called

   (A) Amortization
   (B) Accretion
   (C) Accession
   (D) Prepayment

8. A mortgage which allows the borrower to borrow additional sums up to a certain maximum amount is

   (A) A packaged mortgage
   (B) An open-end mortgage
   (C) A purchase money mortgage
   (D) A wrap around mortgage

9. A mortgage is best defined as

   (A) A document conveying possessory interest
   (B) A general lien
   (C) A special lien
   (D) An involuntary lien

10. To hypothecate is to

    (A) Deliver judicial opinion
    (B) Pledge a thing as security without necessarily giving it up
    (C) Perform services in exchange for the satisfaction of a debt
    (D) None of the above

11. A mortgage is usually accompanied by

    (A) A deed
    (B) Conditional sales contract
    (C) Title policy
    (D) A promissory note

12. When using the fully amortized level payment mortgage,

    (A) The amount of payment on the principal stays the same
    (B) The interest payment is always greater than the principal payment
    (C) Each payment remains the same
    (D) A lump sum payment is made at the end of the mortgage term

13. Which of the following types of mortgage usually contains a partial release clause?

(A) Blanket mortgage
(B) Open-end mortgage
(C) Purchase money mortgage
(D) Junior lien

14. A mortgage is

(A) The amount of money the borrower owes the lender
(B) A pledge of property to secure a debt
(C) The amount of money owed at the time
(D) None of the above

15. a loan is made with real estate as security and not involving government participation in the form of insuring, guaranteeing, or direct lending is known as:

(A) Conventional loan
(B) Standby loan
(C) Bank croft bond
(D) Budget mortgage

16. A balloon payment is usually associated with a

(A) Blanket mortgage
(B) Package mortgage
(C) Variable mortgage
(D) Large payment made at the end of the term of the loan

17. When a mortgage is used in a real estate transaction, the evidence of the principal obligation is the

(A) Warranty
(B) Note
(C) Mortgage
(D) Security

18. The instrument of record to show that a mortgage is paid in full is

(A) Satisfaction piece
(B) Deed release statement
(C) Quitclaim deed
(D) Estoppel certificate

19. Who insures conventional loans?

(A) Federal Housing Administration
(B) Private Mortgage Insurance Companies
(C) Federal Savings and Loan Insurance
(D) Individual state insurance agencies

20. The type of mortgage that covers more than one parcel of real property
    (A) Blanket mortgage
    (B) An inclusive trust deed
    (C) A package mortgage
    (D) A wraparound mortgage

CHAPTER 10 – REAL ESTATE CALCULATIONS

Learning Objectives

    A. Property area calculations
       1. Square footage
       2. Acreage total
    B. Property valuations
       1. Comparative Market Analysis (CMA)
       2. Net Operating Income (NOI)
       3. Capitalization rate
       4. Gross rent multiplier – Broker only
       5. Gross income multiplier – Broker only
       6. Equity in property
       7. Establishing a listing price
       8. Assessed value and property taxes
    C. Division/compensation
    D. Loan Financing costs
       1. Interest
       2. Loan to value (LTV)
       3. Amortization
       4. Discount points
       5. Prepayment penalties
       6. Fees
    E. Settlement and closing costs
       1. Purchase price and down payment
       2. Monthly mortgage calculations – principal, interest, taxes and insurance (PITI)
       3. Net to seller
       4. Cost to buyer
       5. Prorated items
       6. Debits and credits
       7. Transfer tax and recording fees
    F. Investment
       1. Return of investment
       2. Appreciation
       3. Depreciation

4. Tax implications on investment
G. Property management calculations
1. Property management and budget calculations
2. Tenancy and rental calculations

Commission

Commission problem solutions are predicated on understanding of percentages. Percentages are always stated as a percent of something. For example a real estate listing agreement may state that the commission is 6%. The first step to solve any commission problem is the process of converting a percentage to a decimal. Perhaps the easiest way to covert a percentage to a decimal is simply to divide by 100. A 6% commission would result in putting a 6 in the calculator and then press the divide button and then enter 100 and press the equal button. The display should show .06, which is the decimal equivalent of 6%

Most commission problems can be solved with the formula, the part (commission), = percentage times total sales.

$C = \% \times S$

$600,000 =selling price of the home

×6% commission rate

=$36,000 commission paid by the seller

The thirty six thousand dollar amount of commission the seller paid seems to be exorbitant to some people. In most cases there is a selling broker and a buying broker that each split the commission. The buying broker's share would have been $18,000. The buying broker would probably have some commission sharing agreement that would have a 50/50 split between the buying broker, and the salesperson representing the buyer resulting in the salesperson earning $9,000 in which he is responsible for income taxes, social security, automobile expenses, telephone and some office expenses. The large dollar amount of commission seems not so large after all the expenses are deducted, and this does not consider the amount of time the salesperson used to consummate the transaction.

T Method

268

The T-Method for working math problems is a very simple method that can be applied to most of the real estate math problems. The formulas for brokerage, financing, appraising, area and settlement math will also be reviewed.

If an agent sold a property for $100,000 and the broker was paid a 6% commission, what was the commission? Obviously, the answer is $6,000. Using the same example with the T formula is as follows:

Sale Price ×r % Rate of Commission = Commission

Rule 1

In the "T" the total is placed at the bottom left, the rate on the bottom right, and the part at the top. Using the "T" for the above question would look like this:

÷ $6,000 Commission ÷
———————————————
× $100,000   6% ×

When given the two numbers in the bottom of the "T" which are the total and the rate, the mathematical function is multiplication, i.e. $100,000 times .06 = $6,000.

Rule 2

When given the part at the top of the "T" and the rate at the bottom the mathematical function is division. It helps to remember TGIF: Top goes into the calculator first.

For example, if a broker received a $6,000 commission check and the selling price was $100,000, what was the commission rate? The $6,000 is the part that goes at the top of the "T" $100,000 is the sales price or total, and goes into the lower left of the "T." Therefore $6,000 divided by $100,000 = .06 or 6%.

The "T" would look like:

÷ $6,000 = Commission ÷
———————————————
× $100,000 Sale Price   .06 or 6% Commission Rate ×

Rule 3

When given the part at the top of the "T" and the total sales of $100,000 at the bottom. The mathematical function is division. Recall TGIF.

For example, the seller's net was $100,000 and the commission was 6%. What was the sale price of the property?

Notice how this question is different. Is the $100,000 a part or a total? It is a part, so it goes at the top of the "T" it is equal to 94 % of the sale price, 100% - 6% = 94%), so .94 goes in the lower right of the "T" $100,000÷.94 = $106,382.98.

÷ $100,000 Seller's Net ÷	
× $106,382.98	.94 or 94% ×

Rule 4

When solving for the total, take the part and divide by the percent to which that part is equal. For example, the total dollars of commission divided by the commission rate equal the sale price.

Brokerage Math Formulas

Brokerage math questions include computing commissions and determining the sale price when given the seller's net dollars and the commission rate.

÷ Commission $ ÷	
× Sale price commission rate ×	

Sale Price × commission rate = commission $
Commission $ ÷Commission Rate = Sale Price
Commission $ ÷Sale Price = Commission Rate

Property Management Math Formulas

An agent acting as a property manager may be paid a percentage of the gross or net income as commission. Normally, the manager is paid a percentage of the gross income, but in math the questions may not be normal.

For example, the annual gross rent collected on a building is $124,000. If the property manager is paid a 6% commission on the rents collected, how much is he paid annually in commissions?

÷ $7440 Commission $ ÷	
× $124,000	6% or .06 ×

Gross rent × Commission Rate = Commission
Commission $ ÷ Commission Rate = Gross Rent

The commission for the property manager may be computed as so many dollars per square footage of the space leased. For example, a tenant leased a 60' by 100' space for $8 per square foot semi-annually. If the property manager is paid 8% of the rent collected, how much is she paid annually?

Step 1 - 60' × 100' = 6,000 square feet

Step 2 – 6,000 square feet × $8 = $48,000 semi-annual rent

Step 3 - $48,000 semi-annual rent × 2 = $96,000 annual rent

= $7,680 Commission $ =
× $96,000   8% ×

Gross Rent × Commission % = Commission Earned $

Percentage Lease

Although there are several types of percentage leases, the following is the usual method of negotiation: the tenant pays a fixed monthly rent or a base rent, plus a percentage of all income over a certain amount, or the total income. For example, a shop owner entered into a percentage lease with the lessor in which she agreed to pay a fixed rental of $650 per month, and when the gross sales reached $175,000, she pays 5% of the sales over that amount. This year, her gross sales were $225,000. What was the total rent paid at the end of the year?

Step 1 - $650 ×12 = $7,800 fixed rent

Step 2 - $225,000 –$175,000 =$50,000 gross sales over $175,000

Step 3 –

÷ $2,500 Commission $ ÷
×$50,000 .05 or 5%×

Step 4 - $7,800 +$2,500 =$10,300 Total Commission Paid

271

Graduated Lease

In a graduated lease, the rents increase or "step up" on a gradual basis over the life of the lease. For example, a tenant entered into a 12-year graduated lease with the owner of a building. He agreed to pay $400 for the first 4 years of the lease, $450 per month for the next four-year years, and $500 per month for the remaining time of the lease. If the property manager is paid 6 % of the total rent collected, how much will he have collected by the end of the leasing term?

Step 1 –

$400 × 12 × 4 = $19,200
$450 × 12 × 4 = $21,600
$500 × 12 × 4 = $24.000

Step 2 –

$64,800 gross rent collected in 12 years

Step 3
64,800   times 6% commission = $3,888

Mortgage Calculations + State Testing

For test preparation the testing agency cannot require a financial calculator so the test is limited to answering lending questions using only simple interest and mortgage calculation questions using a graph. These two methods are outdated but the student needs to know these applications for testing purposes.

Simple Interest Calculations

The formula for solving simple interest questions is:

Principal times the Interest Rate stated as a percentage per year, times the time, equals the interest.

Principal × Rate × Time = Interest

Principal is the amount of money borrowed. If the rate is stated as 4%, that always means 4% *per year*, and Time is per year, and any fraction of a year must take the time and divide it accordingly.

A typical question will ask:

Last month Britzas' monthly payment for the interest portion of his mortgage amounted to $303.50. Britza pays an interest rate of 9¼%. Based on this information, what is the balance of the loan prior to the last payment?

The monthly mortgage interest payment must be converted to the annual interest payment by multiplying it by 12, resulting in a total of $3,642. Which is the annual interest amount. We then can divide by the interest rate of .0925, the answer being $39,372.93. A check can be made by multiplying $39,372.93 times .0925, dividing by that answer by 12 resulting 303.499 or $303.50.

Financing Math Formulas

Financing math questions include computing the loan amount, annual interest dollars, discount points, loan origination fees and amortization of a loan. The lender negotiates the loan on the sale price or appraised value, whichever is less. For example, a seller agreed to pay $85,000 for a property, but is appraised for $83,500. The lender agreed to negotiate a 90 percent loan to value. What was the loan amount?

÷ $75,150 Loan Amount ÷
_____
× $83,500 Appraised Value   90% ×

Sale price or appraised value divided by the loan to value ratio equals the loan amount.

Loan divided by the sale price or appraised value, (whichever is lower), equals the loan to value ratio.

A question may ask for the annual, semiannual, quarterly, monthly or daily interest that is due on a loan. For example, a buyer negotiated a $125,000 loan at 8.75% annual interest how much interest will be paid the first year?

$\div$ $10,937.50 Annual Interest $ $\div$

$\times$ $125,000 Loan Amount .0875 or 8.75% interest rate $\times$
Loan amount $\times$interest rate = Annual interest $
Annual interest $ $\div$ Loan Amount = Interest Rate
Annual Interest $ $\div$ Interest Rate =Loan

Discount Points

Discount points are computed as a percentage of the loan amount: 1 point = 1% of the loan amount, 2 points = 2% of the loan amount. For example a borrower was charged 3 points on an $89,000 loan amount. How much did he pay?

$\div$ $2,670 Discount Points $ $\div$

$89,000 $\times$ .03 or 3 points =
Loan $\times$ Discount Points% Discount Points $ $\times$
Discount Points $ $\div$Discount Points % = Loan Amount
Discount Points $ $\div$ Loan = Discount Points %

A lender's cash outflow is the loan amount minus the discount points percent.

For example, a borrower secured an $89,000 loan, and the lender required him to pay one point. What was the cash outflow of the lender?

$89,000 loan amount
$-$ 1% Discount Points %

$88,110 Lender's cash outflow

To determine the effective yield to the lender, the rule of thumb is for each discount point that the lender's yield is increased by 1/8 of a percent on a 30-year term loan.

Loan Origination Fee

The loan origination fee is also computed as a percentage of the loan amount. For example the buyer secured a $50,000 loan and had to pay a 1.5 percent loan origination fee. How much did the buyer have to pay for the origination fee?

$\div$ $750 Origination Fee $ $\div$

$\times$ $50,000 .015 or 1.5 % origination fee $\times$
Loan amount $\times$ Origination Fee % = Origination Fee
Origination Fee $ $\div$ Loan Amount = Origination Fee %
Origination Fee $ $\div$ Origination Fee % = Loan Amount

Amortization

The word amortize means to reduce the debt by making payments that include both principal and interest. The principal and interest payment is usually given in a question about loan amortization. For example a borrower negotiated a $100,000 loan at 10% interest for 30 years. The monthly payments are $877,58. What is her loan balance after the first payment?

Step 1

$10,000 Annual Interest $
× $100,000 loan amount   .10 or 10% interest ×

Step 2- $10,000 Annual Interest $ ÷12 months =$833.33 monthly interest

Step 3 - $877.58 Principal and Interest - $833.33 Monthly Interest = $44.25 Principal

Step 4 $100,000 − $44.25 = $99,955.75.   Loan balance after the first payment.

Property Tax Calculations

Property taxes are determined in a three-step procedure.

1. The appraised value is determined by one of the three appraisal methods, (Market Value, Income Approach, or Replacement Cost).
2. The assessed value is determined by multiplying the assessment percentage times the appraised value.
3. The assessed value is multiplied by the tax rate.

Once the taxing authority determines the appraised value of a property, and applies the assessment percentage, then the tax rate is multiplied times the assessment value.

In most states and municipalities the most common method of tax rate is in mills. A mill is defined as a unit of monetary value equal to $.001, or one tenth of one cent.

Some taxing authorities use a tax ratio such as so much per $100 or so much per $1,000. For example a tax ratio of $25 per $1,000 of assessed value on a property appraised at $450,000 with a 30% assessment percentage would have an assessed value of $135,000. The assessed value of $135,000 would be divided by 1,000 with a resulting value of 135 times the $25, with a tax of $3,375. If the tax was quoted in mills of say 35 mills, then the tax would be determined by multiplying the assessed value of $135,000 times the 35 mills or .035, with the resulting tax being $4,725.

As mentioned previously, the calculation of real estate property taxes involves two math formulas. Taxes are computed on the assessed value, which is percentage of the market value. The assessed value is then multiplied by the tax rate to give the annual property tax. For example the market value of a property is $70,000 and it is assessed at 40 percent of the market value. If the tax rate is $5.50 per $100, what is the annual property tax? The word "per" in a math question means divide. Therefore, $5.50 ÷ $100 = .055 tax rate.

÷ $28,000 Assessed Value ÷

× $70,000 .40 or 40% ×

$1,540 Annual Property Tax

$28,000 × .055
Assessed Value × Tax Rate

Mills

As mentioned previously the tax rate can be expressed as mills, which means 1/1000th of a dollar. Therefore, whenever the tax rate appears in mills, divide by 1000 to get the decimal equivalent. For example, if the tax rate is 55 mills, that means 55 ÷ 1,000 the decimal equivalent. If the tax rate is 555 mills, that means 555 ÷1,000 =.555 is the decimal equivalent.

Appraising Math Formulas

The appraising math formulas reviewed in this section are the income approach, and the cost approach. The gross rent multiplier approach to appraising is covered in this section, and includes a review of capital gains, appreciation and depreciation of property.

Income Approach

The income approach to appraising is used to convert the annual net operating income of investment property into a value by dividing it by the capitalization rate. For example, three apartments rent for $450 each per month, three for $500 per month, and two for $550 per month. There is a 5% vacancy rate, $300 in monthly expenses, and $125 per month additional income from the laundry machines. If the owner wants a 10% return on her investment, how much can she pay for the property?

$3 \times 445 \times 12 = \$16,200$
$3 \times 450 \times 12 = \$18,000$
$2 \times \$550 \times 12 = \$13,200$
    $47,400 Potential Gross Income
    −5% vacancy
    $45,030 Effective Gross Income
    $125 \times 12 = \quad +\$1,500$
    $300 \times 12 = \quad -\$3,600$ Expenses

$\div \$42,930$ Annual Net Operating Income $\div$

$\times \$429,300 \quad .10$ or $10\% \times$
Appraised Value using the Income Approach Capitalization Rate

Potential Gross Income
−Vacancy Rate
+Any Additional Income

Effective Gross Income
−Expenses

Annual Net Operating Income
−Expenses

Annual Net Operating Income $\div$

Appraised Value using the Income Approach $\times$ Capitalization Rate

Cost Approach

The cost approach to appraising is used to determine the value of special purposes properties, but it can also be used to appraise new buildings. For example the replacement costs of a building is $125,000. It has an annual depreciation of 10%, and a site value $35,000. What is the value of the property?

$125,000 Replacement Cost
−.10 or 10% Depreciation Rate
─────────────────────────────
= $112,500
+$35,000 Site Value
─────────────────────────────

$147,500 Property Value

Replacement Cost
−Depreciation Rate
+Site value
─────────────────────────────
Property Value using the Replacement Cost Approach

Gross Rent Multiplier

The gross rent multiplier formula is used to appraise small income-producing properties, such as a single family home or duplex that is an investment property. If this method is used to determine the value of a small shopping center, it is called the gross income multiplier and the annual rent is used. For example, an appraiser has determined that the gross rent multiplier of a house that rents for $650 is 110. What is the value of the property?

÷ $71,500 Value ÷
─────────────────────────────
× 110 $650 ×
Gross Rent Multiplier × Rent
Gross Rent Multiplier × rent = Value
Value ÷ Gross Rent Multiplier = Rent
Value ÷ rent = Gross Rent Multiplier

Capital Gains

A capital gain is the profit that an owner makes when selling an asset such as real estate. The payment of tax on the capital gain may be excluded on a principal place of residence under certain conditions. Married homeowners may exclude capital gains profits up to $500,000 if they file jointly. Single filers may exclude from capital gains tax profits up to $250,000. Homeowners whose gain exceeds the maximum for exclusion must pay tax on the amount over the exclusion.

For example a homeowner purchased a property for $90,000. He made $12,500 worth of improvements. Three years later he sold the property for $130,000 and paid a 6% commission. What were his capital gains on the sale?

Step 1

$90,000 Original Investment
+$12,500 Improvement

$102,500 Adjusted Basis
Step 2

$7,800 Commission $

$130,000 .06 = 6%
Sales Price × Commission = Commission $

Step 3

$130,000 − $7,800 = $122,200 Adjusted (net) Sale Price
The sale price minus selling expenses equals the adjusted sale price.
Step 4

$122,200 Adjusted Sale Price
$102,500 Adjusted Basis

$19,700 Capital Gain
Original Investment
+Improvements

Adjusted Basis
Selling Price
− Selling Expenses

Adjusted Sale Price
−Adjusted Basis

Capital Gain

The above formula is for computing the capital gain on an owner's first principal place of residence and must be used a principal place of residence for *two* of the preceding *five* years

279

Appreciation or Depreciation

Appraisal math deals with the appreciation or depreciation of property values. For example a homeowner paid $80,000 for his property. This year, their property appreciated in value 10%. What is the value of the property today?

÷ $88,000 ÷
Original Investment   100% +10% = 110%
$80,000 × 1.10 or 110% =

Appreciated Value
Original   100%
Investment   × Appreciation Rate
Appreciated Amount

The homeowner paid $80,000 for their property. This year their property deprecated in value 10%. What is the value of their property this year?

÷ $72,000 Depreciated Value ÷
× $80,000 Original Investment   100$×
−10%
90% Deprecated %

Settlement Math Formulas

To prorate an expense means to divide or distribute it proportionately. The settlement sheet is a history of the buyer's and seller's debits and credits in a sales transaction. If the entry is a debit, the party owes it at the closing table. If the entry is a credit, the party receives it at the closing table. The following worksheet shows the normal entries on a settlement sheet. Buyer or seller can pay discount points.

	BUYER'S STATEMENT		SELLER'S STATEMENT	
	DEBIT	CREDIT	DEBIT	CREDIT
Purchase Price	X			X
Deposit		X		
Excise Tax			X	
Sales Commission			X	
Pay-Off Existing Loan			X	
Assume Existing Loan		X	X	
New Loan		X		
Purchase Money Loan		X	X	
Title Search	X			
Standard Title Insur.			X	
A.L.T.A. Title Insur.	X			
Loan Discount (Points)			X	
Loan Fee	X			
Property Taxes				
Arrears		X	X	
Current/Not Due		X	X	
Prepaid	X			X
Insurance				
Assume Policy	X			X
New Policy	X			
Interest				
Pay-off Exist. Loan			X	
Assume Exist. Loan		X	X	
New Loan	X			
Reserve Accounts				
Pay-off Exist. Loan				X
Assumption	X			X
Credit Report	X			
Survey	X			
Appraisal	X			
Escrow Fee (Varies)	X		X	
Sale of Chattels	X			X
Misc. Recording Fees	X		X	
Balance Due From Buyer		X		
Balance Due Seller			X	
TOTALS	X	X	X	X

Discount points could be a debit to the seller or a debit to the buyer depending on the type of loan application. To compute proration problems, use a 360-day year, with each month having 30 days, unless stated other wise. Each proration question has a beginning date, prorate date and ending date.

Insurance Proration

Sometimes the buyer assumes the seller's insurance policy. Insurance is always paid in advance, therefore, the entry is a debit to the buyer and a credit to the seller. The beginning date is the date the policy is written. The prorate date is the closing date. The ending date is the same day as the beginning date, for the term of the policy.

Area Math Problems

The area of a rectangle or square is found by multiplying the length times the width.

The area of a triangle is found by multiplying ½ base times width.

The area of a circle is found by multiplying Pi (3.2426) times the radius squared.

The area of a trapezoid is found by adding the parallel lines, dividing by 2, and then multiplying by the height.

- To compute square feet, multiply length times width.
- To compute cubic feet, multiply length times width times height.
- There are 9 square feet in 1 square yard.
- To convert square feet to square yards divide by 9.
- There are 27 cubic feet in 1 cubic yard.
- To convert square feet to square yards divide by 9.
- To convert cubic feet to cubic yards, divide by 27.
- To convert square feet to acres, divide by 43,560.
- To convert acres to square feet multiply by 43,560.
- There are 5,280 linear feet in 1 mile.

Real Estate Calculations Quiz

1. A drop in real estate prices resulted in a 20% loss of value in a home resulting in the house selling for $65,000. What was the original cost of the house?

(A) $65,000
(B) $78,000
(C) $81,250
(D) $117,000

2. If the owner bought the house for $72,000 and now wants to sell it at a 20% profit, what must the selling price be?

(A) $78,000
(B) $79,200
(C ($86,400
(D) $90,000

3. A monthly income of $675 represents an annual return of 7 ½% on an investment of

(A) $,9,000
(B) $90,000
(C) $108,000
(D) $180,000

4. At a 5% return on an investment, what amount would a lender have to lend in order to receive a yield of $125 a month?

(A) $1,500
(B) $15,000
(C) $25,000
(D) $30,000

5. If the listing broker's share of a 6 % commission is 30%, how much will the selling broker realize on the sale of a $90,000 property?

(A) $1,620
(B) $3,240
(C) $3,780
(D) $5,400

6. If space in a warehouse rents for 60¢ per square foot per year, the rent for a space 30 feet by 50 feet would be

(A) $60
(B) $75
(C)$350
(D)$900

7. Lawrence leased a storeroom to Davis on a percentage basis. The lease calls for minimum monthly rental of $425 plus a 5% of the annual gross income over $75,000. How much rent wills Lawrence receives annually if Davis earns annual gross income of $115,000?
8.

(A) $5,100
(B) $7,100
(C) $8,850
(D) $10,850

9. A property manager leases office space with dimensions of 30 feet by 40 feet for $7,25 per square foot per year. The rent per month is

(A) $1,200
(B) $507.50
(C) $8,700
(D) $725

10. The sales commission for selling a house is 8% of the first $75,000 and 5% for the balance of the price. The broker receives a commission of $7,530. What did the property sell for?

(A) $57,923
(B) $86,769
(C) $100,320
(D) $105,600

11. You listed the N ½ of the NE ¼ of the SW ¼ of Section 10 at $9,750 an acre. Your brokerage fee is 9%. Your commission will be

(A) $8,775
(B) $15,600
(C) $17,550
(D) $26,325

12. If a tract of land 1,320 feet by 440 yards sold for $500 per acre, the total sales amount would be

    (A) $10,000
    (B) $20,000
    (C) $25,000
    (D) $40,000

13. If an acre of land has four sides of equal length, the length of each side would be approximately
    (A) 150 feet
    (B) 210 feet
    (C) 330 feet
    (D) 435 feet

13. A property owner has decided to build a cyclone fence around a property. The lot is rectangular, 110 feet by 270 feet. The fence is 7 feet high. Cyclone fencing cost 85¢ per square foot, and the labor costs $1.70 per linear foot. What will the fence cost the property owner?

    (A) $4,667
    (B) $5,814
    (C)$7,497
    (D) $8,979

14. What is the approximate market value of a commercial building with a projected annual gross income of $84,000, if the estimated operating expenses are $38,000, the vacancy factor is 3%, and capitalization rate is 10.5%?

    (A)$414,000
    (B)$425,000
    (C) $438,000
    (D)$449,000

15. What is 18 days of interest on the unpaid balance of a mortgage of $20,000 at 11% simple interest?
    (A)$43.71
    (B)$96.15
    (C)$102.22
    (D)$108.49

16. Mr. Cole borrowed $750 on a straight note at an annual interest rate of 7.2%. These total interest payments were $81. The term of the note was most nearly
    (A) 12 months
    (B) 18 months
    (C) 20 months
    (D) 24 months

17. John borrowed 95% of the appraised value of his house at 8-½% interest. In order to get his loan, he had to pay three discount points. If he had additional closing costs of $1,300, what sum did he need for settlement if the house was valued at $93,000?
    (A) $3,950
    (B) $5,600
    (C) $8,600
    (D) $17,900

18. The property tax on Ms. Jones home is $3,000. What is the assessed value if the tax rate is 1.5%?
    (A)$300,000.
    (B)$250,000
    (C) $200,000
    (D)$250,000

19. A tract of land containing 2,613,600 square feet sold for $375 per half acre. What was the sale price?
    (A)$45,000
    (B)$147,000
    (C) $90,000
    (D)$180,000

20. What would be the taxes for 3 months on a property worth $66,000 if the yearly tax rate was 46 mills, and the assessment percentage was 20% of value?

    (A)$607.20
    (B)$151.80
    (C) $ 302.60
    (D) None of these

GLOSSARY

The following glossary is designed so the reader can look up the term on one page and turn the page to see the definition. Each term is numbered to match the corresponding definition.

1. Accord and Satisfaction	6. Allodial System
2. Acknowledgment	7. American Land Title Association (ALTA)
3. Acre	8. Amortized/ Amortization
4. Ad Valorem	9. Appraisal Report
5. Aliquot	10. APR Annual Percentage Rate

6. The free and full ownership of rights in land by individuals, which is the basis of real property law in the United States. By contrast, under the feudal system, ownership of land was vested in the king or sovereign. The king has allotted select land to his noblemen, chiefs and others. Such allotments were revocable and represented only the right to use the land.	1. The settlement of an obligation. An accord is an agreement by a creditor to accept something different from or less than what the creditor feels he or she is entitled to. When the creditor accepts the consideration offered by the debtor for the accord, the acceptance constitutes a satisfaction and the obligation of the debtor is extinguished.
7. An organization of more than 2,000 Title companies that has standardized forms and coverage on a national basis. Long Beach Mortgage requires this standardized coverage for all loans.	2. A formal declaration made before a duly authorized officer, usually a notary public, by a person who has signed a document; also, the document itself. An acknowledgment is designed to prevent forged and fraudulently induced documents from taking effect. To record a document it must be acknowledged.
8. The gradual repayment of a mortgage loan whereby the borrower makes monthly periodic payments to pay the interest due and part of the principal. A fully amortized loan will completely pay off at the end of the loan term.	3. A measure of land area equal to 43,560 square feet or 208.71 feet by 208.71 feet. A square mile contains 640 acres.
9. Consideration of the Direct Sales Approach. Cost Approach and Income Approach. The reconciliation.	4. 4. Latin for "according to valuation," usually referring to a type of tax or assessment. Real property tax is an ad valorem tax based on the assessed valuation of the property. Assessment – An official valuation of real property for tax purposes bases on appraisals by local government officials; the term is synonymous with assessed value. Sales prices of comparable land are used to estimate land
10. The true interest rate, which includes all prepaid finance charges.	5. A number which, when divided into another number, leaves no remainder. For example, 6 in an aliquot part of 24. Aliquot literally means "contained in something else an exact number of times." An aliquot parts subdivision is used in legal description of large parcels where parts are not less than 10 acres (popular in Alaska).

11. ARM (Adjustable Rate Mortgage)	16. Asset
12. ARM'S Length Transaction	17. Attachment
13. "As Is"	18. Back End Ratio
14. Assemblage	19. Balloon
15. Assessor	20. Bankruptcy/BK

16. Something in value owned by a person; a useful item of property.	11. The interest rate of an ARM loan is comprised of an index rate and a margin percentage that are added together. The index rate fluctuates to match current market rates thus causing the interest rate to adjust. The most important characteristic of an ARM is that the interest rate can adjust on the loan.
17. A legal process whereby the creditor may obtain a lien against the debtor's property.	12. A transaction in which the parties involved are not related in any way.
18. Refers to the debt to income ratio. The back end ratio is calculated by adding principal, interest, taxes, insurance, and consumer credit obligations to arrive at total expenses (debts). The total expense figure is divided by the gross monthly income to arrive at a back end ratio percentage.	13. Words in a contract intended to signify that no guarantees whatsoever are given regarding the subject property. The property is agreed to be purchased in the exact condition in which it is found.
19. A large or "balloon" payment due at the end of a loan term when the repayment term of the loan is less than the amortization term. The balloon payment is equal to the remaining principal balance plus any interest and charges due. Any payment which is greater than twice the amount of regularly scheduled monthly payment.	14. The combining of two or more adjoining lots into one large tract. This is usually done to increase the value of the individual lots because a larger building capable of producing a larger net return may be erected on the larger parcel. The resulting added value is called plottage value. The developer often makes use of option contracts to tie up the right to purchase the desired adjacent parcels. Care must be taken through exact surveys to avoid the creation of gaps or strips between
20. A condition of financial insolvency in which a person's liabilities exceed the assets causing the inability to pay current debts.	15. A public official who appraises property for tax purposes. He or she determines only the assessed value, not the tax rate.

21. Base Line	26. Bilateral Contract
22. Bequeath	27. Bounds
23. Beneficiary	28. Breach of Contract
24. Blanket Mortgage	29. Broker
25. Blockbusting	30. Buy Down

26. A contract in which each party promises to perform an act in exchange for the other party's promise to perform.	21. One of a set of imaginary lines running east and west used by surveyors for reference in locating and describing land under the government survey method of property description
27. A reference to direction, based on terminal points and angles. In a metes-and-bounds legal description, metes is the measurement of length and bounds confines the length to a given area	22. To leave personal property to another by will, as a bequest. To leave real property by will is to devise
28. Violation of any of the terms or conditions of a contract without legal excuse; default; nonperformance. The non-breaching party can usually seek one of three alternative remedies upon a material breach of the contract: rescission of the contract, action for money damages or an action for specific performance	23. The one who is to benefit from a deed of trust. The one to whom the trustee is obligated
29. One who acts as an intermediary between parties to a transaction. A real estate broker is a properly licensed party who, for a valuable consideration or promise of consideration, serves as a special agent to others to facilitate the sale or lease of real property	24. A mortgage secured by several parcels of land. A blanket mortgage is often used to secure construction financing for proposed subdivisions or condominium development projects. The developer normally seeks to have a "partial release" clause inserted in the mortgage so that he or she can obtain a release from the blanket mortgage for each lot as it is sold, according to a specified release schedule
30. A buy-down occurs when a higher loan fee (points) is charged in exchange for a lower interest rate. (If the loan fees are reduced, the opposite may occur and it is referred to as a buy-up.)	25. An illegal and discriminatory practice whereby one person induces another to enter into a real estate transaction from which the first person may benefit financially by representing that a change may occur in the neighborhood with respect to race, sex, religion, color, handicap, familiar status or ancestry of the occupants, a change possibly resulting in the lowering of the property values, a decline in the quality of schools or an increase in the crime rate. Blockbusting generally violates

31. CAP	36. Chattel
32. Capital Gain	37. Closing
33. Cash Out	38. Closing Statement
34. CC&R's	39. Cloud on Title
35. Chain of Title	40. Collateral

36. The word chattel comes from the word cattle, one of the early important possessions, and is personal property. Chattels are transferred by a bill of sale.	31. The highest rate that an adjustable rate mortgage may adjust.
37. The consummation of a real estate transaction, when the seller delivers title to the buyer in exchange for payment (purchase price of the property) by the buyer.	32. The taxable profit derived from the sale of capital asset. The capital gain is the difference between the sale price and the original purchase price of the property after making appropriate adjustments for closing costs, capital improvements and allowable depreciation.
38. A detailed cash accounting of a real estate transaction prepared by a broker, escrow officer, attorney or any other person designate to process the mechanics of a sale, showing all cash received, all credits and charges made and all cash paid out in the transaction.	33. Any funds being refunded directly to the borrower including consolidation of consumer debt.
39. An encumbrance on real property, which if valid, would affect the ownership of the property.	34. The written contract stating and explaining the covenants, conditions and restrictions imposed by the members of association of owners, such as that of condominiums of PUC.
40. Something of value given as a basis for a loan.	35. The recorded history of matters that affect the title to a specific parcel of real property, such as ownership, encumbrances and liens, usually beginning with the original recorded source of the title. The chain of title shows the successive changes of ownership, each linked to the next so that a "chain" if formed.

41. Collection Account	46. Compliance	56. Conversion
52. Consideration		57. Cooperative Ownership
53. Construction Loan		58. Covenant
54. Consumer Credit		59. Credit Scoring
55. Conventional Loan		60. Curtsey

56. The appropriation of property belonging to another. Taking a clients money and spending it	51. An association of owners of condominium units
57. Ownership of an apartment unit in which the apartment owner has purchased shares in the corporation (or partnership or trust) that holds title to the real estate	52. An act or the promise thereof, which is offered by one party to induce another to enter into a contract that which is given in exchange for something from another; also the promise to refrain from doing a certain act, like filing a justifiable lawsuit (the forbearance of a right)
58. An agreement or promise between two or more parties in which they pledge to perform (or not perform) specified acts on a property; or a written agreement that specifies certain uses or nonuse of the property. Covenants are found in real estate documents such as leases, mortgages, contracts for deed and deeds. Damages may be claimed for breach of a covenant	53. A short-term or interim loan to cover the construction costs of a building or development project, with loan proceeds advanced periodically in the form of installment payments as the work progresses (called draws)
59. A financial snapshot of a borrower's credit history and current usage of credit at a given point in time. The information comes from credit bureaus and other sources. Because the credit score is numerical, it is helpful with computer analysis of a borrower's credit rating. Sample scores range from 400 to 900, and the lower the number, the greater the risk of default. Freddie Mac favors scores of 620 or higher	54. Credit owned by the individual, not secured by real estate
60. The interest, recognized in some states, of a husband in property owned by his wife at the time of her death. Has been replaced by community property in most states	55. A loan not underwritten by HUD, SBA, or FHA. LBMC's loans are conventional loans

61. Debt Ratio (DR)	66. Deed Restrictions
62. Deed	67. Deferred Maintenance
63. Deed of Trust	68. Deficiency Judgment
64. Deed In Lieu of Foreclosure	69. Delivery
65. Deed of Reconveyance	70. Depreciation

66. Provisions placed in deeds to control future uses of the property	61. The customers monthly obligations divided by their monthly gross income
67. Refers to damage or wear to a property that has not been repaired at the time of the appraisal	62. A written instrument by which a property owner, a "grantor", conveys and transfers to a "grantee" an ownership interest in real property
68. The lender may seek a deficiency judgment, or court ruling requiring payment of the remaining debt, against the borrower. This judgment is possible under the terms of the note. The note terms state that the borrower is personally liable for the full amount of the obligations	63. This document, also known as a trust deed or trust indenture, secures an interest in property used as collateral for a loan. A deed of trust differs from a mortgage in that the power of sale, or right to sell the property, is held in trust during the term of the loan. While the mortgage only involves two parties, the deed of trust involves three
69. The legal act of transferring ownership. Documents such as deeds and mortgages must be delivered and accepted before becoming valid	64. When a borrower defaults on the mortgage and cannot reinstate it, he/she will offer to give the property back to the lender rather than go through a foreclosure. This is referred to as a deed in lieu. The deed in lieu is voluntary and transfers title from the current owner or title holder to the lender
70. The reduction of property value due to such sauces as deterioration, obsolescence or normal wear and tear	65. A document used to transfer legal title from the trustee back to the borrower (trustor) after a debt secured by a deed of trust has been paid to the lender (beneficiary.)

71. Derogatory letter	76. Dower
72. Devise	77. Due-On- Sale Clause
73. Discharge	78. Durable
74. Discount Points	79. Earnest Money
75. DOCS	80. Easements

76. The legal right or interest recognized in some states that a wife acquires in the property her husband held or acquired any time during their marriage. During the husband's life, the dower is an expectant, or inchoate, interest that does not actually become legal estate until the husband's death. Has been replaced by community property in most states.	71. A letter written by the borrower explaining any derogatory credit.
77. A form of acceleration clause found in most mortgages, requiring the mortgager to pay off the mortgage debt when the property is sold.	72. A transfer of real property under a will. The donor is the devisor, and the recipient is the devisee
78. A power of attorney will continue beyond the physical or mental incapacity of the principal.	73. Following a completed bankruptcy proceeding, discharged debts are no longer owned or collectable. For all bankruptcies, LBMC requires a copy of the Discharge of Debts document to continue with the loan
79. The cash deposit (including initial and additional deposits) paid by the prospective buyer of real property, as evidence of good faith intentions, to complete the transaction.	74. An added loan fee charged by a lender to make the yield higher on a loan. One discount point is equal to 1 percent of the loan amount
80. An interest in property, owned by another, that entitles the holder to a specific limited use or privilege, such as the right to cross or to build adjoining structures on the property.	75. Abbreviation for mortgage loan documents

81. Easement Appurtenant	86. Emblements
82. Easement by Necessity	87. Eminent Domain
83. Easement by Prescription	88. Encumbrance
84. Easement in Gross	89. Escrow
85. ECOA (Equal Credit Opportunity Act)	90. Escrow Closings

86. A growing crop, such as grapes or corn, which is produced annually through labor and industry. Emblements are regarded as personal property even before harvest; thus, a tenant has the right to take the annual crop resulting from his or her labor, even if the harvest does not occur until after tenancy has ended	81. An easement that runs with the land
87. The right of government (both state and federal), public corporations (school districts sanitation districts), public utilities and public service corporations (railroads, power companies) to take private property for a necessary public use, with just compensation paid to the owner.	82. An easement created by a court of law in cases where justice and necessity dictate it, especially in a classic landlocked situation.
88. Any claim, lien, charge or liability, attached to and binding on real property that may lessen its value, burden, obstruct or impair the use of a property, but not necessarily prevent transfer of title; right or interest in a property held by one who is not the legal owner of the property.	83. A right acquired by adverse possession, the use that results in an easement by prescription must be adverse, hostile, open, notorious and continuous for the statutory period.
89. A financially disinterested third party used to hold funds, documents and title delivery deeds until the fulfillment of all transaction contingencies.	84. The limited right of the one person to use another's land (servient estate) when such right is not created for the benefit of any land owned by the owner of the easement.
90. An escrowee is a disinterested third party who has no financial interest in the transaction and is usually title insurance company representative, often referred to as an escrow office.	85. In 1974, federal legislation was passed to ensure that various financial institutions and other firms engages in the extension of credit, exercise their responsibility to make credit available with fairness, impartiality and without discrimination on the basis of; race, color, religion, national origin, sex, marital status, age economic situation or good faith under the Consumer Credit Protection Act.

91. Escrow Instructions	96. Fannie Mae (Federal National Mortgage Association)
92. Estate	97. Federal Fair Housing
93. ET AL	98. Fee Simple Estate
94. Exclusive Agency	99. Feudal System
95. Exclusive Right to Sell	100. FHA (Federal Housing Administration)

96. A quasi-governmental corporation which buys mortgages and packages them for sale on the secondary market. They are then sold as securities to individual investors	91. Issued by the escrow company detailing the instructions provided by the lender. These instructions indicate the parameters and contingencies involved in the transaction as agreed upon by both parties. Escrow instructions must be accurate to the final transaction and signed by the escrow company and the borrowers
97. In 1968 Congress enacted Title VIII of the Civil Rights Act, called the federal Fair Housing Act, which declared a national policy of providing fair housing throughout the United State (reference Sections 3601-3631 of Title 42, United States Code). This law makes discrimination based on race, color, sex, familial status, handicap, religion or national origin illegal in connection with the sale or rental of most dwellings	92. Describes the extent and character of a person's rights and interest in real property. Two types of estates frequently financed by mortgage lenders are the fee simple and the leasehold estate
98. Complete ownership in which the owner or owners are entitled to all the rights connected with the property. This means that the owners can do anything allowed by law with their land. The owners may sell, mortgage, lease or give away the property	93. And others
99. An ancient system of land ownership. Under old English common law the government or king held title to all lands. The individual was merely a tenant whose rights of use and occupancy of real property were held at the sufferance of an overlord	94. A written listing agreement giving a sole agent the right to sell a property for a specified time, but reserving to the owner the right to sell the property himself without owing a commission. The exclusive agent is entitled to a commission if he or she personally sells the property or if it is sold by anyone other than the seller
100. A federal agency which sets guidelines and insures loans on residential housing	95. A written listing agreement appointing a broker the exclusive agent for the sale of property for a specified period of time. The listing broker is entitled to a commission if the property is sold by the owner, by the broker or by anyone else

101. Fiscal Year	106. Free and Clear
102. Fixed-Rate Loan	107. Front End Ratio
103. Flood Insurance	108. Fructus Naturales
104. Foreclosure	109. Full Reconveyance
105. Freddie Mac (Federal Home Loan Mortgage Corporation)	110. Functional Obsolescence

106. Property that is completely paid for and has no liens or encumbrances attached	101. The accounting year used by corporations for tax purposes. A fiscal year runs 12 months, but does not necessarily begin in January or end in December
107. Refers to the debt to income ration calculations by adding the housing expenses (principal, interest, taxes, insurance, (flood and hazard, and Homeowner Association Dues), to arrive at a housing expense (debt) total	102. A loan with the same rate of interest for the life of the loan. Until the late 1970s and early 1980s, the fixed-rate loan was the predominant real estate loan. With the arrival of highly volatile interest rates, lenders attempted to adjust interest rates with a variety of new and different loans
108. Uncultivated crops and perennial plantings, such as trees and bushes, which are generally classified as real property	103. Insurance against loss due to flood
109. Upon payment in full of the debt secured by a deed of trust, reconveyance of the property by the trustee to the person or persons entitled thereto on written request of the grantor and the beneficiary, upon satisfaction of the obligation secured and written request for reconveyance made by the beneficiary or assignee thereof	104. A non-voluntary procedure to sell real property according to the terms and conditions of the security instrument which identified the subject property as security for the loan
110. Loss in desirability of the style, layout or function of an element of a property (overtime)	105. (See FANNIE MAE definition.) Freddie Mac buys "A" paper loans from banks and mortgage companies

111. Funding	116. Hazard Insurance
112. Gift Letter	117. HOA (Home Owners' Association)
113. Ginnie Mae	118. Holdback
114. Grant Deed	119. Holographic Will
115. Hard Money Mortgage	120. Homestead

116. Insures the property against damage causes by fire, wind or other hazards. Unless specifically stated, does not cover earthquake, riot, or flood damage	111. Process of disbursing money to the title company or attorney to fund a loan
117. An association of people who own homes in a given area, formed for the purpose of improving or maintaining the quality of the area	112. A letter provided to a lender or government agency acknowledging that the money being used (often the down payment) to purchase real property was a gift from a relative with no obligation to repay
118. A portion of the loan proceeds (cash out) allowed to be held back by a lender until a contingency set forth by the lender is met	113. A federal agency created in 1968 when the Federal National Mortgage Association (FNMA), now Fannie Mae, was partitioned into two separate corporations. Ginnie Mae is a corporation without capital stock and is a division of HUD. Ginnie Mae operates the special assistance aspects of federally aided housing programs and has the management and liquidating functions of the old FNMA loans
119. A will that is written, dated and signed in the testator's handwriting, but not witnessed. Some states consider a holographic will to be valid even though it was not witnessed, presumably on the theory that the handwriting can be analyzed	114. A type of deed in which the grantor warrants that he/she has not previously conveyed the estate being granted to another, that he/she has not encumbered the property except as noted in the deed, and that he/she will convey to the grantee any title to the property he/she may later acquire
120. The house and adjacent land of the head of the family	115. A mortgage loan given to a borrower is exchange for cash, as opposed to a mortgage given to finance a specific real estate purchase. Often, a hard money mortgage will take the form of a second mortgage given to a private mortgage company in exchange for the cash needed to purchase an item of personal property or solve some personal financial crisis. The borrower in this case would pledge the

121. Hypothecate	126. Intestate
122. Impound Account	127. Interstate Land Sale Full Disclosure
123. Indemnification	128. Joint Tenants
124. Index	129. Land Contract
125. Interest	130. Lateral and Subjacent Support

126. Dying without a will or having left a will that is defective in form. An intestate decedent's property passes to his or her heirs according to the laws of descent in the state where such real property is located. These laws of descent vary from state to state and determine who is entitled to the decedent's property, which then must pass through probate in the state	121. To pledge specific real or personal property as security for an obligation without surrendering possession of it
127. A federal law created in 1968. That regulates state land sales by requiring registration of real property with the Office of Interstate Land Sales Registration (OILSR) of the U.S. Department of Housing and Urban Development (HUD)	122. Account held by the lender for future payment of property taxes, hazard insurance and flood insurance. The borrower contributes to the escrow account with the monthly payment which includes allowances for this purpose
128. A form of co-ownership by two or more persons each with equal shares and the right of survivorship upon death of a co-tenant	123. To protect against loss, damage or liability and is obtained from a title company when a lien has not been reconveyed, but the title company is willing to insure the Bank against harm from that lien
129. An installment contract for sale with the buyer receiving equitable title (right to possession) and the seller retaining legal title (record title)	124. A measure of fluctuations in certain factors of economic activity and serves as an indicator of past and current financial market conditions
130. The support a parcel of real property receives from the land adjoining it is called lateral support. It is not a right in the land of an adjoining owner, rather a right incident to ownership of the property entitled to the support. Subjacent support is that support the surface of the earth receives from its underlying strata	125. An amount, usually expressed as a percentage that a person borrowing money pays in addition to the amount originally borrowed

121. Hypothecate	126. Intestate
122. Impound Account	127. Interstate Land Sale Full Disclosure
123. Indemnification	128. Joint Tenants
124. Index	129. Land Contract
125. Interest	130. Lateral and Subjacent Support

126. Dying without a will or having left a will that is defective in form. An intestate decedent's property passes to his or her heirs according to the laws of descent in the state where such real property is located. These laws of descent vary from state to state and determine who is entitled to the decedent's property, which then must pass through probate in the state	121. To pledge specific real or personal property as security for an obligation without surrendering possession of it
127. A federal law created in 1968. That regulates state land sales by requiring registration of real property with the Office of Interstate Land Sales Registration (OILSR) of the U.S. Department of Housing and Urban Development (HUD)	122. Account held by the lender for future payment of property taxes, hazard insurance and flood insurance. The borrower contributes to the escrow account with the monthly payment which includes allowances for this purpose
128. A form of co-ownership by two or more persons each with equal shares and the right of survivorship upon death of a co-tenant	123. To protect against loss, damage or liability and is obtained from a title company when a lien has not been reconveyed, but the title company is willing to insure the Bank against harm from that lien
129. An installment contract for sale with the buyer receiving equitable title (right to possession) and the seller retaining legal title (record title)	124. A measure of fluctuations in certain factors of economic activity and serves as an indicator of past and current financial market conditions
130. The support a parcel of real property receives from the land adjoining it is called lateral support. It is not a right in the land of an adjoining owner, rather a right incident to ownership of the property entitled to the support. Subjacent support is that support the surface of the earth receives from its underlying strata	125. An amount, usually expressed as a percentage that a person borrowing money pays in addition to the amount originally borrowed

131. Lead Poisoning	136. Lessor
132. Leasehold	137. Leverage
133. Lease Option	138. LIBOR (London Interbank Offered Rate)
134. Legal Description	139. Lien
135. Lessee	140. Life Estate

136. The person who rents or leases property to another. In residential leasing, he or she is often referred to as a landlord	131. A serious illness caused by high concentrations of lead in the body, discovered by a blood test. Lead can cause major health problems, especially learning disabilities in young children
137. The impact of borrowed funds on investment return. The use of borrowed funds to purchase property with the anticipation that the acquired property will increase in return so that the investor will realize a profit not only on his or her own investment but also on the borrowed funds	132. Created when the owner of a property (lessor), grants the tenant (lessee), the right to a parcel of land for a period of time. A lease is both a conveyance of land and a contract
138. The basic interest rate paid on deposits between banks in the Eurodollar market	133. A lease containing a clause that allows the tenant the right to purchase the property under specified conditions
139. A charge or claim that an individual has upon the property of another as security for a debt or obligation	134. A description that legally describes the real property or interest being conveyed. Usually accomplished by lot/tract, metes and bounds, or US Government Survey type of legal description
140. Any estate in real or personal property that is limited in duration to the life of its owner or the life of some other designated person. If the estate is measured by the lifetime of a person other than its owner, it is called a *life estate pur autre vie*. Although the classified as a freehold estate because it is a possessory estate of indefinite duration, a life estate is not an estate of inheritance	135. The person to whom property is rented or leased; called a tenant in most residential leases

141. Liquidated Damages	146. Local Improvement District
142. LIS Pendens	147. Margin
143. Loan Origination	148. Mechanic's Lien
144. Loan Origination Fee	149. Metes and Bounds
145. Loan to Value	150. Mill

146. A separate legal entity, activated under state law by the inhabitants of a particular geographic area. The district is governed by a board of directors and possesses many of the characteristics of a city, particularly in terms of taxation. As a rule, the district issues its own bonds to finance particular improvements, such as water distribution systems, drainage structures, irrigation works and a host of other types of developments	141. An amount predetermined by the parties to an agreement as the total amount of compensation an injured party should receive if the other party breaches a specified part of the contract. Often in building contracts the parties anticipate the possibility of a breach (for example, a delay in completion by a set date) and specify in the contract the amount of the damages to be paid in the event of the breach. To be enforceable, the liquidated damages clause must set forth an amount that bears a reasonable relationship to the actual damages as estimated by the parties perform.
147. A constant percentage added to an index to determine the interest rate charged on an adjustable rate mortgage. While The index rate may vary throughout the adjustment period, the margin remains constant for the life of the loan	142. A Latin term meaning "action pending" and takes on the nature of a "quasi lien". A recorded legal document providing constructive notice that an action affecting a particular piece of property has been filed in a state or federal court
148. A lien created by statue for the purpose of securing priority of payment for the price or value of work performed and materials furnished in construction or repair of improvements to land and/or structure	143. The fee paid to the company originating a mortgage loan to cover the costs of creating, processing and closing a loan. Usually 1% of the loan amount.
149. Measurement, angles, boundaries and distance used in describing land perimeters	144. An ancient ceremony of transferring title to real property. In the Middle Ages, conveyance was accomplished by a formal process known as an *enfeoffment*, with livery of seisin literally a handing over of the fee with delivery of the seisin (possession of a freehold estate). The transfer was often symbolized by the simple ritual of transferring a handful of the soil, a piece of the turf, or a twig from a
150. One-tenth of one cent. Some states use a mill rate to compute property taxes and sales taxes. Example: if the mill rate is 52 and the property is assessed at $40,000, the tax would be 0.052 x $2,080	145. The loan amount in relationships to the appraised value or selling price expressed as a percentage (for example, a loan amount of $80,000 divided by the appraised value of $100,000 equals an 80% LTV)

151. Mixed Use	156. Mortgage-Backed Security (MBS)
152. Month-to-Month Tenancy	157. Mortgage Banker
153. Monument	158. Multiple Listing
154. Moral Turpitude	159. Mutual Mortgage Insurance Fund
155. Mortgage	160. Negative Amortization

156. A security guaranteed by pools of mortgages and used to channel funds from securities markets to housing markets. Ginnie Mae has a popular MBS program recognized for its low risk and high yield. The Ginnie Mae MBS security is a pool of VA and FHA mortgages put together as a bond. Freddie Mac and Fannie Mae also have MBS programs	151. A property (such as a commercial store with an apartment located above the commercial store). In which a portion of the property is used for commercial or retail purposes. A property can also be considered mixed use if different combinations of uses are present such as commercial/industrial or residential/industrial
157. A type of financial institution that does not directly attract funds such as deposit accounts, instead, it borrows funds from other sources such as banks or savings institutions to make mortgage loans	152. A periodic tenancy where the tenant rents for one period at a time. In the absence of a rental agreement (oral or written), a tenancy is generally considered to be month-to-month or, in the case of boarders, week-to-week. Under such a tenancy, the estate continues for an indefinite period of time until either lessor or lessee gives the statutory notice of termination
158. A listing agreement used by a broker who is a member of a multiple-listing organization. The multiple-listing agreement is in effect an exclusive right to sell with an additional authority and obligation on the part of the listing broker to distribute the listing to other brokers making up the multiple-listing organization	153. A visible marker, either a natural or artificial object, set by the government or surveyors, used to establish the lines and boundaries of a survey. Monuments include artificial immovable like stakes, iron pins or posts, and metal or stone markers, as well as natural objects like marked trees, streams, and rivers. A possible problem with natural monuments is that they sometimes move from their
159. One of four FHA insurance funds into which all insurance premiums and other specified FHA revenues are paid, and from which any losses are meet	154. Example, embezzlement, perjury, robbery and larceny are generally crimes of moral turpitude, whereas failure to pay income tax, speeding or possession of small amounts of marijuana probably are not
160. A method of amortization that limits the monthly payment increase at the time of the adjustment by placing a "cap" on the payment amount, and the difference between the true payment needed to amortize the loan and the discounted payment is added to the principal loan amount. The cap is usually expressed as a percentage of the previous payment	155. A legal instrument in which real property is pledged by the borrower (mortgagor) to the lender (mortgages) as security for the repayment of a loan or the performance of a duty. This pledge ends when the debt or duty is discharged

161. Net Disposable Income	166. Notary Public
162. Non-Conforming Use	167. Notice of Default (NOD)
163. Non-Owner Occupied	168. Nuncupative Will
164. Non-Recourse Loan	169. Obligations
165. Non-Recurring Closing Costs	170. Offer and Acceptance

166. A public officer authorized to administer oaths, attestations and certifications of certain documents, including security instruments. This office can also take depositions and perform other civil functions	161. Money left after subtracting the principal, interest, taxes and insurance (housing expenses) and all other obligations from the monthly net income. The amount the borrower has available for living expenses after housing expenses are subtracted
167. A recorded notice of a borrower's failure to repay an obligation under a deed of trust. It is the document filed at the beginning of the foreclosure proceedings	162. A permitted use of real property that was lawful at the time of its original construction but that no longer conforms to the current zoning law
168. An oral will declared by the testator just prior to his or her death, made before witnesses and shortly afterward reduced to writing by the witnesses. Such a will is not valid in most states and is usually limited to military personnel or to disposition of personal effects	163. A property not used as the "primary" residence of the owner
169. Any debt or recurring payment the borrower is obligated to pay	164. A loan in which the borrower is not held personally liable on the note. Also called a dry mortgage
170. The two components of a valid contract; a meeting of the minds. An offer is a manifestation of an intention to enter into an agreement	165. Fees associated with the closing of a loan that occur only one time in the transaction and do not recur

171.Open Listing	176. Piggy Back Loan
172. Owner Occupied	177. PITI
173. Per Auitre Vie	178. Planned Unit Development (PUD)
174. Percentage Lease	179. Point of Beginning (POB)
175. Periodic Tenancy	180. Points

176. Financing obtained, subordinate to the first mortgage, to facilitate closing the first mortgage. Also known as Secondary Financing	171. A listing given to any number of brokers who can work simultaneously to sell the owner's property. An open listing need not contain a definite termination date
177. Principal, interest, taxes, and insurance. The complete monthly mortgage cost associated with a property	172. A property used as the owner's "primary: residence
178. Property owned as a group, where individuals own the specific piece of land and structure they occupy, but also have a divided interest in a common area. The development is governed by a board of homeowners	173. A life estate measured by the life of another person other than the owner of the real estate.
179. The starting point in a metes-and-bounds description of property – usually a street intersection or a specific monument. To be complete, a legal description of a property must always return to the point of beginning to describe the area accurately	174. A lease whose rental is based on a percentage of the monthly or annual gross sales made on the premises. Percentage leases are common with large retail stores, especially in shopping centers
180. Charged as a part of the prepaid finance charge. Points may be used to buy down the rate or to pay a broker's commission. One point equals one percent of the gross loan amount	175. A leasehold estate that continues from period to period, such as month-to-month or year-to-year. All conditions and terms of the tenancy are carried over from period to period and continue for an uncertain time until proper notice of termination is given

181. Police Power	186. Prepaid interest
182. Power of Attorney (POA)	187. Prepayment Penalty
183. Power of Sale	188. Principal
184. Preliminary Title Report (Prelim or Commitment)	189. Principal and Interest (P&I)
185. Prepaid Finance Charge	190. Private Mortgage Insurance (PMI)

186. The portion of interest, collect at loan closing, which covers the time period between funding and the first of the month preceding the first payment due	181. The constitutional authority and inherent power of a state to adopt and enforce laws and regulations to promote and support the public health, safety, morals and general welfare
187. A lender need not accept payment in advance of the state maturity of a loan, even if the borrower offers to pay all interest to the date of maturity with the full principal	182. A written instrument authorizing a person, the attorney-in-fact, to act as the agent on behalf of another to the extent indicated in the instrument
188. The net balance or the amount due less interest, impound and late charges	183. A clause in a mortgage authorizing the holder of the mortgage to sell the property at public auction without a judicial action in the event of the borrower's default
189. The principal and interest portions of the monthly mortgage payment	184. The title report generated at the beginning of the application process. It disclosed all liens on the property and contains the properties legal description. The Preliminary Title Report also indicates outstanding issues to resolve in order to gain a clear title prior to recording our trust deed
190. A special form of insurance designed to permit lenders to increase their loan-to-market-value ratio, often up to 97% of the market value of the property	185. Any fees charged to the borrower as a cost of obtaining the loan. A prepaid finance charge is paid directly to the lender or the broker and is a onetime cost to the borrower

191. Procuring Cause	196. Purchase Agreement
192. Profit and Loss (P & L)	197. Quitclaim Deed
193. Promissory Note	198. Real Estate Investment Trust (REIT)
194. Prorate	199. Real Estate Settlement Procedures Act (RESPA)
195. Public Offering Statement	200. Real Property

196. The agreement made between the buyer and seller of a property. The agreement contains the purchase price and contingencies of the sale	191. That effort which brings about the desired result. Also called the predominant efficient cause or the contributing cause
197. A deed operating as a release; intended to pass any title, interest, or claim which the grantor may have in the property, but not containing any warranty of a valid interest or title in the grantor	192. A statement of a business' gross income, cost of goods, operating costs and net profit or loss
198. A method of pooling investment money using the trust form of ownership	193. A written promise by the borrower to pay a debt owed, within a specified time, to the private or institutional lender under conditions mutually agreed upon. The chief function of the promissory note is to make the borrower personally liable for the payment of the mortgage debt
199. Requires lenders to provide borrowers with information on known or estimated settlement costs anticipated to close a loan. Under the law, lenders give residential mortgage loan applicants detailed information about settlement services and costs at the time of application	194. To divide or distribute proportionately. With the exception of principal payments on a mortgage, most real estate expenses such as rent, insurance which is frequently prepaid for several years coverage and the like are paid in advance
200. Land and all attachments to the land, such as buildings, crops or mineral rights. Ownership of real property can be divided into various types of interest and rights	195. The document prepared by a sub divider in accordance with individual state subdivision laws that disclose all material facts about a subdivision to be offered for sale to the public. No sale is valid unless the purchaser receives a copy of the current public offering statement, is given a reasonable time in which to examine it and signs a receipt for it

201. Realtor	206. Rescission
202. Receiver	207. Reversion
203. Reconveyance (RECON)	208. Riparian Rights
204. Reliction	209. Sale Leaseback
205. Remainderman	210. Salvage Value

206. The legal remedy for canceling, terminating or annulling a contract and restoring the parties to their original positions; a return to status quo	201. A registered trade name that may be used only by members of the state and local real estate boards affiliated with the National Association of Realtors (NAR)
207. The estate remaining in the grantor, or the estate of a testator, who has conveyed a lesser estate from the original	202. An independent party appointed by a court to impartially receive, preserve and manage property that is involved in litigation, pending final disposition of the matter before the court
208. Those rights and obligations that are incidental to ownership of land adjacent to or abutting on watercourses such as streams and lakes. Riparian rights do not attach except where there is a water boundary on one side of the particular tract of land claimed to be riparian	203. The release of a recorded lien, upon fulfillment of all obligations of the deed of trust, with the county recorder by the trustee
209. An arrangement where one party sells a property to a buyer, and the buyer immediately leases the property back to the seller.	204. The gradual recession of water from the usual watermark and, therefore, an increase of the land. Reliction refers to a situation where land that once was covered by water becomes uncovered. The uncovered land is treated as allusion, and the rules of the accretion apply to the ownership of this new land. This new land usually belongs to the riparian owner
210. It is the estimated value of an asset after the end of its useful life. In accounting it is the asset's remaining value after depreciation. Also know as residual value and scrap value.	205. One entitled to take an estate in remainder. The remainderman has the right to bring court action against the current possessor for committing waste

211. Satisfaction	216. Security Deposit
212. Second Mortgage	217. Senior Mortgage
213. Secondary Financing	218. Servient Tenement
214. Secondary Mortgage Market	219. Severalty
215. Section	220. Shared Appreciation Mortgage

216. Money deposited by or for the tenant with the landlord	211. It is an instrument for recording and acknowledging the final payment of a mortgage loan. The lender acknowledges the debt has been paid.
217. A real estate loan that is in the first priority in case of default.	212. A mortgage that is junior or subordinate to a first mortgage. Typically an additional loan imposed on top of a first mortgage. Because of the risk to the lender usually requires a shorter term and higher interest rate than the first mortgage.
218. Land on which easement exists in favor of an adjacent property (called a dominant or estate). If property A has a right of way across property B, property B is the servient tenement.	213. Any financing other than a first mortgage that creates a lien against the property is considered secondary financing.
219. Sole ownership of a property.	214. A market for the purchase and sale of existing mortgages designed to provide greater liquidity for selling mortgages and is also called the secondary market.
220. A mortgage loan in which the lender in exchange for a loan with a favorable interest rate participates in any profits the borrower incurs at some future date.	215. As used in the government survey method, a land area of one square mile. A section is 1/36th of a township. Sections are numbered starting in the upper northeast corner or upper right hand corner.

221. Sheriff's Deed	226. Special Assessment
222. Sheriff's Sale	227. Specific Performance
223. Short Sale	228. Square Foot Method
224. Simple Interest	229. Statute of Frauds
225. SITUS	230. Statute of Limitations

226. A tax or levy imposed on specific on specific properties that will benefit from a proposed public improvement. Examples of special assessments include bringing water, sewer, and/or to the property.	221. The deed given at a sheriff's sale.
227. An action brought in a court in special cases to compel to carry out the terms of a contract.	222. An auction sale of a property held by a sheriff pursuant to a court order to seize and sell the property to satisfy or pay a judgment after notice to the public.
228. A method of estimating construction, reproduction, or replacement cost, whereby the structure square footage floor area is multiplied by an appropriate construction cost per square foot.	223. A sale occurs where the proceeds fall short of the balance owed on the property.
229. State laws that require certain contracts to be in writing and signed by a party to be charged or held to the agreement to be legally enforceable.	224. Interest compounded on the balance only, and disregards previously accumulated interest.
230. The law pertaining to the period of time within which certain actins must be brought before the court.	225. An alternate word for site.

231. Straight Note	236. Takeout Loan
232. Straw Man	237. Tax Base
233. Subordination Agreement	238. Tax Deed
234. Subsurface Rights	239. Tax Lien
235. Syndicate	240. Tax Out Commitment

236. The "permanent" (long term) financing of real estate after completion of construction	231. A promissory note evidencing a loan in which payments of interest only are made periodically during the term of the note
237. The assessed valuation of real property, which is multiplied by the tax rate to determine the amount of tax due	232. One who purchases property for another so as to conceal the identity of the real purchaser; a dummy purchaser; a nominee; a front
238. Deed from tax collector to governmental body after a period of non-payment of taxes according to statute. Deed to a purchaser at a public sale of land taken for delinquent taxes. The purchaser receives only such title as the former owners had, and strict procedures must be followed to prevent attachment of prior liens	233. An agreement by which an encumbrance is made subject (junior) to a junior encumbrance. For example: A loan on vacant land is made subject to a subsequent construction loan
239. A lien for nonpayment of property taxes. Are unpaid. A federal income tax lien. May attach to all property of the one owning the taxes	234. The rights, whether by fee or easement, to oil, gas, or mineral, below a certain depth beneath the surface of land. The right of surface entry may or may not be excluded, and is important to the value of the surface land for improvement purposes
240. Agreement by a lender to place a long term (take out) loan on real property after completion of construction	235. An association of individuals, formed for the purpose of carrying on some particular business venture in which the members are mutually interested

241. Tax Rate	246. Tenancy in Common
242. Tax Sale	247. Tender
243. Teaser Rate Mortgage	248. Time is of the Essence
244. Tenancy by the Entirety	249. Torrens System
245. Tenancy for Years	250. Township

246. A form of concurrent ownership of property between two or more persons, in which each has an undivided interest in the whole property. This form is frequently found when the parties acquire title by descent or by will	241. Traditionally the ratio of dollars of tax per hundred or per thousand dollars of valuation. Modernly, has become to be expressed as a percentage of valuation
247. An unconditional offer by one of the parties to a contract to perform his or her part of the bargain	242. Public sale of property at auction by governmental authority, after a period of nonpayment of property tax
248. A contract clause that emphasizes punctual performance as an essential requirement of the contract. Thus, if any party to the instrument does not perform within the specified time period (the "drop-dead" date), the party is in default, provided the non-defaulting party has made a valid tender of performance	243. An adjustable rate-mortgage with an interest rate initially set below the market rate
249. A legal system for the registration of land used to verify the ownership and conditions (except tax liens), without the necessity of an additional search of the public records	244. A form of ownership by husband and wife whereby each owns the entire property. In the event of the death of one, the survivor owns the property without probate. Used only in states that are not community property states
250. A division of territory, used in the government (rectangular) survey system of land description, that is six miles square; contains 36 sections, each of which is one mile square; and consists of 23,040 acres.	245. A less-than-freehold estate (or tenancy) in which the property is leased for a definite, fixed period of time be it for 60 days, any fraction of a year, a year or 10 years.

251. Truth-in-Lending Act	256. Unilateral Contract
252. Undisclosed Principal	257. Unity of Title
253. Undue Influence	258. Unmarketable Title
254. Unencumbered	259. Usury
255. Uniform Commercial Code	260. Vacancy Factor/Rate

256. A contract where one party expressly makes a promise. The other party although having made non reciprocal promise may be obligated by law or may be required to give consideration	251. A body of federal law effective July 1969 as part of the Consumer Credit Protection Act, and implemented by the Federal Reserve Board's Regulation Z. The main purpose of this law is to ensure that borrowers and customers in need of consumer credit are given meaningful information with respect to the cost of credit
257. In joint tenancy, the holding by the joint tenants under the same title	252. A principal whose identity is not revealed by an agent
258. Not saleable. Having serious defects	253. Influence used to destroy the will of another so that his decision is not of his free will
259. Charging an interest rate greater than the rate permitted by law	254. Free of liens and other encumbrances. Free and clear
260. The estimated percentage of vacancies in a rental project. Derived from historic records, a professional guess, or from the average of surround buildings	255. A code/law which regulates the transfer of personal property; it took the place of the various state statutes covering chattel mortgages, conditional sales, trust receipts, etc.

261. Valid	266. Vendor
262. Valuation	267. Veteran's Administration Loans (VA Loans)
263. Variable Interest Rate	268. Void
264. Variance	269. Voluntary Lien
265. Vendee	270. Walk-Through

266. Legally binding. Carried out properly in accordance with legal procedures	261. Legally binding. Carried out properly in accordance with legal procedures
267. A home loan guaranteed by the Department of Veterans Affairs. Enables a veteran to buy a home with no money down	262. The estimating of value. Appraisal. Assessment
268. Having no force or binding effect	263. An interest rate that fluctuates as the prevailing rate moves up or down. In mortgages there are usually maximums as to the amount and frequency that rate can change. Most have lifetime caps
269. A lien placed on a property with the knowledge and consent of the property owner	264. Permission obtained from governmental zoning authorities to build a structure or conduct a use that is expressly prohibited by the current zoning laws; an exception from the zoning laws
270. A final inspection of a property just before closing. This assures the buyer that the property has been vacated, that no damage has occurred and that the seller has not taken or substituted any property contrary to the terms of the sales agreement	265. The buyer of real estate under a land contract

271. Warranty	276. Wrap-Around Mortgage
272. Warranty Deed	277. Zero Lot Line
273. Waste	278. Zoning
274. Waver	279. Zoning Ordinance
275. Without Recourse	280. Zoning Variance

276. A method of financing in which the new mortgage is placed in a secondary or subordinate position. The new mortgage includes both the unpaid principal balance of the first mortgage and whatever additional sums advanced by the lender.	271. A promise that certain facts are true.
277. When a house is built on a lot so that one wall is on the property boundary line.	272. A deed in which the grantor fully warrants good, clear title to the property.
278. The regulation of structures and uses of property within designated districts or zones.	273. An improper use of abuse of property by a landowner who holds less than the fee ownership, such as a tenant, life tenant, mortgagor or vendee. Waste thus impairs the value of the land or the interest of the one holding the title or the reversion
279. The exercise of police powers by a municipality to regulate and control uses of property.	274. To give up a right voluntarily
280. A zoning variance permits a change in the specifications required by the present zoning	275. It is a clause in a sales contract by which a lender/seller sells loans to an investor. It means the lender/seller is under no obligation to reimburse the buyer for any losses resulting from the purchased loan.

Made in the USA
San Bernardino, CA
03 December 2019